The Family Camping Guide to Wisconsin Michigan Illinois & Indiana

Frazier M. Douglass

D1215590

Trails Books

BOULDER

Published by Trails Books
a Big Earth Publishing company
3005 Center Green Drive, Suite 225
Boulder, Colorado 80301
1-800-258-5830
E-mail: books@bigearthpublishing.com
www.bigearthpublishing.com

Cover and text design by D.K. Luraas
ISBN: 978-1-934553-51-0

Library of Congress Control Number: 2014941745

9   8   7   6   5   4   3   2   1

Printed in the United States of America

For
Ernest (Ernie) L. Grinder
November 15, 1926–

Caretaker and Park Manager, Dane County (Wisconsin) Parks 26 years
Expert auto and small engine mechanic
Retired dairy farmer
Devoted husband and father
Compassionate Christian and lifetime member of
Perry Lutheran Church
One of my life mentors

Ernie Grinder stands in the Brigham County Park campground where he served as property manager for several years.

Other Books by Frazier Douglass

Lightweight Camping for Motorcycle Travel (2009)

The Tent Camper's Handbook (2012)

Contents

Preface

My first camping trip occurred over half a century ago when I was about ten years old. My father and his wife Kitty bought a small motorboat and took the family on what they called a "water skiing vacation." From our home in Birmingham, Alabama, we drove seventy miles down to Wind Creek Park near Alexander City and spent one glorious week camping on the shores of Lake Martin, swimming in the lake, relaxing in our hammocks, eating home-cooked meals, and skiing until my little legs became too tired to do anything but collapse into my cot at the end of the day. Over the next seven years, my father took the family on several more of these skiing vacations to different lakes around central Alabama. Inspired by these wonderful childhood memories, I wanted to continue taking vacations after entering Auburn University in 1963—but had little money. So, I bought a cheap Army surplus canvas tent with no floor, and spent many weekends exploring various lakes and popular tourist destinations around south Alabama, west Georgia, and the Florida Gulf Coast. By camping in state parks, I was able to visit these destinations on a shoestring budget. In fact, cheap gas prices in the summer of 1969 even allowed my young bride and me to take a memorable three-week camping vacation to the Grand Canyon, northern Utah, Colorado Rockies, and the Great Plains of Kansas.

By the age of twenty, I had begun camping on a regular basis and since then, have taken hundreds of camping trips—mainly in the southeastern and midwestern sections of the country. I have camped in about two hundred campgrounds in twenty different states. During the 1970s, '80s, '90s, and early 2000s, I traveled through the Midwest dozens of times and thought I had become an expert on public campgrounds in that region until I realized in 2010 that my knowledge of public campgrounds in these states was still very limited. Although I had camped in a few state and private campgrounds, I was completely unfamiliar with some of the most popular state parks, national parks, recreation areas, forests, Army Corps of Engineers Recreation Areas, state forest preserves, state wildlife areas, county parks, and municipal parks. Furthermore, my understanding of how to plan vacation trips and travel routes to fit available camping areas, how to evaluate campground amenities and activities, and most importantly, how to reserve campsites so that comfortable spots would be waiting on the day of my arrival was very limited. In consequence of my poor planning, I frequently encountered "campground full" signs, and had to spend many nights in nasty, crowded private campgrounds or pricy motel rooms.

When I searched for resources that could help me identify the best campgrounds in each state and explain how to secure campsites in these campgrounds, I found little help. Although a few guidebooks were available, they had notable limitations and provided little guidance for evaluating the safety, comfort, and recreational opportunities of possible destinations in a particular area.

State park guidebooks provide brief descriptions of state parks but include limited information about their campgrounds and do not include nice federal, county, and municipal campgrounds. Furthermore, most of these books are now outdated. *The Best in Tent Camping* books, published for Wisconsin, Michigan, Illinois, and several other states, describe fifty quiet, secluded campgrounds in each state, but do not name some of the largest, most popular, and safest campgrounds in the state. The Internet provides useful information about virtually every public campground in any state, but provides much less help for identifying the names of specific campgrounds in unfamiliar destinations or along unfamiliar travel routes.

Conversations with other campers have revealed that my limited knowledge about public campgrounds was not unique. Without a complete and well-organized guide to public campgrounds, veteran campers planning camping vacations in the Lake Michigan states frequently have difficulty finding the names of many public campgrounds located more than a hundred miles away from their homes and, consequently, often decide to stay in motels when traveling to unfamiliar destinations. In this regard, tent campers differ from RVers who have learned how to identify RV parks, trailer parks, public parks, residential driveways, Walmart parking lots and other places to park overnight as they travel around the country. If they do not like the first place they stop, they can easily crank up the truck or motor home and drive to another.

Because no comprehensive guide to public campgrounds in Wisconsin, Michigan, Indiana, and Illinois exists, I decided to compile and organize such a guidebook and present tent camping as an economical, safe, and comfortable means of vacationing in these states. I decided to include all developed public (state, federal, county, and municipal) campgrounds in the four states for families who want to travel anywhere in the area—regardless of the particular type of campground they prefer. I also felt that it was necessary to explain current procedures for planning tent camping vacation trips because these procedures have changed radically in the past ten years. This guidebook stands apart from other midwestern guidebooks in eight respects:

- It is written for family (or tent) campers who typically prefer public campgrounds with large, level, grassy and shady camp-sites, rather than for RVers who prefer private campgrounds with 30- or 50-amp electrical service, wide roads, few trees, paved parking pads, and dump stations.
- It provides critical information for all 721 state, federal, county, and municipal camping destinations in the four Lake Michigan States, rather than a few arbitrarily selected "favorite" camp-grounds. Details needed to evaluate each property as a possible destination, make reservations, and navigate to it are presented in the campground listings at the end of each chapter.
- It organizes public campgrounds by geographic location, man-agement authority, and number of campsites rather than by al-phabetical (or random) order. Families who prefer large popular campgrounds with lots of activities will always find these camp-grounds at the top of the lists while families who prefer small remote campgrounds where they can get away by themselves will always find these campgrounds at the end of the lists.
- It names campgrounds that have been cited by other authorities as good camping destinations in addition to the campgrounds that the author prefers.
- It recognizes that most families select camping destinations on the basis of location and recreational activities rather than re-moteness and quietness.
- It uses a unique system of reference towns, highways, and land-marks to locate campgrounds on a highway map, rather than an alphabetical and numerical grid system.
- It describes how to select and reserve campsites in chosen camp-grounds several days or weeks in advance rather than waiting until the day of arrival and hoping that a site will be available.
- It emphasizes the importance of using the Internet, tourist bro-chures, and other resources to explore local vacation attractions rather than waiting until the day of arrival.

Regardless of your past camping experience, this guide to family camping vacations will help you plan more enjoyable camping trips to the Lake Michigan states. If you want to save a little money, see more tourist attractions, and fully enjoy the great outdoors on future family vacations, pack a little camping gear and stay in some of the more than seven hundred public campgrounds scattered around Wisconsin, Michi-gan, Illinois, and Indiana.

Lake Michigan States

1
Overview

My first camping experience in the Lake Michigan states occurred in 1970. At the age of twenty-four, I had completed a master's degree in psychology from Auburn University in south Alabama and accepted a college teaching position in Richland Center, Wisconsin. In August of that year, my young expectant wife and I packed our few possessions and three dogs in a small U-Haul truck and struck out on a new adventure. Since we had been students all of our lives, never had full-time jobs, and accrued considerable debt, we decided to camp out along the way to save money. My wife drove our old Chevy Impala and I drove the truck. The trip took three days because we had to stop often and drive through several large cities before Interstate highways had been completed. Our second overnight stop was at Turkey Run State Park just north of Terre Haute. I do not remember much about that night other than the fact that the campground provided a safe and economical respite from the long day's journey. We eventually reached our Wisconsin destination, established our home, gave birth to two sons, and lived in Richland Center five years before moving to Milwaukee for further graduate study.

In total, we lived in Wisconsin nine years and, during those years, took dozens of camping vacations around the state and to neighboring states. We also took a few longer camping excursions to Manitoba, Canada, Denver, Colorado, Manhattan, Kansas, and the Florida Gulf Coast. In 1979, we moved back to Alabama and although the marriage did not survive, my love for camping in the Midwest did. For the past thirty-four years, I have traveled back to Wisconsin several times a year and camped in dozens of campgrounds in the state and along the way. In the summer of 2013, my wife Eva and I completed two touring trips through Illinois, Wisconsin, Michigan, and Indiana during which we set up camp in seventeen different campgrounds and visited another thirty-eight campgrounds along the way.

After many hours of research, I have been able to identify 721 state, federal, county, and municipal public campgrounds in the four Lake Michigan states. To date, I have visited over a hundred of these campgrounds and plan to visit many more in the next few years. My approach to selecting camping destinations is to divide each state into geographic regions and then identify the largest and most popular campgrounds in each region. This approach has allowed me to experience some of the best tent camping destinations and tourist attractions in the Midwestern United States.

From my vacation and camping trips over the past forty-three years, I have come to love the Lake Michigan region and believe that it is one of the most exciting camping and vacation destinations in the country. Interesting facts about these four states and suggestions for planning trips to this region are presented throughout this book.

History

Numerous midwestern camping and tourist destinations are located near topographical features created by giant glaciers that slowly advanced down from Canada many years ago. At least five of these glacial periods (or Ice Ages) are believed to have occurred since the earth's creation. The most recent period, named the Wisconsin Glaciation, reached its maximum advance about 21,000 years ago and ended about 10,000 years ago. During these glacial periods, mile-high glaciers leveled hills in the midwestern region, gouged out lakes, and pushed boulders, rocks, gravel, sand, silt, and other debris to distant places. Each glacier moved tons of rock and material about the area.

Moraine View State Park (Illinois) is located near the Bloomington Moraine left by mile-high glaciers that covered the area many years ago.

When the glaciers melted, rivers of melting ice moved smaller sand and silt to even more distant locations. After each glacier melted and receded, the largely flattened land had numerous *kettle lakes*, elongated hills and ridges (*drumlins*), accumulations of boulders and other materials (*moraines*), layers of rocks, sand and gravel (*tills* and *outwash*), long stratified ridges or sandbars (*eskers*), and dunes of fine wind-blown soil (*loess*). Today, many midwestern lakes, hills, hiking trails, and scenic vistas are the products of these giant glaciers and many of these glacial features can be found in and around state and national parks. Popular midwestern camping destinations near glacial features include campgrounds on thousands of small kettle lakes throughout Michigan and the upper Midwest, Bloomington Moraine (Illinois), glacial boundaries (southern Indiana), and three Kettle Moraine Forest Units (Wisconsin).

Lake Michigan states have thousands of kettle lakes carved by giant glaciers that covered the area thousands of years ago. Big Muskellunge Lake in the Northern Highland/American Legion State Forest (Wisconsin), like most of these kettle lakes, offers great paddling and fishing opportunities.

Several Midwestern tourist destinations are located near mounds and archeological sites left by early nomadic people who roamed through the area for ten to eleven thousand years after the glaciers receded. The first of these early Native American people, identified by their tools and spear points, is called the *Clovis culture.* Following the Clovis Culture, several progressively advanced cultures occupied the land. Recent inhabitants include the *Adena culture* (about 1000 BCE to 500 BCE), *Hopewell culture* (200 BCE to about 400 CE), *Mississippean culture* (500 to 1500 CE), and *Effigy Mounds culture* (650 to 1200 CE). These recent cultures built ceremonial and burial mounds or earthworks throughout the Midwest, and many of these earthworks and archeological sites are now protected by state and federal parks. Popular camping and tourist destinations include Aztalan Mounds (Wisconsin), Missaukee Mounds (Michigan), Angle Mounds (Indiana), Mounds State Park (Indiana), and Cahokia Mounds Historic Site (Illinois).

Midwestern vacationers will notice that numerous towns, rivers, lakes, and geographical features have French names. From 1500 to 1830, French explorers and settlers traveled though the area by canoe and named many places they visited. The first explorers (Joliet, Marquette, and LaSalle) entered the region trying to find a water travel route to the Gulf Coast. Subsequently, traders came into the area seeking beaver pelts and other valuable items that could be sold for fur hats and coats. These French traders built trading posts, married and

Many Great Lakes towns, rivers, and parks, such as Ouabache Trails County Park (Indiana), have French names dating back to early French settlement in the region.

socialized with the native people, spread Catholicism, and maintained a strong presence in the area until a series of Indian wars, international treaties, and colonial expansionism gradually shifted control of the area over to American settlers. Examples of midwestern places with French names include Ouabache—pronounced Wabash—Park (Indiana), Au Sable River and Lighthouse (Michigan), Prairie Du Chien (Wisconsin), and Bourbonnais (Illinois).

Throughout the Midwest, tourists will find many towns, rivers, and lakes that have names derived from Native American languages. Over thirty tribes, including the *Chippewa, Pottawattamie, Winnebago,* and *Sauk* once lived in the four midwestern states. Most of these tribes

Shabbona Lake State Park (Illinois) was named after a Potawatomi Tribal Chief who lived in the state many years ago.

were pushed out of the area to western states during the 1830s and 1840s. Today, many museums and historical markers around the Midwest reflect the life and culture of these early Native American people. One popular camping and tourist destination, for example, is the Tippecanoe Battlefield (Lafayette, Indiana) where Chief Tecumseh and his brother—the Prophet—tried to establish an Indian Confederacy in 1811 to resist American settlers who were pushing the *Shawnee* and other Native American people out of the eastern states. In Northern Illinois and Southwestern Wisconsin, tourists will find several sites that commemorate Chief Black Hawk—a *Sauk* chief who led an unsuccessful effort in 1832 to reclaim tribal lands in northern Illinois and southern Wisconsin. Other notable places with Native American names include Museum of Native American History (Rock Island, Illinois), Mississinewa Lake, (Indiana), Oswego (Michigan), and Menominee (Wisconsin).

We enjoyed learning about the Adena-Hopewell culture at Mounds State Park in Anderson, Indiana.

Old World Wisconsin, like many other towns and tourist attractions in the Lake Michigan states, demonstrates the lifestyle and survival tactics of hearty pioneers who settled this area during the early 1800s.

Throughout the region, tourists will find numerous towns, shops, restaurants, and festivals that reflect the food, dress, and customs of various ethnic groups that settled in the Midwest between 1800 and today. In Vincennes and Terre Haute, Indiana, tourists will find reminders of the early Jewish merchants who were some of the first settlers in the area. Mineral Point in southwestern Wisconsin preserves the buildings and customs of Cornish miners who moved to the area to work in lead mines during the 1830s. Throughout the Midwest, dozens of towns including Milwaukee (Wisconsin), Frankenmuth (Michigan), and Germantown (Illinois) preserve the food, language, and customs of German immigrants who flooded the area. Mount Horeb (Wisconsin) and Decorah (Iowa) preserve food and traditions of Norwegian immigrants who moved to the area to escape poverty and overcrowding in Norway. New Glarus (Wisconsin) and Tell City (Indiana) preserve Swiss dress and traditions. Holland (Michigan) preserves Dutch traditions. Many more towns throughout the area feature restaurants, festivals, and cultural activities that offer food and customs of several more immigrant groups including Polish, Jewish, Finish, Swedish, and Irish. Detroit and other large cities have African American events as reminders of those who moved up from the south to find better paying jobs in Midwestern factories. More recently, Chicago, Milwaukee, Green Bay, and other Midwestern cities are establishing restaurants and festivals that feature Hispanic, Asian, and Muslim foods and traditions.

In the early 1900s, many state and national parks were created by conservation groups as an effort to protect large scenic tracts of land from devastation by mining and lumbering companies. In the late 1800s, lumber barons and mine owners gained enormous political power in the country, bought large tracts of land throughout the upper Midwest for small sums of money, and clear-cut thousands of acres of timber with little regard for the future uses of the land. When they finished logging or mining a particular tract of land, they walked away from it—leaving their devastation and soil erosion for others to clean up. Conservation-minded citizens objected to this wide-scale ravishing of their forests and gradually built coalitions that gained the political strength needed to purchase large land tracts and establish state parks and forests. The Sierra Club, founded by John Muir and others in 1892, was one of the first of these coalitions. The battle between these two forces over land usage raged for half a century until the lumber and mining interests gradually lost their political muscle. Today, campers will find a few parks with stands of "old-growth" or virgin forests that survived the lumberjack's ax and many more parks with "second-growth" forests that were rehabilitated and replanted after the timber and mining companies abandoned the land

During the 1930s, many buildings, roads, bridges, hiking trails, and other improvements were constructed in state and federal parks by the Civilian Conservation Corps (CCC) and most of these structures still stand today. In fact, these old structures provide the infrastructure for many state and federal parks today.

This old log building at Lincoln State park (Indiana) was built by the CCC in the 1930s.

Safety

Public campgrounds, as a general rule, are safe and enjoyable places suited for families and their children. Most public campgrounds have entrance control stations and gates to prevent unwelcomed visitors from entering the property, campground hosts that watch for inappropriate behavior in the campground, rules that require campers and their guests to be quiet after 10 P.M., park patrols that monitor activities in

Most large state and federal parks have entrance control stations that prevent unwanted people from entering the campground.

Most large state and federal parks, such as Turkey Run State Park (Indiana), provide a safe and comfortable family atmosphere.

the campground after dark, law enforcement officers and park personnel who are trained to remove disorderly people and dangerous critters, and other security measures. By virtue of these efforts, virtually all state and national parks are safe for families and their children. But a few smaller campgrounds, especially national forest and county park campgrounds, have occasional problems with drunkenness and disorderly behavior. Therefore, campers should investigate these campgrounds before deciding to spend the night in them.

Best Campgrounds

Veteran campers hold a wide range of opinions regarding the best campgrounds. For example, *The Best in Tent Camping* series published by Menasha Ridge Press recommends remote and private campgrounds where tent campers can escape RVs, concrete slabs, generator noise, and loud radios. National Geographic has recognized about five parks in each state as having exceptional historical or scenic significance. Reserve America, TripleBlaze, Yahoo Sports, and Lumberjack websites use various criteria to rank parks and campgrounds in terms of their overall popularity and recreational opportunities. Horse riders prefer campgrounds that have bridle trails, tack shops, hitching posts, and stables. Fishermen prefer campgrounds that are located near good fishing spots with boat ramps. And RVers prefer open campgrounds with few trees, pull-through sites, 50-amp electrical service, and dump stations.

Eva and I prefer large family campgrounds near our travel route or destination with good overnight security, large level and widely spaced sites, plenty of trees providing shade and anchor points for our hammocks, clean bathrooms with flush toilets, hot showers, and plenty of recreational opportunities. Our camping trips are typically touring trips during which we travel around 2,000 miles through the Lake Michigan states, stop for a night or two at selected campgrounds, visit local tourist attractions, and then move on to the next destination. On a typical trip, we spend two to three weeks on the road, sleep in a small four-person tent, camp in five to ten different campgrounds, and cook most of our meals in the campsite. We would rather camp near other tent campers but frequently find that the best campsites are in the modern camp-grounds that attract numerous RVs. Over the past few years, we have discovered that large state and federal campgrounds with at least fifty campsites plus a few larger county and municipal campgrounds meet our expectations better than smaller more remote campgrounds.

In view of these diverse opinions, each chapter in this book will sum-marize all public campgrounds in the state and indicate campgrounds

that have been named by other authorities as some of the best. In addition, I will note those campgrounds that are our per-sonal favorites. These opinions are presented to help readers nar-row their campground choices down to the ones that best fit their particular preferences. As readers will notice, many of the public campgrounds in the four states have been praised by one authority or another.

In addition to flush toilets and hot showers, many large state parks now offer WiFi connectivity. Photo by Eva Douglass.

Campground Listings

At the end of each chapter, all public campgrounds in the state are listed and organized by geographic location, management authority, and number of campsites. For each campground, key details such as location, amenities, and recreational opportunities are provided to help readers make informed judgments about their suitability as possible vacation destinations. To save space, the following abbreviations will be used.

CG   Campground
COE   U.S. Army Corps of Engineers
CP   County Park
CR   County Road

DNR	Department of Natural Resources
FP	Forest Preserve
FWA	State Fish and Wildlife Area
MP	Municipal or City Park
NF	National Forest
NLS	National Lakeshore
NP	National Park
NRA	National Recreation Area
NSR	National Scenic River
NWR	National Wildlife Refuge
P sites	Primitive sites with pit or vault toilets and no showers
PUA	Public Use Area
RA	Recreation Area
RD	Road
SF	State Forest
SHS	State Historic Site
SP	State Park
SRA	State Recreation Area
SR	State Road

GPS Coordinates

Navigating with a GPS receiver is an easy way to find new campgrounds in unfamiliar regions. To help readers find their selected campgrounds, the campground listings at the end of each chapter include GPS coordinates in the decimal degree format. These GPS coordinates were compiled in a variety of ways. Many were copied directly from the campground's official website. More were copied from websites that handle campground reservations. For example, coordinates for several federal properties were copied from www.Recreation.gov and coordinates for several state parks were copied from www.ReserveAmerica.com. Coordinates for Army Corps of Engineers recreation areas were copied from the book, *Camping with the Corps of Engineers*.

When coordinates were not available, street addresses were entered into www.itouchmap.com. When street addresses were unavailable for smaller campgrounds in rural areas, campground coordinates were approximated by using published driving directions to locate the property on www.itouchmap.com. About one hundred of these coordinates have been personally verified. Although reasonable efforts were made to assure the accuracy of all GPS coordinates, errors are possible when copying and transposing over seven hundred coordinates. Therefore, readers should cautiously use given coordinates in conjunction with state highway maps and posted highway signs when navigating to a particular property.

Planning

Over my lifetime, I have encountered dozens of problems during various camping trips. Whenever problems emerged, I tried to solve them in camp but sometimes did not have the knowledge or equipment needed to solve them and had to cut my trip short. In talking with other campers, I have learned that I am not the only person to encounter problems on camping trips. Most of my experienced tent camping friends tell numerous stories about essential items left at home, arriving at planned destinations only to discover that all campsites were occupied, spending several days in awful campsites located next to smelly trash dumpsters or high traffic areas, having food eaten and equipment damaged by animals, spending hours drying clothing and sleeping bags that were soaked by heavy rains, and other common camping problems. Over the past forty plus years, I have learned many tricks and procedures to assure safe and enjoyable camping trips. Perhaps the most important lesson I learned is that advance planning is the key to avoiding most camping disasters.

Planning is especially important for long-distance trips since camping problems—coupled with an inability to get home quickly—can be especially traumatic. As a consequence, many people—including those with considerable tent camping experience—choose to sleep in motels and eat in restaurants during their long-distance trips. Until now, finding safe and comfortable motel rooms in unfamiliar regions of the country has been much easier than finding safe and comfortable campgrounds—and staying in motels requires much less planning. For most of my life, I was one of these part-time campers. While I took frequent camping trips to state and national parks near my home and in Wisconsin, I spent many more nights in motel rooms during my trips to and from various vacation destinations.

Had we not made advance reservations, we would have been disappointed to see this "Lot Full" sign at Charles Mears State Park (Michigan).

Unfortunately, these motel-based vacation trips have now become pro-hibitively expensive, costing thousands of dollars each week.

Within the past five years, planning has become even more impor-tant for safe and comfortable tent camping vacations. Many popular state and federal campgrounds have revised their procedures for assign-ing campsites and enforcing appropriate behavior. Popular campgrounds now offer few, if any, campsites for last minute arrivals and require that all campsites be set up before 10 P.M. To secure a good campsite in popular tourist destinations, families must go to the Internet several days or weeks before their trip dates, select an available campsite, and make their reservations before actually viewing the campground or its campsites. After arriving at many campgrounds, families will discover increased emphasis upon park rules and appropriate behavior. Many campgrounds now have entrance control stations, restrictions on pos-session of alcoholic beverages, and stronger law enforcement presence designed to protect park property and discourage disorderly behavior, reckless driving, and other inappropriate behaviors that were often over-looked only ten years ago.

To avoid common problems and secure the best sites in the most popular campgrounds, families must plan their tent camping vacations weeks, if not months, before the actual departure date. Here are my sug-gestions for planning these trips:

- Acquire camping equipment and skills. To acquire these skills, talk with experienced camping authorities and read books such as my *The Tent Camper's Handbook* available from Amazon.com.
- Gather additional information about possible destinations. Use-ful sources include state DNR websites, state tourism publica-tions, published guidebooks, and YouTube (www.youtube.com) videos.
- Understand differences between state parks, state forests, na-tional parks, national forests, national wilderness areas, county park campgrounds, and municipal park campgrounds.
- After gathering as much information as possible, select camp-ground destinations that offer the amenities and recreational opportunities that match your family's interests.
- Set trip dates early so that you can secure a good campsite in your selected campground.
- Use campground maps and campsite photos on the Internet to select the best available campsite within your chosen camp-ground.

- Make reservations as soon as possible to assure that your site will be available on the day of your arrival. Go to the park's website and follow directions. Most state park websites will redirect you to www.ReserveAmerica.com and most federal park websites will redirect you to www.recreation.gov.
- Plan travel route and overnight camps. Get state highway maps and consult websites such as MapQuest to decide which highways to take and which campgrounds to select for overnight camps. When traveling more than four hundred miles, such as from Alabama to Wisconsin or Michigan, plan at least one overnight camp along the way to the destination and another camp on the way back home.
- Plan meals and food storage so that you can save money by preparing a few meals in the campsite and protect your food from animal access. Squirrels, raccoons, and mice will eat food, damage storage containers, and shred paper wrappers around the campsite. In a few parks, skunks can cause unpleasant consequences and bears can pose a danger when food is left unattended in campsites. To prevent animal problems, pack food in sealable plastic containers and keep it in your car trunk as much as possible. Never bring food, candy, or clothing with food odors into your tent!
- Pack several days before the trip so that you will have time to restock supplies such as toothpaste, soap, and batteries and remember items that may have been initially forgotten. Use packing guides such as the one at the end of this chapter to assist packing.
- Depart early in the morning so that you will have time to reach your destination by early afternoon and explore nearby activities and attractions.
- Pack clothing and gear for weather extremes and monitor weather forecasts so that you can adjust your clothing and activities accordingly. On daily excursions, pack warm clothes and rain gear in small daypacks.
- Limit alcohol consumption and obey park rules so that public campgrounds will be safe and enjoyable vacation destinations for other families and their children.
- Observe Leave-No-Trace Guidelines to help preserve beautiful scenery, wildlife, and other natural resources in the park for future generations. If you are unfamiliar with these guidelines, please visit www.lnt.org.

Conclusion

Basic tent camping offers a safe and economical way to travel that provides opportunities to experience unique and exciting attractions plus
innumerable intangible benefits that help to improve overall mental
health. Well-planned camping vacations allow people to escape the
constant pressures of their jobs, family stresses, friends' problems, daily
household chores, needed home repairs, and so on. Camping trips allow
people to communicate with their spouses, re-bond with their children,
and appreciate the glory of God's creation. Campers can relax in their
hammock or chair, read books, listen to music, enjoy peaceful walks
or hikes, learn about history and ecology, become more self-sufficient,
observe wild animals, smell exotic aromas drifting through the campground, stare into crackling campfires, and hear owls or a gentle rain
falling on the tent at night. All of these experiences combine to refresh
the spirit and help people return to their daily routine with renewed
strength and enthusiasm.

For more information about the equipment, clothing, and skills
needed to plan safe and comfortable tent camping vacations, consider
reading my other book, *The Tent Camper's Handbook.*

*Peninsula State Park (Wisconsin) has been my primary
vacation destination for the past eighteen years.*

Many parks in the Lake Michigan states, such as Brigham County Park (Dane County, Wisconsin), display vivid yellow, red, and orange fall colors during September.

There is no telling what campers might see next. One afternoon this large snapping turtle meandered through our Peninsula State Park (Wisconsin) campsite while we were eating supper.

This sandhill crane and two of its companions were enjoying a warm summer afternoon in the Ottawa Campground of Kettle Moraine State Forest— Southern Unit (Wisconsin). Photo by Eva Douglass.

One of life's greatest pleasures is taking a mid-day siesta in a hammock. Photo by Eva Douglass.

Spending several hours staring into the flickering flames of a cozy campfire is another one of life's great pleasures.

This wild hen turkey and her brood could be seen strolling around Rock Cut State Park (Illinois) campground one summer morning.

Fort Mackinac on Mackinac Island (Michigan), in the straits connecting Lakes Michigan and Huron, demonstrates life during the War of 1812.

Many parks such as Lincoln State Park (Indiana) offer boat rentals and other recreational opportunities.

Camping Gear Packing Guide

Shelter—packed in a large duffle bag.
- Essential: tent with ground cloth (or footprint), poles, & doormat(s).
- Optional: kitchen shelter.

Bedding—packed in a large duffle bag.
- Essential for each person: mattress & sleeping bag.
- Optional: ground blanket, sheet, small blanket, pillowcases, & pillows.

Tools—packed in small tool bag.
- Essential: cord, multi-tool/knife, hatchet, tent stakes, channel lock pliers, duct tape, gloves, & microfiber towel.
- Optional: screw drivers, crow bar, 6 carabineers, 6 spring clips, 6 small marbles (for making emergency tarp attachment points), pole repair tube, sewing kit, & whisk broom.

Furniture—packed in a large duffle bag.
- Essential: tablecloth with two tie-down cords.
- Optional: folding chairs for each person, folding table, & 2 bath mats.

Clothing—packed in soft duffle bags & daypack.
- First day: underwear, shirt, pants/shorts/dress, travel vest, socks, shoes or boots, & hat.
- In cool weather add: base layer pants, extra shirts, insulated jacket, & gloves.
- Essential for each person: knit cap, underwear (2), socks (2), shirts (3), pants/shorts/dress (1), athletic pants, rain jacket, & laundry detergent.
- Optional for each person: laundry bag, extra underwear, socks, shirts, pants/shorts/dresses, hats, & shoes.

Personal Items—packed in pockets & soft ditty bags.
- Essential: highway map, pocket knife, sunglasses, cell phone, folded paper towel, camera, medicine, daypack, 2 headlamps with extra batteries, shower bag, bath towel, wash cloth, soap, shower shoes, toothbrush, toothpaste, floss, razor, hair brush, nail clips, & liquid hand soap.

- Optional: GPS receiver, hammocks, weather radio, digital audio player, computer, DVD player, chargers, hair dryer, extension cord, books, games, movies, bug net, water shoes, fishing tackle, tennis racquets, hitch-mounted bike rack, bikes, roof rack system, canoes, golf clubs, & solar charger.

Protection & First-Aid—packed in vehicle.
- Essential: sun screen, insect repellent, hand sanitizer, Band-Aids, 3 sterile pads, elastic bandage, Ibuprofen, aspirin, Benadryl, antibiotic ointment, burn jell, itch eraser, & poison ivy cream.

Kitchen—packed in milk crates.
- Essential: water bottle, cup, & spoon for each person, tongs, 3 butane cigarette lighters, small "GI" can opener, paper towels, dish cloth, & dish detergent.
- Basic options: aluminum foil, spatula, nylon stirring spoon, kitchen knife, 2 dish towels, & cooking grate.
- Motorcycle options: backpack stove, fuel canister, 1-quart boiler, small bowl for each person, small soft-side cooler, & 1 water jug.
- Small car options: backpacking stove, fuel canister, small cook set, 8-inch frying pan, small salad plate & bowl for each person, medium hard-side cooler, & 2 water jugs.
- Large car options: 2-burner propane stove, fuel cylinder, large cook set, 10-inch frying pan, 4 dinner plates and bowls, large hard side cooler, 4 water jugs, charcoal, cooking tripod, Dutch oven.

Non-perishable foods—packed in a bucket and a milk crate.
- Essential: instant oatmeal packs, tea bags, hot chocolate, honey, salt, garlic salt, & onion.
- Optional: tortillas, olive oil, hamburger buns, pancake mix, bagels, dry cereal, breakfast bars, breakfast pastries, peanut butter, canned tuna or chicken, dehydrated rice & pasta meals, packaged seasonings for spaghetti, sloppy joes, & fettuccine alfredo, hamburger helper meals, Ramen Noodles, jalapeño peppers, canned vegetables, canned fruit, fresh vegetables, fresh fruit, chips, snacks, & cookies.

Perishable foods—packed in a cooler.
- Essential: milk, cheese, mayonnaise, eggs, & butter.
- Optional: Italian salad dressing, pickles, syrup, bacon, kielbasa, steaks, ketchup, mustard, cream cheese, sour cream, juice, & pop.

Wisconsin

2

Wisconsin

This guide to family camping vacations begins with the state of Wisconsin for four important reasons. First, Wisconsin occupies the central position within the midwestern states and serves as the primary vacation destination for many people living around the midwestern, eastern, and southern United States. Second, Wisconsin has historically been a leader in developing public recreational areas and social services for average working-class families. Third, the state attracts *many* more tent camping families than other midwestern states. And finally, Wisconsin was my home for nine years and my primary summertime camping destination for the past thirty-four.

Wisconsin's nickname, "The Badger State," reportedly was based upon survival strategies used by Cornish immigrants who came to southwestern Wisconsin during the 1820s and 1830s to work in the lead mines. To survive the brutal Wisconsin winters, these immigrants dug holes into the hillsides, similar to badger holes, to survive the winter weather. In effect, these Cornish miners were some of the first European campers to visit in Wisconsin, and they did so in the harshest winter conditions. Anyone who wants to learn more about the lives of these early immigrants can ride over to Mineral Point in the southwestern corner of the state and visit the Pendarvis Historical Area.

Wisconsin could just as easily have been nicknamed, "The Festival State." Throughout the summer and fall camping season, parties and festivals are held every weekend all over the state. These parties and festivals usually combine food (such as bratwurst or fish), alcoholic beverages (usually beer), music (frequently polka bands), games (including pool, Euchre, and bar dice), zany Wisconsin one-liners, cheese curds, and lots of fun. Many years ago, Friday nights became a popular party night because it was the time when dairy farmers and their families "cleaned up" and came into town to shop and socialize. Furthermore, since about half of Wisconsin's population was Catholic, taverns began offering Friday night fish fries, and these fish fries along with Friday night tavern socialization became a well-established Wisconsin tradition.

Most towns have at least one special festival or event every year. Milwaukee offers several. Summerfest is scheduled during the first week of July and books many well-known popular entertainers. State Fair falls during the first week of August and appeals to people from rural areas, families, and older folks. German Fest, Irish Fest, Mexican Fiesta and other ethnic festivals are scheduled other weekends. Chippewa Falls hosts the Frenchtown Annual Tube Float and Regatta (FATFAR) every June. New Glarus features polka music and dancing at the New Glarus Hotel every Friday and Saturday night, the Heidi Fest every June, and the Wilhelm Tell Festival every September. La Crosse stages an Oktoberfest every fall. Furthermore, many more cities sponsor such events as baseball games and football games that provide the occasion for tailgating and partying before and sometimes long after the game.

Mexican Fiesta in Milwaukee (2013).

Wisconsin was one of the first states in the nation to consider establishing a state park. In 1878, the Wisconsin legislature authorized the creation of The State Park, to be located in Vilas County, about 200 miles north of Madison. The intent of the park was to protect the fragile headwater area from the lumberjack's ax. Unfortunately, lumber barons were more powerful than park supporters at the time and eventually gained control over the land. In 1895, the Wisconsin state legislature tried again to create a state park and passed a bill authorizing the creation of Interstate Park to protect the Dalles (or dells) area of the St Croix River. This Interstate Park was finally established in 1900. Seven years later, John Nolin drafted a master plan for a Wisconsin State Parks System. Within the next five years, he led efforts to establish Peninsula and Devil's Lake parks. In 1925, the state tried again to establish a park in northern Vilas County and successfully created the Northern Highland/ American Legion State Forest a few miles north of the location of the previously proposed state park.

Today, the Wisconsin Department of Natural Resources (DNR) manages thirty-seven state parks, nine state forests, two state recreation areas, and two state trails with campgrounds.

Several of these parks and forests have two or more separate campgrounds, and most of these campgrounds have their own unique character. As a general rule, campgrounds tend to be more rustic than campgrounds in the other three Lake Michigan states. Campsites are typically large and well spaced with considerable understory vegetation (including poison ivy) between most sites providing partial or full privacy from neighboring sites. Park employees and park visitors tend to be exceptionally friendly and eager to talk with fellow campers whenever the occasion presents itself. My primary complaint of many Wisconsin state parks is that many campgrounds have smelly outhouses and a few small bathrooms that are unable to handle the large numbers of people who camp in many parks. On busy weekends, bathrooms in many campgrounds are damp, dingy, and smelly.

The state DNR website (www.dnr.wi.gov) provides brief overviews of all parks and recreation areas along with a link to the *Reserve America* website to reserve campsites. The *Reserve America* website provides additional information about each property, campground maps, and photos of individual campsites. Reservations may also be made by calling ReserveAmerica's Customer Service line, listed in the Useful Resources section at the end of this chapter, during normal business hours. In addition to campsite rental fees, the Wisconsin DNR requires park visitors to purchase a park pass. In 2014, Wisconsin park admission fees are: residents over age 64, $3 daily or $10 annual; residents, $7 daily or $25 annual; non-residents, $10 daily or $35 annual.

Three federal agencies manage seven properties with campgrounds in the state of Wisconsin. The U.S. Forest Service manages two national forests in the northern half of the state, and each forest has over a dozen campgrounds. The National Park Service (NPS) manages the Apostle Islands National Lakeshore with canoe-in campsites on fifteen islands located in Lake Superior, as well as the Saint Croix National Scenic Riverway along the banks of the Saint Croix and Namekagon rivers with several canoe-in campsites. The U.S. Army Corps of Engineers manages three public-use areas (PUA) on the western side of the state, and each PUA has a nice campground.

County and municipal governments in the state manage eighty-nine additional parks with developed campgrounds suited for tent camping. Most of these campgrounds provide safe and comfortable camping destinations but a few may not. Campers should investigate these properties before deciding to stay.

Wisconsin also has seven U.S. wilderness areas. The Gaylord Nelson Wilderness Area is located in the Apostle Islands and is managed by the National Park Service. Blackjack Springs, Headwaters, Porcupine Lake, Rainbow Lake, and Whisker Lake are located in the two national forests and are managed by the U.S. Forest Service. Wisconsin Islands are three small islands located in Lake Michigan adjacent to Door County and are managed by the U.S. Fish and Wildlife Service.

In total, Wisconsin has 187 public campgrounds spread across the state. To summarize these campgrounds and their respective recreational activities, I shall divide the state into four geographic regions. Within each region, I will summarize popular tourist attractions and feature a few recommended campgrounds. At the end of this chapter, I will list all of Wisconsin's public campgrounds along with key details needed to evaluate their location, popularity, amenities, and activities.

Southwestern Region: The Driftless Area

The southwestern region, frequently called the Driftless or unglaciated area, is defined as the area that is south of a line running from La Crosse to Coloma (along I-90 and State Road 21), and west of I-39. The western border of this southwestern region is defined by the Mississippi River and the southern border is defined by the Illinois state line. Reference cities in this region include Madison (the state capital) located on the eastern edge of the region, La Crosse, Prairie Du Chien, and Dubuque, Iowa, located on the Mississippi River, and Janesville located in the southeastern corner. Through the middle of this region, the Wisconsin River flows out to the Mississippi River. Topographically, this region has miles of rolling hills and valleys that were spared by past glacial advances. Within these rolling hills, campers will find many dairy farms and small rivers. Lakes Mendota, Monona, Waubesa, Kesonga, and Wingra, located in the city of Madison, provide many recreational opportunities as does Dutch Hollow Lake, Yellowstone Lake, and Blackhawk Lake scattered across the region.

The state's top rated tourist attraction, Wisconsin Dells, is located on the Wisconsin River in the northeastern corner of this region. The Dells is a narrow gorge carved by glacial ice sheets thousands of years ago. Today, the area has numerous public campgrounds, private campgrounds, hotels, souvenir shops, and tourist attractions that draw thousands of visitors every year. The main attractions of the area are scenic boat tours through the upper and lower Dells featuring unusual rock formations. Excursions on amphibious ducks that travel on both land and water are also popular.

Another popular vacation destination in this region is the Madison area, which features several summer festivals plus numerous cultural, sporting, and political events. Spring Green, located about forty miles west of Madison, features numerous Frank Lloyd Wright–styled buildings, art galleries, unique shops, restaurants, and a live Shakespeare theatre. Several towns host ethnic festivals throughout the summer. Madison and Waunakee feature German restaurants and festivals. Mineral Point displays their Cornish traditions. New Glarus features Swiss-German food and traditions in many ways. Mount Horeb and Westby feature Norwegian traditions.

Southwestern Wisconsin's extensive bike trails and rivers draw many more tourists. The Military Ridge, Sugar River, Cheese Country, and Elroy-Sparta bike trails are four of the more popular trails in the Midwest. Bike riders must secure trail passes before entering the trails. The Wisconsin River with its lazy current and shifting sandbars plus several smaller rivers such as the Pine, Kickapoo, or Pecatonica draw thousands of paddling enthusiasts every year. Hikers can tackle any of the state trails or the Ice Age Trail that runs along the eastern edge of the region.

The Wisconsin Department of Natural Resources manages sixteen state parks and one state bicycle trail with campgrounds in this region. Tent campers planning vacations in this region may want to consider one of the following destinations.

Devil's Lake State Park (407 sites)**,** in the northeastern corner of this region near Baraboo, was established in 1911 as the third oldest park in the state and has been named by *National Geographic* and *Reserve America* as one of the best state parks in the United States. With three family campgrounds and nine group campsites, Devil's Lake is the largest and most popular state park in the region. It is one of my favorite camping destinations because it is located near Wisconsin's most popular tourist destination—Wisconsin Dells—and has many challenging hiking trails. The park features a small lake surrounded by quartzite bluffs, large boulder fields, loess hills, and a terminal moraine created by a combination of prehistoric geologic events and glacial advances.

Devil's Lake State Park's balanced rock is a frequently photographed landmark along the Balanced Rock Trail.

Within the park, campers can enjoy swimming, canoeing, fishing, scuba diving, mountain biking, hiking, rappelling, rock climbing, and geological educational programs at the nature center. The Balanced Rock Trail and East Bluff Trail are moderately strenuous but well worth the effort. Their rewards are beautiful views of glacial rock formations, Devil's Lake, and the rolling hills of southwestern Wisconsin. In addition to the Dells, visitors can easily ride to the Ringling Brothers Circus World Museum in Baraboo.

Governor Dodge State Park (270 sites), just north of Dodgeville in the center of the Driftless Area, is the second most popular park in the region. The park, named by both *The Best in Tent Camping: Wisconsin* and *TripleBlaze* as one of the best camping destinations in the state, is also one of my favorite camping destinations because it is located in the middle of several tourist attractions in the area. It features over

Governor Dodge State Park, located in the center of the Driftless Area, is a popular camping destination. This is site #61 in the Cox Hollow Campground.

five thousand acres of steep rolling hills with intermittent forested and prairie areas. Two family campgrounds (Cox Hollow and Twin Valley) are located within the park along with a group camp, six backpacking campsites, and eleven equestrian sites. Most sites in the family campgrounds are large and well suited for tents. Sites #1 through # 44 in the Cox Hollow Campground are particularly well suited, being large, level, and shady sites. When I first camped in this park during the early 1970s, most campsites were open prairie lands with virtually no vegetation, but today, trees and understory vegetation provide abundant shade and privacy between sites.

The park offers forty miles of trails suited for hiking, mountain biking, and horseback riding, plus a short bike lane along State Highway 23 that connects with the forty-mile long Military Ridge Bicycle Trail running from Dodgeville to Verona. In addition to the trails, campers will find two swimming beaches and concession areas. Near the park, campers can enjoy horse rentals, canoeing on the Wisconsin River, touring the Lands' End telephone and distribution center, browsing artists' shops in Spring Green, and watching great plays at The American Players Outdoor Theatre. Visitors in the park should be warned to avoid contact with the wild parsnip that grows near many campsites because brief contact can produce severe skin irritation.

Yellowstone Lake State Park (128 sites), on a man-made lake near the center of the Driftless Area, is another popular camping destination in this region. Early plans to build the lake were proposed in 1949, but the lake was not completed until 1954. The family campground, located on a hill above the lake, has two camping loops. The East Campground seems to be a little more popular but both campgrounds offer large, level sites with partial shade and considerable privacy. Shower buildings in the campground are especially nice. Within the park, campers can enjoy relaxing on the beach, swimming in

Yellowstone Lake State Park is a popular fishing destination in southwestern Wisconsin.

the lake, or fishing for walleye, muskie, bluegill, or catfish. Just outside the park, bikers will enjoy the Cheese Country Trail whereas history enthusiasts will enjoy touring Mineral Point and the Pendarvis Historic Site. A little farther away from the park, campers may enjoy touring the first state capital near Belmont, Swiss towns of New Glarus and Monroe, and the Norwegian town of Mount Horeb.

Blue Mound State Park (78 sites), atop the highest hill in southern Wisconsin about twenty-five miles west of Madison, has been one of my favorite camping destinations for the past fifteen years. For campers who value both privacy and hot showers, this is the park to visit. The large secluded campsites are widely spaced along a winding road in a heavily forested area. Thick understory plus space between campsites gives the feeling of isolation. Inside the park, campers can enjoy a large swimming pool and observation tower that offers spectacular views of the Driftless Area or unglaciated hills of southwestern Wisconsin. For those who bring bicycles, the short trail down the hill connects with the forty-mile-long Military Ridge Bike Trail. A left turn at the trail gives bikers the opportunity to explore Mount Horeb, Riley's Tavern, and Verona. A right turn takes riders to Barneveld, Ridgeway, and Dodgeville. But be warned—after a long day of biking, the ride back up the hill to the campground is a killer! Within a few miles of the park, campers will find Cave of the Mounds, Little Norway's Niessedahle (a Norwegian homestead and church), Mount Horeb's Troll Stroll, and weekend Norwegian festivals.

Blue Mound State Park offers many large, widely spaced, and secluded sites. This is site #26.

Blue Mound State Park sits atop the highest hill in southern Wisconsin. This photo was taken from the Military Ridge Bicycle Trail.

New Glarus Woods State Park has a small rustic campground in a popular tourist area. This is site #16.

New Glarus Woods State Park (34 rustic sites), about twenty-five miles southwest of Madison, is another one of my favorite camping destinations. Although the park lacks flush toilets and showers, it is located near the town of New Glarus that features Swiss shops, restaurants, music, and festivals all summer long. The campground is spread across a heavily forested ridge top. Drive-in campsites offer considerable space, shade, and privacy but walk-in (or bike-in) sites tend to be small, shady, and damp. The park has a short bike trail that goes into the town of New Glarus and connects with the twenty-four-mile long Sugar River Trail. On Friday and Saturday nights, campers can check out the Swiss fondue or Swiss buffet and polka music at the New Glarus Hotel. Visitors to the area should also sample one of the award-winning beers brewed at the New Glarus Brewery. During the day, area visitors may explore the many unique European-style shops and listen for the Glockenspiel (a German-styled bell tower that plays music on the hour) or drive down to Monroe and visit the Huber Brewery and Brennan's Market for an outstanding selection of produce cheese, meats, beer, and wine.

The U.S. Army Corps of Engineers manages two campgrounds in this southwestern region. Both campgrounds are located near the Mississippi River. **Blackhawk Campground** (173 sites) located twenty-five miles south of La Crosse is the largest COE campground. **Grant River Recreation Area** (63 sites) is located fifteen miles north of Dubuque.

County and municipal governments in the southwestern region manage fifteen additional public campgrounds. **Goose Island Park** (400 sites), located in Lacrosse County on an island in the Mississippi River about three miles south of La Crosse, is the largest of these county parks and one of my favorite camping destinations. The campground is spread along the riverbank and offers many amenities, including a swimming beach, canoe and kayak rentals, camp store, fishing supplies, laundry, and WiFi connectivity. Near the park, visitors will find many cultural and recreational activities in La Crosse and the surrounding area. Popular tourist attractions include the Heileman Brewery and the *La Crosse Queen* river cruise. A few tourists may want to spend a day at the Riverside Amusement Park. During the early 1970s, my wife and I spent several weekends here and especially enjoyed camping trips during the La Crosse Oktoberfest weekends. Although the weather was frosty and other campers were rowdy, I have great memories of this park. Campers who prefer a smaller campground near La Crosse may want to consider **Veterans Memorial Park** located on the La Crosse River a few miles east of the city.

Castle Rock County Park (300 sites) in Juneau County near Mauston, and **Castle Rock Park** (200 sites) in Adams County near Friendship are two large county campgrounds located on Castle Rock Lake along the Wisconsin River. **Sidie Hollow Park** (73 sites) in Viroqua and **Blackhawk Memorial Park** (38 primitive sites) near Argyle were both named by *The Best in Tent Camping: Wisconsin* as two of the more private campgrounds in the region. Several smaller municipal park campgrounds are located along the Pecatonica River for canoe enthusiasts who want to take overnight trips down the river. Other county parks in this region that I have personally visited are briefly described below.

Brigham Park (25 primitive sites) is located in Dane County on a second hill adjacent to Blue Mound State Park. A large stand of maple trees provides ample shade for all sites and thick understory vegetation provides privacy for the sites in the back of the campground. A camp host is on duty most nights and weekends through the summer camping season. Other than the lack of showers and flush toilets, Brigham offers the same activities as the adjacent Blue Mounds State Park. On the north side of the park, visitors can enjoy spectacular views of the Driftless rolling hills of southern Wisconsin. Campers can ride over to the state park to swim and shower for a minimal fee. Bicyclists can ride down the hill and connect with the Military Ridge Bike Trail. Campers who want to tour the surrounding area can easily drive to Mount Horeb, Dodgeville, Mineral Point, Prairie du Chien, Spring Green, Madison, and various attractions located in southwestern Wisconsin. Although it is not a very popular camping destination in the region, I wanted to feature Brigham Park because I served as its campground host for three summers during the mid-1990s and dedicated this guide to its park manager—Ernie

Grinder—who became a good friend and life mentor. Unfortunately, the park and campground has attracted fewer and fewer campers over the past five years.

Mendota, Babcock, and Token Creek are three other Dane County parks with safe and comfortable campgrounds. In contrast to Brigham, all three of these county parks have showers and flush toilets in the campground. Furthermore, all three are located near Madison and, thus, offer economical places to stay while touring the state capitol, people watching on State Street, or enjoying various museums, plays, concerts, and sporting events at the University of Wisconsin. Of the three, Mendota Park, located on the shores of Lake Mendota on the north side of town, is my favorite campground because of its scenic lakeshore and proximity to Madison. My only complaint is that it, compared with the other two Dane County Parks, is farther away from the state Capitol and university. Babcock, located on the southeast side of town, is much closer to the Capitol and university plus it offers a lot of amenities for boaters and fishermen. Token Creek, located on the eastern side of Madison, is conveniently located near the I-90/94 expressway.

Southeastern Region: Milwaukee Attractions

The southeastern region is defined as the area that is south of a line running from Coloma east to Manitowoc (along State Road 21 and US Highway 151) and east of I-39 running south from Coloma to Rockford, Illinois. The eastern border of this region is defined by Lake Michigan and the southern border is defined by the Illinois state line. Reference cites in this region are Milwaukee, Racine, and Sheboygan, located on the shores of Lake Michigan, plus Fond du Lac located in the northern edge of the region, and Madison and Janesville located on the western edge. The southern tip of Lake Winnebago extends down into this region from the northeastern region. Long years ago, this region was covered by glaciers. As a result, it has a flat topography that is the home of many immaculately manicured dairy farms mixed with glacial fields, small kettle lakes, and large population centers.

Recreational activities and attractions in the southeastern region are largely based in the Milwaukee area. Milwaukee offers professional sports, an outstanding zoo, theatre, concerts, museums, cultural festivals almost every weekend through the summer, shopping, boat tours, and various water sports. Summerfest, scheduled about the first week in July and State Fair, scheduled about the first week in August, are two of the more popular festivals. Tourists who plan to visit either of these two events or one of the other summer festivals should plan to spend six to eight hours at the festival grounds to be able to enjoy all of the many activities. Milwaukee also has many great restaurants, but my favorite is Karl Ratzsch's located in the downtown area. This restaurant is world renown and offers an excellent selection of authentic German cuisine, including sauerbraten and kasseler rippchen.

Other popular tourist destinations near Milwaukee include the Ice Age National Scenic Trail that meanders through the Kettle Moraine State Forest and other parts of this region, Six Flags Great America Amusement Park, about forty miles to the south, the Alpine Valley Music Theatre thirty-five miles to the southwest, Old World Wisconsin living history museum about twenty-five miles to the southwest, Horicon Marsh wildlife viewing areas about fifty miles to the northwest, fishing charters into Lake Michigan, Johnson's Wax Headquarters designed by Frank Lloyd Wright in Racine, and beaches located along the shores of Lake Michigan. About fifty miles west of Milwaukee, the Fireside Dinner Theatre in Fort Atkinson hosts many fine plays during the year.

The Wisconsin Department of Natural Resources manages five state parks, three state forests, one state recreation area, and one state trail with campgrounds within this southeastern region. The largest of these state properties are the Kettle Moraine State Forest—Northern Unit and Kettle Moraine State Forest—Southern Unit. These two units, along with other units, were established to create a publicly owned forest in southeastern Wisconsin and preserve numerous glacial features in the area. Tent campers planning vacations in this region may want to consider one of the following destinations.

Kettle Moraine State Forest—Northern Unit (335 sites), about forty miles north of Milwaukee, is the largest state camping area in the southeastern region and one of my favorite camping destinations because it has nice bathrooms, a nice beach, a nice bike trail, and is conveniently located near Milwaukee. This part of the forest has two large family campgrounds with showers. Mauthe Lake Recreation Area is the more popular of the two. Sites 215 to 223 feature lake views while sites 300 to 314 are located near the showers. Near the campground is a large playground/beach and concession area that attracts hundreds of visitors on nice summer weekends. The Long Lake Recreation Area, arranged as five loops along a forest road, is the larger of the two campgrounds in terms of the number of campsites and the number of shower buildings. The forest also offers a six-mile-long bike trail that connects the two family campgrounds, a backpacking area, and an equestrian campground. Activities within the forest include fishing, hiking, and exploring vari-

Kettle Moraine State Forest—Northern Unit has a beautiful picnic area and beach.

ous glacial formations. Thirty-one miles of the Ice Age National Scenic Trail travels through the forest and past glacial eskers and moraines. Visitors should also plan to tour the Ice Age Visitor Center. Outside the park, campers can enjoy day trips into Milwaukee and shorter trips over to parks on the shores of Lake Michigan.

Kettle Moraine State Forest—Southern Unit (201 sites), about thirty miles southwest of Milwaukee, is the second largest camping area in the region. This state forest, named by *TripleBlaze* and *The Best in Tent Camping: Wisconsin* as one of the best camping destinations in Wisconsin, has two family campgrounds with showers (Ottawa and Pinewoods, which share a common registration station) plus a primitive campground (Whitewater) with sixty-three campsites. Campsites in the Ottawa Campground are large, shady, and widely spaced. In addition, the

Kettle Moraine State Forest—Southern Unit is conveniently located just west of Milwaukee. This is site #358 in the Ottawa Lake Campground.

park offers several walk-up sites and an equestrian campground. Inside the forest, campers can enjoy two beaches plus opportunities for canoeing and fishing. Just outside the park, campers can rent horses and enjoy over eighty miles of bridle trails that weave through the park. Visitors to this area can enjoy the interesting exhibits, lectures, and demonstrations at the Old World Wisconsin museum and should plan to spend at least four hours there. Since the Southern Unit is only thirty miles away from Milwaukee, this park can be used as a base camp for visiting various tourist attractions in the city.

Richard Bong State Recreation Area (217 sites), about thirty miles south of Milwaukee, is the third largest camping destination in southeastern Wisconsin. The property has two family campgrounds (Sunrise and Sunset). Sunrise is closer to the entrance station and appears to be the more popular of the two campgrounds. Sites 1 through 30 in the first loop are best suited for tent campers because they have more trees and shade. The other sites in Sunrise and all of the sites in Sunset have full sun with few trees. Sunset, however, has a very nice bath and shower facility. Within the park, campers can enjoy swimming, fishing, hiking, viewing wildlife, and visiting the Molinaro Nature Center. Large groups may be able to reserve a special use area for horseback riding, off-road vehicles, hunting, or other activities. On the day of our visit, we saw a dozen children riding trail bikes on a dirt oval trail and several dozen hunters with their dogs. Outside the park, visitors can easily ride over to Lake Michigan and visit attractions in Racine or Kenosha, or they can ride up to Milwaukee.

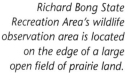
Richard Bong State Recreation Area's wildlife observation area is located on the edge of a large open field of prairie land.

Kohler-Andrae State Park (137 sites), on Lake Michigan about forty-five miles north of Milwaukee, initially began as two separate parks. The land for Terry Andrae State Park, donated to the state in 1927, was named in memory of the president of Julius Andrae and Sons' Electric Supply Company in Milwaukee. The land for John Michael Kohler State Park, donated to the state in 1966, was named in memory of the founder of the Kohler Plumbing manufacturing company. In subsequent years, the state acquired several more acres of land and merged the two parks. In addition to relaxing on the beach and swimming in Lake Michigan, campers may take time to visit the Sanderling Nature Center, hike the Creeping Juniper Nature Trail through the sand dunes, hike the Woodland Dunes Nature Trail through the sand dune forest, and visit the Black River Marsh Boardwalk. This park was one of my favorite camping destinations in the late 1970s and I fondly remember my two small sons playing in the sand near our campsites. As we recently discovered, campers who want to camp in this park on summer weekends must now make reservations several weeks ahead.

Big Foot Beach State Park (100 sites), on Lake Geneva near the Illinois state line, was named for a Potawatomie tribal chief who resided in the area about a century ago. This park is one of my favorite camping destinations because thirty years ago, while camping in this park, I decided to continue my education at the University of Wisconsin—Milwaukee rather than returning to the south where I grew up and where my extended family still lived. As a result of that decision, I spent four more years in Wisconsin and developed a love for the state and its camping destinations that has continued until this day. In many respects, that decision was one of the most important of my life. The park, located in an urban area, offers a very popular beach and swimming area on a crystal clear lake. The campground has a walk-in tent section and a car/ RV camping section with

Big Foot Beach State Park picnic and beach area is a popular destination on warm summer weekends. Photo by Eva Douglass.

electricity. In August 2013, the old shower building was closed and a temporary trailer with showers was parked in sites 98 and 100.

On nice summer weekends, hundreds of visitors flock to the beach area to moor their boats, bask in the sun, swim, and picnic. While camping at the park, visitors may want to take a scenic boat cruise around the lake, visit the Yerkes Observatory, and explore historical sites in the city of Lake Geneva that were frequented by Al Capone and other Chicago mobsters during the 1920s and '30s. Many campers also like to wander around the small shops in the town of Lake Geneva and enjoy some of the concerts presented around the lake. Big Foot Beach State Park is close enough to Milwaukee to permit day trips up to the city.

Cliffside County Park also has some of the cleanest campground bathrooms I have ever seen.

Cliffside County Park (Racine County) offers a safe and comfortable campground conveniently located near Milwaukee. This is site #23.

County and municipal governments in the southeastern region manage thirteen additional public campgrounds. **Cliffside Park** (92 sites), located in Racine, has the largest campground of these and is one of my favorite camping destinations. It is conveniently located near Milwaukee, with a family-friendly atmosphere, several large grassy sites, ample shade, and some of the nicest bathrooms I have ever seen in a public campground. The campground is divided into two sections—one has reservable sites while the other only accepts walk-ups. Since it frequently fills on summer weekends, campers must either reserve a site and pay an extra $11 or plan to arrive before Friday.

Muskego Park (24 sites), in Waukesha County about five miles southwest of Milwaukee, was one of my favorite places to camp near the Milwaukee area for several years. Campsites in this park are offered on a first-come, walk-up basis. Inside the park, campers will find a small swimming lake with a beach and showers. The primary reason for selecting this park is its close proximity to Milwaukee attractions. It allows campers to stay in the Milwaukee area for a fraction of the cost of staying in area hotels. In addition to visiting various Milwaukee attractions, campers may want to visit the Alpine Valley Music Theatre that has hosted many popular performers, the Old World Wisconsin living history village, and the Johnson's Wax building in Racine that features innovative architectural designs of Frank Lloyd Wright.

Naga-waukee Park (33 primitive sites) is another small Waukesha County park located near Milwaukee. This park provides a convenient base camp for visiting various activities and attractions on the western side of Milwaukee, such as the Milwaukee Zoo, Miller Park, and State Fair Park. Golfers may enjoy this park because its golf course is considered to be one of the best to be found anywhere in the Midwest. After camping here on two different trips, I concluded that it was a little too rustic and unsupervised for my tastes and decided to camp in other parks when visiting the Milwaukee area.

Mukwonago Park (30 sites), located about twenty miles southwest of Milwaukee, and **Menomonee Park** (33 sites), located about ten miles northwest, are two other Waukesha County parks that could be used as base camps when visiting the Milwaukee area. **Horicon Ledges Park** (46 sites) in Dodge County was named by *The Best in Tent Camping: Wisconsin* as one of the most secluded campgrounds in the state.

Northeastern Region: Door County

The northeastern region of Wisconsin is defined as the area north of a line running from Coloma to Manitowoc (along State Road 21 and US Highway 151) and east of a line that runs from Coloma north to the Michigan state line (along US Highway 51 to Woodruff). Within this region, Lake Michigan defines the eastern border and the Door County Peninsula is perhaps the most prominent feature of the shoreline. The peninsula juts out into the lake and forms Green Bay on its western shore. Lake Winnebago is located on the southern edge of the region and hundreds of small lakes are scattered around the area. The Menominee and Oneida Indian reservations can be found near Green Bay and the Nicolet National Forest plus many acres of state forest lands are located along the northern border. Reference cities in the region include Appleton near the southern edge, Stevens Point and Wausau on the western edge, and Green Bay near the center.

Within this region, campers will find at least five popular tourist and camping destinations. Perhaps the most popular of these destinations is Door County, located at the tip of Wisconsin's "thumb" that juts out into Lake Michigan. Four state parks and dozens of private campgrounds spread along the shores of Green Bay and Lake Michigan welcome thousands of campers every summer. Many people, including Eva and myself, return to this area year after year to enjoy the mild summer weather, live theatre, concerts, art galleries, unique specialty shops, and fish boils. The city of Green Bay is a second popular tourist destination. Packer fans come to tour Lambeau Field and eat at Curly's Pub—but be advised that one meal at this restaurant provides enough food for two out-of-state adults. Also located in Green Bay is the Heritage Hill living history museum. Marinette County is a third popular tourist destination. Campers and tourists come to see many beautiful waterfalls in the area. Canoe enthusiasts and kayakers enjoy paddling the Peshtigo River and various small lakes in the region. The Minocqua-Arbor Vita-Woodruff area is a fourth popular tourist destination in the region. Campers come here to fish and savor the real Northwoods experience. Finally, several popular parks and campgrounds are located along the Lake Michigan shore. Throughout the region, tourists will find Indian reservations, museums, powwows, and other Native American attractions. Hikers will find the eastern terminus of the Ice Age National Scenic Trail in southern Door County.

The Wisconsin Department of Natural Resources manages two state forests and seven state parks in this northeastern region. Tent campers planning vacations in this region may want to consider one of the following destinations.

The Northern Highland—American Legion (NHAL) State Forest (871 sites), in the Minocqua-Arbor Vita-Woodruff area near the Michigan border, was established in 1925 as one of Wisconsin's early state parks and is one of my favorite camping destinations. With over 230,000 acres, NHAL is the largest property in the state. Within the forest, campers will find four developed campgrounds with showers. Crystal Lake (100 sites), Big Muskellunge Lake (81 sites), and Firefly Lake (70 sites) are clustered together near the center of the forest. Clear Lake

Gene Tiser, retired superintendent of Peninsula State Park, joined us for a two-day camping and fishing trip to the Northern Highland/American Legion State Forest. This is site #308 in the Musky Lake Campground.

(98 sites) is located in the southern part of the forest. In 2013, we enjoyed camping in the Big Muskellunge Lake campground for a few days and paddling around the lake. Although our site was shown on the map as a lakeside site, the understory vegetation was so dense that we could not see the lake. In addition to these four developed campgrounds, the forest has fourteen primitive campgrounds ranging from 18 to 72 sites, two group campgrounds, 78 canoe campsites, and 12 wilderness campsites. Fishing, canoeing, bike riding, boat rentals, and water sports are popular activities around the forest. Outside the forest, campers can find a few shops and restaurants in Boulder Junction but a much better selection plus dozens of tourist activities in Minocqua, Arbor Vitae, and Woodruff. When traveling to campgrounds and recreational areas within this forest, use a map and GPS if possible because many highway directional signs are small and sometimes difficult to read.

Peninsula State Park (471 sites), on the Door County Peninsula that juts out into Lake Michigan, was established in 1910 as Wisconsin's second state park and currently ranks as the state's most popular camping destination. The park was named by *National Geographic* as one of the most scenic and historically significant state parks in the United States and is my all-time favorite camping destination. Two supervised entrance stations, dozens of friendly park employees, several campground hosts, visible park rangers and frequent park patrols help to create a safe and comfortable family environment. Five separate campgrounds are scattered about the park and each has its own unique character. Weborg Point is preferred by RVers while Welckler's Point

Over the past seventeen years, I have camped in about twenty different campsites in Peninsula State Park. In 2013, we stayed in site #612 in the North Nicolet Bay Campground.

Peninsula State Park's South Nicolet Bay campground is our favorite because it is close to the beach, concession area, WiFi pavilion, and theatre. This is site #782.

Peninsula State Park's beach is a popular destination on warm summer days.

Peninsula State Park's Nicolet Bay Store and Snack Bar are located in the middle of the picnic and beach area.

Peninsula State Park offers several pull-off points where visitors can enjoy scenic views of Green Bay. This one is on Skyline Road.

Peninsula State Park's Eagle Harbor and Eagle Bluff set the backdrop for spectacular sunsets almost every summer evening.

appeals to those who enjoy rustic camping experiences. South Nicolet Bay is my favorite because it is conveniently located near the beach, snack bar, and amphitheatre, but campsites, especially water-front sites, must be reserved as much as eleven months in advance. Most campsites in the park are large and shady with dirt, gravel, or grass floors but a few, especially in Tennison Bay, are open and crowded.

The park offers a swimming beach, canoe/kayak rentals, bicycle rentals, over twenty miles of bicycle trails, an operational lighthouse museum, an observation tower, a well-organized nature center, fabulous live plays almost every night of the summer, a golf course, and beautiful sunsets every evening. Visitors in the park should look for the elusive pileated woodpecker. Campers might want to eat a meal or two at the snack bar and shop in the camp store where coffee is available early every morning. Peter and Sue manage the store and snack bar and make cheeseburgers that are as good as any you can find outside the park. The primary limitations of the park are the small, old, over used bathrooms and shower facilities. Near the park, visitors will find charter fishing boats, charter cruises, kayak rentals, live theatre, concerts, art galleries, fish boils, many great restaurants, and so much more. My favorite restaurants near the park are Pelletier's in Fish Creek and Al Johnson's Swedish Restaurant in Sister Bay. To get a visual image of the park, watch the YouTube video—it is especially well made.

Point Beach State Forest (127 sites), on the shore of Lake Michigan about eighty miles north of Milwaukee, is the third largest camping destination in the northeastern region. The family campground is close to beautiful sandy beaches that stretch for six miles along the lakeshore. Within the park, campers can enjoy relaxing at the beach, swimming in the frigid lake, taking photos of the Rawley Point Lighthouse, visiting the nature center, bike riding, kayak training, and hiking seventeen miles of trails that meander through diverse beach and forest habitats. During Halloween, campers compete in a campsite-decorating contest. Outside the park, campers can shop in Two Rivers or Manitowoc. While in Manitowoc, most tourists make a stop at Beerntsen's Confectionary. Campers can also take a day trip up to Green Bay about thirty miles to the north.

Potawatomi State Park (123 sites), on the southern edge of Door County just west of the city of Sturgeon Bay, was established in 1928 as one of Wisconsin's early state parks and is one of the most popular camping destinations in the region. It is also one of my favorite camping destinations because it is located on the southern edge of one of Wisconsin's most popular tourist destinations—Door County. The largely shaded campground, located on the shore of Sturgeon Bay, consists of two loops with a shower building, nature center, and camp store located between the loops. Inside the park, campers can rent bicycles, canoes, and kayaks. They can also fish in the bay and hike part of the Ice Age Trail that begins in the park. Outside the park, campers can enjoy the Maritime Museum, plays, concerts, charter fishing trips, and other activities in the city of Sturgeon Bay. Campers who would like to enjoy a good fish or steak dinner should visit the Sunset Bar and Grill, located at Riley's Point on Green Bay about five miles south of the park. The restaurant offers fantastic sunset views every evening and a genuine Wisconsin Northwoods atmosphere.

High Cliff State Park (112 sites), on the northeastern shore of Lake Winnebago, is another popular camping destination in the region. The wooded family campground, located on a high cliff of the Niagara escarpment above Lake Winnebago, is neatly arranged as two sections, each with two internal loops. Most sites have full shade, ample space, and partial privacy. Within the park, campers can enjoy swimming, boating, fishing, hiking roughly twenty-six miles of trails, visiting effigy mounds, attending nature programs, climbing the observation tower, and enjoying panoramic views of the lake and surrounding area. Campground roads are level for short bicycle rides but the rest of the park is too hilly for all but the most dedicated bicyclists. The park also operates a marina located on Lake Winnebago and loans fishing equipment. Outside the park, campers may enjoy playing golf at the nice course adjacent to the park or taking short day trips over to Lake Michigan or up to Green Bay.

The U.S. Forest Service manages nineteen campgrounds in the Nicolet National Forest. Most of these campgrounds are located on small kettle lakes with swimming and fishing opportunities. **Boulder Lake Campground** (99 sites), located near Langlade about fifty miles northwest of Green Bay, is the largest of the campgrounds and the only one with showers. **Luna-White Deer Lake** (35 primitive sites) and **Bear Lake** (27 primitive sites) were named by both the *TripleBlaze* website and *The Best in Tent Camping: Wisconsin* as among the best places to camp in the state. Furthermore, **Franklin Lake** (77 primitive sites) and **Boot Lake** (33 primitive sites) were named by *TripleBlaze* while **Laura Lake** (41 primitive sites), **Bagley Rapids** (30 primitive sites), and **Lost Lake** (27 primitive sites) were named by *The Best in Tent Camping: Wisconsin*.

County and municipal governments in the northeastern region manage twenty additional public campgrounds that are suitable for tent camping. **Holtwood Municipal Campground** (130 sites), located in the town of Oconto about thirty miles north of Green Bay, and **Bay Shore Campground** (115 sites), located in Brown County near New Franken about five miles northeast of Green Bay, are the largest of these county and municipal campgrounds. **Dells of the Eau Claire Park** (28 primitive sites), **Goodman Park** (15 primitive sites) and **Twelve Foot Falls Park** (11 primitive sites) were all named by *The Best in Tent Camping: Wisconsin* as some of the most secluded and private camping areas in the state.

Northwestern Region: The Northwoods

The northwestern region of Wisconsin is defined as the area north of the line from La Crosse to Coloma and west of the line from Coloma up to the Michigan state line. The western border of the region is defined by the Mississippi and Saint Croix Rivers, and the northwestern border is defined by the shoreline of Lake Superior and Michigan's Upper Peninsula. Reference cities in this area are La Crosse in the southwestern corner, Superior in the northwest corner, Wausau and Stevens Point on the eastern edge, and Eau Claire in the center of the region. Minneapolis-Saint Paul is just eighteen miles west of the Wisconsin border. Over 5,000 small lakes can be found throughout this region. In addition, the Chequamegon National Forest, three Indian reservations, and the Apostle Islands National Lakeshore in Lake Superior are also located in the region.

This area of the state has also been called Indian Head Country because the twists and turns of the Saint Croix River on the western border resemble the profile of an older Native American male looking to the west. The small curves near Saint Paul resemble his mouth and lips, the larger sweeping curve near Grantsburg resembles his nose, the border south of Duluth form his eyes and forehead, and the Apostle Islands form his headdress.

Major tourist attractions in this region center on fishing, hunting, and logging or lumberjack history. Visitors to this region will find dozens of museums celebrating everything from accordions and cooperage to rural life. In Eau Claire, tourists will find Paul Bunyan Logging Camp Museum with statues of Paul and his blue ox Babe. During the last week in July, visitors in Hayward are astounded by the skills displayed at the Lumberjack World Championships, where hundreds of male and female lumberjacks compete in the 60-foot speed climb, underhand block chop, boom run, log rolling, and other events.

Other visitors to this area enjoy exploring Native American museums, cultural exhibits, reservations, and powwows. In Lake Superior, many tourists are drawn to the Apostle Islands National Lakeshore. Hikers can explore the western terminus of the Ice Age National Historic Trail in the Interstate State Park. Campers who make the short trip across the state line to the twin cities will find many sporting events, museums, plays, concerts and other cultural activities in the twin cities. In addition, shoppers can shop at the Mall of America—one of the largest and most popular malls in the United States.

The Wisconsin Department of Natural Resources manages twelve state parks, four state forests, and one state recreation area in the northwestern region of the state. Interstate State Park, located on the western edge of the region, was the first state park established in Wisconsin. Pattison State Park, located in the extreme northwestern corner of the region, has the highest waterfall in Wisconsin. Part of the Northern Highland—American Legion State Forest, discussed previously in the northeastern region, actually lies on the border of these two regions and a few campgrounds are physically located in this northwestern region. Tent campers planning vacations in this area may want to consider one of the following destinations.

Black River State Forest (98 sites), just off of I-94 about midway between Madison and Minneapolis, is the largest of the state properties in the northwestern region. This forest has three family campgrounds: Castle Mound (35 sites), East Fork (24 primitive sites), and Pigeon Creek (38 primitive sites). The park also offers a group camp, an equestrian camp, two canoe campsites, and several primitive backcountry campsites. Permits are required before setting up camp in a backcountry or primitive area. Recreational activities in the area revolve around hunting, fishing, and Native American events. A great day trip from this forest would be a short ride up to Chippewa Falls where one can tour the historic Leinenkugel Brewery. Several years ago, I enjoyed camping in one of the dispersed camping areas with my wife, two small children and another family.

Big Bay State Park (60 sites), on Madeline Island (the largest of the Apostle Islands in Lake Superior), was named by both *Reserve America* and *The Best in Tent Camping: Wisconsin* as one of the best camping destinations in the state. To get to the park, campers must catch a ferry that departs from Bayfield every half hour during the summer. The cost of a round trip for two adults and a vehicle is about fifty dollars. After landing on the Island, campers must drive six miles to the park. The campground has sixty campsites located near the shore of Lake Superior. A town park with additional campsites is located next to the park. Activities in the area include swimming, kayaking, biking, and hiking. In Bayfield, the primary activity is exploring the Apostle Islands National Lakeshore. Most tourists to the area book guided cruises through the islands, but a few hearty souls prefer to kayak through the islands. Other activities include shopping and touring the maritime museum.

Copper Falls State Park (55 sites), on the Bad River about twenty miles south of Lake Superior, was established in 1929 as one of Wisconsin's early state parks and was recently named by *National Geographic* as one of the most scenic and culturally significant state parks in the United States. The park has two small campgrounds and a unique log concession building. Activities in this park center primarily on hiking scenic trails and visiting beautiful waterfalls. Swimming, fishing, and canoeing opportunities are also available. Overall, the park and the campground offer unique opportunities to see and enjoy nature that cannot be found in many other places.

Council Grounds State Park (55 sites), on the Wisconsin River about eighteen miles north of Wausau, reportedly served as a central meeting area for Chippewa and other Native American tribes living many years ago in north central Wisconsin. It is one of my favorite camping destinations because of its history, its beach on the Wisconsin River, and its paddling and canoe rental opportunities. The campground is neatly arranged in symmetrical loops and campsites typically are large, level, fully shaded, and partially private. My primary complaint about this campground is that standing water after rains and considerable shade breed lots of mosquitoes. Inside the park, campers can enjoy swimming, hiking, bike riding, fishing, and paddling.

Three federal agencies manage public campgrounds in this northwestern region. The U.S. Army Corps of Engineers manages the **Highland Ridge Campground** (45 sites) near Spring Valley about forty miles west of Eau Claire. The National Park Service manages primitive, canoe-in campsites along the **Saint Croix National Scenic Riverway** and Namekagon River, and several primitive, canoe-accessible campsites located on fifteen small islands in Lake Superior within the **Apostle Islands National Lakeshore**.

The U.S. Forest Service manages twenty-one campgrounds in the **Chequamegon National Forest. Two Lakes Campground** (93 primitive sites), located near Drummond about fifty miles southeast of Superior, is the largest of these campgrounds and was named by *Reserve America* as one of the top family campgrounds in America. **Chippewa Campground** (78 sites), located near Perkinstown about forty-five miles northeast of Eau Claire, is one of the few campgrounds in the

Council Grounds State Park has a small picnic and swimming area on the Wisconsin River.

Nicolet National Forest with showers. **Day Lake** (66 primitive sites), **Black Lake** (29 primitive sites), **Spearhead Point** (26 primitive sites) and four other campgrounds were named by *The Best in Tent Camping: Wisconsin* as among the most secluded camping destinations in the state.

County and municipal governments in the northwestern region manage forty-one additional public campgrounds suited for tent camping. **Petenwell County Park** (500 sites), located on Lake Petenwell (Wisconsin River) in Arkdale about forty miles southwest of Stevens Point, is the largest of these county parks. **Russell Memorial County Park** (230 sites), located near Merrillan and **Rock Dam County Park** (150 sites), located near Willard, also have large campgrounds. **Gordan Dam County Park** (33 primitive sites), located near Gordon, and **Harstad County Park** (28 primitive sites), located near Eau Claire, were named by *The Best in Tent Camping: Wisconsin* as two of the most secluded campgrounds in the state.

Useful Resources

After reading this chapter, readers should consult additional resources to determine specific destinations and campgrounds that best fit their family's particular interests and expectations. Some helpful resources are listed below.

- The Wisconsin Department of Natural Resources website (www. dnr.wi.gov) contains information about all state managed properties.
- The official Wisconsin state highway map, available from the Wisconsin Department of Transportation (www.dot.wisconsin. gov) and at highway rest areas, shows approximate geographic locations of each state and most federal properties. The map also has a table that summarizes phone numbers and amenities for each state property.
- *Wisconsin State Park System* (brochure), available in rest areas, lists the names of all state properties and provides brief descriptions of each one.
- *Wisconsin State Parks, State Forests, and Recreation Areas* (older book) provides detailed descriptions of state properties. Some of the details are out of date, but most are still accurate.
- *The Best in Tent Camping: Wisconsin* (book) provides detailed descriptions of Wisconsin's most secluded campgrounds, including a few county and municipal parks.
- Travel Wisconsin (www.travelwisconsin.com) is a website that describes major tourist attractions in the state.
- Reserve America (www.reserveamerica.com/campgroundSearch. do, 888-947-2757) is a private organization that makes reservations for Wisconsin state parks and recreation areas. The website also shows photos of individual campsites.
- Recreation.gov (www.Recreation.gov, 877-444-6777) is a private organization that makes reservations for all federal properties.

Wisconsin's Public Campgrounds

Campgrounds are listed by number of campsites available from most numerous to least. The following abbreviations are used to note public campgrounds that have been named by various authorities as among the best in the state:

FD   This property is one of my favorite camping destinations.
TB   This property was named by the *TripleBlaze* website as one of the fifteen best campgrounds in the state.
RA   This property was named by *Reserve America* as having one of the top 100 family campgrounds in America.
BTC This property was named and described in *The Best in Tent Camping: Wisconsin* as having one of the fifty most quiet and most private campgrounds in the state.
NG   This property was named and described by *National Geographic's Guide to State Parks in the United States* as one of America's most historic and scenic state parks.
(P = primitive)

Southwestern Region: The Driftless Area

State DNR Parks, Recreation Areas, and Forests

Devil's Lake SP
407 sites, showers, beach, rock
  climbing, Wisconsin Dells
  attractions, Circus World
S 5975 Park Rd, Baraboo
35 m NW of Madison, 14 miles W
  of I-90

FD, TB, RA, BTC, NG
608-356-8301
43.43158, -89.73157

Governor Dodge SP
270 sites, showers, beach, canoe &
  horse rental, live theatre, bike trails
4175 SR 23 N, Dodgeville
40 m W of Madison, 5 m N of US
  Hwy 18

FD, TB, BTC
608-935-2315
43.01679, -90.14171

Mirror Lake SP
151 sites, showers, Wisconsin Dells
    attractions, Circus World Museum
E 10320 Fern Dell Rd, Baraboo
45 m N of Madison, 1 m S of I-90/94

TB, BTC
608-254-2333
43.56, -89.820

Yellowstone Lake SP
128 sites, showers, beach, boat
    rentals, Pendarvis Historic Area
8496 Lake Rd, Blanchardville
38 miles SW of Madison, 20 miles E
    US 151

608-523-4427
42.75899, -89.94892

Wyalusing SP
109 sites, showers, canoe rental,
    Villa Louis
13081 State Park Lane, Bagley
On Mississippi River, 40 m NW of
    Dubuque

BTC
608-996-2261
42.98000, -91.12091

Rocky Arbor SP
89 sites, showers, hiking, Wisconsin
    Dells attractions
Wisconsin Dells
40 m NW of Madison, 1 m E of
    I-90/94

608-254-8001
43.64336, -89.80717

Lake Kegonsa SP
80 sites, showers, beach, Madison
    attractions
2405 Door Creek Rd, Stoughton
10 m SE of Madison, 1 m S of I 90

608-873-9695
42.97535, -89.23481

Blue Mounds SP
78 secluded sites, showers, pool, bike
    trail, Norwegian heritage sites
4350 Mounds Park Rd, Blue Mounds
25 m W of Madison, 3 m N of US 151

FD
608-437-5711
43.02596, -89.84464

Capital Springs Centennial SP
54 sites, showers, fishing, Madison
    attractions
3101 Lake Farm Rd, Madison
2 m S of Madison, 2 m S of US 12/18
    Beltline

608-873-2100
43.02727, -89.34544

Buckhorn SP
53 P sites, beach, Wisconsin River,
    fishing, canoe rental
W 8450 Buckhorn Park Ave, Necedah
60 m E of La Crosse, 10 m NE of
    I-90/94

RA, BTC
608-565-2789
43.93812, -90.00655

Nelson Dewey SP
48 sites, showers, fishing, bluff views
CR VV, Cassville
On Mississippi River, 25 m NW of
    Dubuque

BTC
608-725-5374
42.73482, -91.02271

Roche-A-Cri SP
41P sites
1767 SR 13, Friendship
80 m E of La Crosse, 20 m W of I-39

BTC
 608-339-6881
44.00310, -89.82006

New Glarus Woods SP
32 P sites, Swiss-German festivals,
    bike trail
New Glarus
22 m SW of Madison, 13 m S of
    US 151

FD
608-527-2335
42.78273, -89.63222

Wildcat Mountain SP
30 sites, showers, canoe rental,
    horse rentals
E 13660 SR 33, Ontario
35 m E of La Crosse, 25 m S of I-90

BTC
608-337-4775
43.69846, -90.56834

Mill Bluff SP
21 P sites, beach, hiking, unusual
    glacial rock formations
Camp Douglas, Mauston
50 m E of La Crosse, 1 m S of I-90/94

608-427-6692
43.95039, -90.31602

Tower Hill SP
15 P sites, canoe rental, live theatre,
    House on the Rock
Spring Green
30 m W of Madison, 2 m S of US 14

BTC
608-588-2116
43.14927, -90.04548

**Sparta CG, Elroy–Sparta State
    Bicycle Trail**
13 P sites, bike trail
Sparta
25 m E of La Crosse, 2 m N of I-90

608-463-7109
43.91026, -90.75874

Elroy CG, Elroy–Spa rta State Bicycle Trail
608-463-7109
43.74444, -90.27598
11 P sites, bike trail
SR 71, Elroy
21 m E of La Crosse, 2 m N of I-90

U.S. Army COE Campgrounds

Blackhawk CG, Mississippi River Pool 9
608-648-3314
43.46080, -91.2231
173 sites, showers, fishing, boating
E 590 CR B1, De Soto
On Mississippi River, 25 m S of
La Crosse

Grant River RA, Mississippi River PUA
608-763-2140
42.65940, -90.7097
63 sites, showers, fishing, boating
River Lane Rd, Potosi
On Mississippi River, 15 m N of
Dubuque

County and Municipal Campgrounds

Goose Island Park, La Crosse CP
FD
608-788-7018
43.72545, -91.23150
400 sites, showers, Wi-Fi, laundry
W 6488 CR GI, Stoddard
On Mississippi River, 5 m S of
La Crosse,

Castle Rock Park, Juneau CP
608-847-7089
43.90825, -90.03072
300 sites, showers, fishing
650 Prairie, Mauston
70 m NW of Madison, 10 m NE of
I-90/94

Castle Rock Park, Adams CP
608-339-7713
43.90668, -89.93116
200 sites, showers, beach
2397 CR Z, Friendship
75 m NW of Madison, 25 m W of
US 51

Blackhawk Lake RA, Iowa CP   608-623-2707
150 sites, showers, fishing, paddling,   43.01368, -90.28564
    miniature golf
2025 CR BH, Highland
45 m W of Madison, 5 m N of US 18

Wilderness Park, Juneau CP   608-565-7285
128 sites, showers, beach   44.15560, -89.98214
N14054 21st Ave, Necedah
70 m E of La Crosse, 20 m NE of
    I-90/94

Veterans Memorial Park,   608-786-4011
   La Crosse CP   43.89472, -91.11551
120 sites, showers, boating, fishing
N 4668 CR VP, West Salem
5 m E of La Crosse, 1 m N of I-90

Sidie Hollow Park, Vernon CP   BTC
73 sites, showers, fishing   608-637-5480
220 Airport Rd, Viroqua   43.57482, -90.89450
30 M SE of La Crosse, 5 m w of US 14

White Mound CG, Sauk CP   608-546-5011
59 sites, showers, paddling   43.36275, -90.08840
S 7995 White Mound Dr, Hillpoint
40 m NW of Madison, 12 m N of
    US 14

Token Creek Park, Dane CP   608-242-4576
43 sites, showers, disc golf, nature   43.17994, -89.31557
    area, Madison attractions
6200 US 51, Deforest
8 m NE of Madison, 2 m E of I-90/94

Blackhawk Memorial Park,   BTC
   Lafayette CP   608-776-4850
38 P sites, paddling, fishing,   42.66217, -89.87968
2995 CR Y, Argyle
40 m SW of Madison, 25 m SE of
    US 151

Riverside CG, Muscoda MP   608-604-7094
36 sites, showers, pool, Wisconsin   43.19688, -90.44526
    River
E River Road, Muscoda
60 m W of Madison, 10 m W of US 14

Mendota Park, Dane CP
30 sites, showers, fishing, beach,
   Madison attractions
5133 CR M (Century Ave), Middleton
5 m N of Madison, 3 m NE of US 14

FD
608-242-4576
43.11865, -89.44845

Babcock Park, Dane CP
25 sites, showers, fishing, Madison
   attractions
4601 Burma Rd, McFarland
5 m S of Madison, 3 m S of US
   12/14/18

608-242-4576
43.00685, -89.30599

Brigham Park, Dane CP
25 P sites, Norwegian festivals,
   Madison attractions
3160 CR F, Blue Mounds
20 m W of Madison, 2 m N of US 151

608-242-4576
43.02692, -89.81906

Banker Park, Viola MP
12 P sites
321 W Commercial St, Viola
40 m SE of La Crosse, 8 m N of US 14

608-627-1831
43.50567, -90.67270

Southeastern Region: Milwaukee Attractions

State DNR Parks, Recreation Areas, and Forests

Kettle Moraine SF—Northern Unit
335 sites, showers, beach, boat rental,
   horse rental, fishing, Milwaukee
   attractions
N 1765 CR G, Campbellsport
40 m N of Milwaukee, 15 m E of
   US 41

FD
262-626-2116
43.61522, -88.15275

Kettle Moraine SF—Southern Unit
265 sites, showers, beaches, Old
   World Wisconsin, Milwaukee
   attractions
S 91 W39091 SR 59, Eagle
20 m W of Milwaukee, 12 m S of I-94

FD, TB, BTC
262-594-6200
42.86718, -88.55203

Richard Bong SRA   262-878-5600
217 sites, showers, beach, fishing,   42.63623, -88.12711
   Milwaukee attractions
26313 Burlington Rd., Kansasville
15 m S of Milwaukee, 10 m W of I-94

Kohler-Andre SP   FD, TB
109 sites, showers, beach, nature   920-451-4080
   programs   43.66843, -87.71728
1020 Beach Park Lane, Sheboygan
On Lake Michigan, 35 m N of
   Milwaukee

Big Foot Beach SP   FD
100 sites, showers, beach, boat   262-248-2528
   rentals, shopping, concerts, 42.57090, -88.43190
   festivals, cruises
1452 S Wells St, Lake Geneva
3 m W of Racine, 15 m S of I-43

Harrington Beach SP   TB
66 sites, showers, beach   262-285-3015
531 CR D, Belgium   43.49398, -87.80338
On Lake Michigan, 30 m N of
   Milwaukee

Kettle Moraine SF—Pike Lake   BTC
32 sites, showers, Milwaukee   262-670-3400
   attractions   43.32130, -88.31360
Hartford
20 m NW of Milwaukee, 5 m W of
   US 41

Sandhill Station State CG, Glacial—   920-648-8774
   Drumlin State Bicycle Trail 43.04606, -88.91351
15 sites, showers, bike trail
Mud Lake Rd, Lake Mills
20 m E of Madison, 1 m S of I-94

County and Municipal Campgrounds

Cliffside Park, Racine CP   FD
92 sites, showers, amusement park   262-886-8440
3515 CR X, Racine   42.81883, -87.81895
On Lake Michigan, 20 m S of
   Milwaukee

Astico Park, Dodge CP
70 sites, showers, paddling
N 3620 CR TT, Columbus
55 m NW of Milwaukee, 5 m E of
    US 151

920-623-5274
43.32568, -88.95618

Broughton Sheboygan Marsh Park,
    Sheboygan CP
64 sites, showers, wildlife viewing,
    observation tower
W 7039 CR SR, Elkhart Lake
55 m N of Milwaukee, 15 m W of I-43

920-876-2535
43.84097, -88.10030

Horicon Ledges, Dodge CP
46 sites, showers aquatic center
N 7403 Park Rd, Horicon
35 m NW of Milwaukee, 10 m W of
    US 41

BTC
920-387-5450
43.46176, -88.58124

Waupun Park, Fond du Lac CP
42 sites, showers
825 County Park Rd, Waupun
20 m SW of Fond du Lac, 3 m W of
    US 151

920-929-2933
43.64291, -88.75678

Columbia Park, Fond du Lac CP
40 sites, showers, boating
N 10340 Calumet Harbor Rd, Malone
On Lake Winnebago, 10 m NE of
    Fond du Lac

920-929-3135
43.91560, -88.32822

Sanders Park, Racine CP
39 sites, showers, Lake Michigan
4809 Wood Rd, Racine
In Racine, 8 m E of I-90/94

262-886-8440
42.67411, -87.84526

Riverside CG, Sullivan MP
36 sites, showers
W Water St, Sullivan
30 m W of Milwaukee, 5 m S of I-94

608-739-3786
42.98816, -88.62993

Menominee Park, Waukesha CP
33 sites, beach, Milwaukee attractions
W220 N7884 Townline Rd,
    Menominee Falls
15 m NW of Milwaukee, 10 m N of
    I-94

262-548-7801
43.15913, -88.18116

Naga-waukee Park, Waukesha CP   262-548-7801
33 P sites, beach, golf, Ice age Trail,   43.05867, -88.35089
   Milwaukee attractions
651 SR 83, Delafield
25 m W of Milwaukee, 2 m N of I-94

Mukwonago Park, Waukesha CP   262-548-7801
30 sites, showers, beach, amusement   42.86344, -88.38826
   park, Milwaukee attractions
CR LO, Mukwonago
20 m SW of Milwaukee, 3 m W of I-43

Derge Park, Dodge CP   920-887-0365
25 sites, showers, fishing, boating   43.49803, -88.88059
N8379 CR CP, Beaver Dam
50 m NW of Milwaukee, 5 m W of
   US 151

Muskego Park, Waukesha CP   262-548-7801
24 sites, showers, beach, Milwaukee   42.89665, -88.16694
   attractions
S 83 W 20370 Janesville Rd, Muskego
15 m SW of Milwaukee, 2 m E of I-43

Northeastern Region: Door County

State DNR Parks, Recreation Areas, and Forests

Northern Highland—American   FD, BTC
   Legion SF   715-385-2727
871 sites, showers, paddling, fishing   46.00172, -89.62203
8770 CR J, Woodruff
70 m N of Wausau, on US 151

Peninsula SP   FD, NG
471 sites, showers, beach, bike rental,   920-868-3258
   boat rental, live theatre, Door   45.12677, -87.23629
   County attractions
9462 Shore Rd, Fish Creek
On Green Bay, 60 m NE of Green Bay

Point Beach SF   BTC
127 sites, showers, beach   920-794-7480
9400 CR O, Two Rivers   44.20695, -87.52474
On Lake Michigan, 80 m N of
   Milwaukee

Potawatomie SP
123 sites, showers, boat rentals,
    Ice Age National Scenic Trail,
    Door County attractions
3740 CR PD, Sturgeon Bay
On Green Bay, 40 m NE of Green Bay

FD
920-746-2890
44.86109, -87.41331

High Cliff SP
112 sites, showers, beach, golf, horse
    rental, Green Bay attractions
N 7630 State Park Rd, Sherwood
On Lake Winnebago, 25 m S of
    Green Bay

920-989-1106
44.16763, -88.29025

Hartman Creek SP
101 sites, showers
N 2480 Hartman Creek Rd, Waupaca
45 m W of Appleton, 5 m SW of US 10

BTC
715-258-2372
44.32568, -89.21343

Governor Thompson SP
50 sites, showers, fishing, boating
N10008 Paust Lane, Crivitz
70 m N of Green Bay, 13 m W of
    US 141

715-757-3979
45.33751, -88.23928

Rock Island SP
40 P sites, remote campsites, scenic
    views, Door County attractions
1924 Indian Point Rd, Washington
    Island
In Lake Michigan, 90 m NE of
    Green Bay

BTC, NG
920-847-2235
45.41740, -86.81896

Newport SP
16 P sites, Door County attractions
475 CR NP, Ellison Bay
On Lake Michigan, 75 m NE of
    Green Bay

BTC
929-854-2500
45.22698, -86.98961

National Forest Campgrounds

Boulder Lake, Nicolet NF
99 sites, showers, beach, kayaking,
    fishing, white water rafting,
    mosquitoes
Langlade
50 m NW of Green Bay, 28 m N of
    SR 29

TB
715-276-6333
45.13944, -88.63944

Franklin Lake, Nicolet NF
77 P sites, beach, nature programs
Eagle River
75 m N of Wausau, 20 m E of US 51

TB
715-479-2827
45.93190, -88.99373

Laura Lake, Nicolet NF
41 P sites, fishing
Armstrong Creek
90 m N of Green Bay, 4 m N of US 8

BTC
715-674-4481
45.70240, -88.50916

Luna-White Deer Lake, Nicolet NF
35 P sites, beach, fishing, loons
Eagle River
80 m NE of Wausau, 10 m E of US 45

TB, BTC
715-479-2827
45.9108, -88.94810

Boot Lake, Nicolet NF
33 P sites, beach, lakefront sites,
    fishing, mosquitoes
Townsend
60 m NW of Green Bay, 30 m W of
    US 141

TB
715-276-6333
45.26148, -88.64430

Spectacle Lake, Nicolet NF
33 P sites, beach, fishing, paddling
Eagle River
70 m N of Wausau, 8 m E of US 51

715-479-2827
45.86854, -89.56020

Lac Vieux Desert, Nicolet NF
31 P sites, beach
Land O' Lake
On Michigan border, 3 m E of US 45

715-479-2827
46.11252, -89.11877

Kentuck Lake, Nicolet NF
31 P sites, fishing
Eagle River
10 m S of Michigan border, 12 m E of
    US 45

715-479-2827
45.99100, -88.97591

Bagley Rapids, Nicolet NF
30 P sites, fishing
Mountain
45 m NW of Green Bay, 20 m w of
    US 141

BTC
715-276-6333
45.14945, -88.46676

Sevenmile Lake, Nicolet NF
27 P sites, beach, fishing, paddling
Eagle River
70 m N of Wausau, 15 m E of US 51

715-479-2827
45.89435, -89.43386

Lost Lake, Nicolet NF
27 P sites, beach, fishing
Florence
7 m S of Michigan border, 35 m E of
  US 45

BTC
715-528-4464
45.92462, -88.63346

Bear Lake, Nicolet NF
27 P sites, beach, boating
Blackwell
70 m NW of Green Bay, 8 m E of US 8

TB, BTC
715-674-4481
45.52000, -88.53036

Richardson Lake, Nicolet NF
19 P sites, beach, fishing
Wabeno
75 m NW of Green Bay, 15 m S of
  US 8

715-674-4481
45.43668, -88.71217

Ada Lake, Nicolet NF
19 P sites, beach, paddling
Wabeno
70 m NW of Green Bay, 28 m E of
  US 45

715-674-4481
45.37989, -88.73936

Anvil Lake, Nicolet NF
18 P sites, beach, fishing, loons, bears
Eagle River
70 m N of Wausau, 10 m E of US 51

715-479-2827
45.93247, -89.07908

Morgan Lake, Nicolet NF
18 P sites, beach, paddling, fishing
Long Lake
18 m S of Michigan border, 10 m N of
  US 8

715-528-4464
45.7704, -88.54317

Laurel Lake, Nicolet NF
12 P sites, fishing
Three Lakes
65 m NE of Wausau, 3 m E of US 45

715-479-2827
45.80682, -89.12353

Brule River, Nicolet NF
11 P sites, paddling, river sites
Iron River
On Michigan border, 22 m E of US 45

715-528-4464
46.01971, -88.81817

Pine Lake, Nicolet NF
11 P sites, beach, fishing
Hiles
65 m NE of Wausau, 10 m E of US 45

715-674-4481
45.69545, -88.98550

County and Municipal Campgrounds

Holtwood CG, Oconto MP   920-834-7732
130 sites, showers, pool, laundry   44.88819, -87.88749
400 Holtwood Way, Oconto
30 m N of Green Bay, on US 41

Bay Shore CG, Brown CP   920-448-4466
115 sites, showers, Green Bay activities   44.63313, -87.80361
5637 Sturgeon Bay Rd, New Franken
On Green Bay, 10 m NE of Green Bay

Chute Park, Oconto CP   920-834-6800
74 sites, showers, beach   45.13062, -88.44235
SR 32, Mountain
60 m NW of Green Bay, 22 m W of
   US 141

Calumet Park, Calumet CP   920-439-1008
71 sites, showers, Lake Winnebago   44.10169, -88.31184
CR EE, Stockbridge
35 m S of Green Bay, 30 m W of I-43

Veterans Memorial Park, Forest CP   715-478-2040
66 sites, showers, fishing   45.51807, -88.90243
County Park Road, Crandon
100 m NW of Green Bay, 12 m E of
   US 45

Lake Emily Park, Portage CP   715-346-1433
66 sites, showers, beach, fishing   44.47131, -89.33228
3968 Park Dr, Amherst Junction
15 m SE of Stevens Point, on US 10

Wausaukee Evergreen Park,   715-856-5341
   Wausaukee MP   45.38029, -87.94988
49 sites, showers, concerts
Wausaukee
60 m N of Green Bay, on US 141

Veterans Memorial Park,   715-623-6214
   Langlade CP   45.23357, -89.15566
48 sites, showers, beach, boat rental
N8375 Park Rd, Deerbrook
35 m NE of Wausau, 25 m E of US 51

Cecil Lakeview Park, Cecil MP
40 sites, showers, fishing
111 E Hofman St (SR 22), Cecil
30 m NW of Green Bay, 8 m N of
    SR 29

715-745-4428
44.80999, -88.45232

Kewaunee Marina CG,
    Kewaunee MP
36 sites, showers, boating, fishing
Kewaunee
On Lake Michigan, 25 m E of
    Green Bay

920-388-3300
44.46649, -87.50138

North Bay Shore CP, Oconto CP
33 sites, showers
Y Rd, Oconto
On Green Bay, 30 m N of Green Bay

920-834-6995
44.96881, -87.78187

Village of Hancock CG, Hancock MP
30 sites, beach, fishing, boating,
    laundry, Wi-Fi
CR GG, Hancock
75 m N of Madison, 1 m E of I-39

715-249-5496
44.12879, -89.49843

Marathon Park, Marathon CP
28 sites, showers, concerts festivals
Wausau
In Wausau, east of US 51

715-261-1566
44.95690, -89.65163

Dells of the Eau Claire Park,
    Marathon CP
28 P sites, beach, scenic views,
    Ice Age Trail
Wausau
12 m E of Wausau, 9 m N of SR 29

BTC
715-261-1566
45.00386, -89.32848

Collins Park, Portage CP
27 sites, showers, beach, fishing
2711 CR I, Rosholt
20 m NE of Stevens Point, 10 m N of
    US 10

715-346-1433
44.60183, -89.34226

Jordan Park, Portage CP
22 sites, showers, beach
8500 Jordan Rd, Stevens Point
2 m N of Stevens Point, 2 m E of I-39

715-346-1433
44.56251, -89.59522

Goodman Park, Marinette CP   BTC
15 P sites, paddling, fishing   715-732-7530
N 15201 Goodman Park Rd,   45.52024, -88.33951
    Athelstane
65 m N of Green Bay, 12 m W of
    US 141

Twelve Foot Falls Park, Marinette CP BTC
11 P sites, scenic waterfalls, fishing   715-732-7530
Beecher Rd, Pembine   45.57827, -88.13736
80 m N of Green Bay, 5 m W of
    US 141

City Park, Oconto MP   920-834-7706
9 P sites, showers, laundry, fishing   44.85886, -87.85712
CR N, Oconto
30 m N of Green Bay, on US 41

Marinette City Park, Marinette MP   715-732-5140
A few overnight sites, showers   45.09059, -87.63694
Marinette
On Michigan border, 50 m N of
    Green Bay

Northwestern Region: The Northwoods

State DNR Parks, Recreation Areas, and Forests

Black River SF   BTC
98 sites, showers, beach, fishing   715-284-4103
910 SR 54 E, Black River Falls   44.30304, -90.62041
50 m SE of Eau Claire, 15 m E of I-94

Perrot SP   BTC
98 sites, showers, boating, fishing,   608-534-6409
    Mississippi River   44.01763, -91.47005
W 26247 Sullivan Rd, Trempealeau
On Mississippi River, 18 m NW of
    La Crosse

Interstate SP   45.39166, -92.66527
85 sites, showers, beach, boating,
    fishing
SR 35, St Croix Falls715-483-3747
On St Croix River, 40 m NE of St Paul,
    MN

Lake Wissota SP
81 sites, showers, beach, canoe rental,
    Leinenkugel Brewery
18127 CR O, Chippewa Falls
15 m NE of Eau Claire, 7 m E of US 53

BTC
715-382-4574
44.96937, -91.29391

Willow River SP
78 sites, showers, beach, fishing
1034 CR A, Hudson
On St Croix River, 3 m N of I-94

BTC
715-386-5931
45.02000, -92.67832

Brunet Island SP
69 sites, showers, canoe rental, bike
    trail
23125 255th St, Cornell
30 m NE of Eau Claire, 20 m E of
    US 53

BTC
715-239-6888
54.18341, -91.15489

Merrick SP
69 sites, showers, boating, fishing
S 2965 SR 35, Fountain City
On Mississippi River, 35 m NW of
    La Crosse

608-687-4936
44.15736, -91.75753

Pattison SP
62 sites, showers, beach, waterfalls
6294 S SR 35, Superior
12 m S of Superior, 15 m W of US 53

715-399-3111
46.52794, -92.12171

Big Bay SP
60 sites, showers, beach, water
    activities
2402 Hagen Rd, La Pointe
In Lake Superior, 80 m E of Superior

RA, BTC
715-747-6425
46.79896, -90.69602

Flambeau River SF
60 P sites, canoe and kayak areas,
    fishing
W 1613 County Rd, Winter
75 m NE of Eau Claire, 18 m N of US 8

BTC
715-332-5271
45.69280, -90.75231

Copper Falls SP
55 sites, showers, beach, fishing,
    water falls
36764 Copper Falls Rd, Mellen
16 m S of Lake Superior, 75 m SE of
    Superior

TB, BTC, NG
715-274-5123
46.36545, -90.64578

Council Grounds SP
55 sites, showers, beach, canoe rental
N 1895 Council Grounds Dr, Merrill
55 m N of Stevens Point, 5 m W of
    US 51

FD
715-536-8773
45.18308, -89.74221

Amnicon Falls SPTB
36 P sites, fishing, scenic views
4279 CR U, South Range
10 m SE of Superior, 1 m E of US 53

BTC
715-398-3000
46.61867, -91.89549

Brule River SF
35 P sites, paddling and kayaking
6250 S Ranger Rd, Brule
25 m E of Superior, 12 m E of US 53

TB, BTC
715372-5678
46.59185, -91.59815

Governor Knowles SF
31 P sites, paddling and kayaking
324 SR 70, Grantsburg
On St Croix River, 60 m N of
    St Paul, MN

BTC
715-463-2898
45.92656, -92.61034

Rib Mountain SP
30 sites, showers, hiking
4200 Park Rd, Wausau
5 m S of Wausau, 2 m W of US 51

715-842-2522
44.92023, -89.68632

Chippewa Moraine Ice Age SRA
3 P sites, hiking
13394 CR M, New Auburn
28 m N of Eau Claire, 10 m E of US 53

715-967-2800
45.20773, -91.36814

U.S. Army COE, National Park Service, and National Forest Campgrounds

**Highland Ridge CG, Eau Galle Lake
    COE Project**
45 sites, showers, movies
Spring Valley
40 m W of Eau Claire, 4 m S of I-94

715-778-5562
44.86722, -92.24417

Apostle Islands NLS
Canoe-in P sites on 15 islands
415 Washington Ave, Bayfield
On Lake Superior, 80 m E of Superior

715-779-3397
46.92775, -90.63240

Saint Croix NSR
Walk-in and canoe-in P sites, paddling
401 N Hamilton St., Saint Croix Falls
On St Croix River, 70 m N of
   St Paul, MN

715-483-2274
45.96108, -92.55703

Two Lakes, Chequamegon NF
93 P sites, beach, boating
Drummond
50 m SE of Superior, on US 63

RA
715-373-2667
46.29625, -91.18229

Chippewa CG, Chequamegon NF
78 sites, showers, beach, boating
Perkinstown
45 m NE of Eau Claire, 20 m N of
   SR 29

715-748-4875
45.23356, -90.68574

Day Lake, Chequamegon NF
66 P sites, beach, wildlife viewing
Clam Lake
70 m SE of Superior, 20 m E of US 63

BTC
715-634-4821
46.17359, -90.90581

Namekagon, Chequamegon NF
33 P sites, beach
Cable
60 m SE of Superior, 12 m SE of US 63

715-634-4821
46.24831, -91.08058

Black Lake, Chequamegon NF
29 P sites, beach
Hayward
80 m SE of Superior, 20 m W of SR 13

BTC
715-634-4821
45.98068, -90.94308

Spearhead Point, Chequamegon NF
26 sites, showers nearby
Westboro
65 m NE of Eau Claire, 10 m W of
   SR 13

BTC
715-748-4875
45.34077, -90.43196

Eastwood, Chequamegon NF
21 sites, showers, Ice Age Trail,
   wildlife viewing
Westboro
60 m NE of Eau Claire, 15 m S of US 8

715-748-4875
45.33308, -90.43580

Wanoka Lake, Chequamegon NF
20 P sites, fishing, paddling
Iron River
40 m E of Superior, 1 m S of US 2

715-373-2667
46.54670, -91.28140

Sailor Lake, Chequamegon NF   715-762-2461
20 P sites, boating, fishing, ATV trail   45.84889, -90.27270
Fifield
70 m N of Wausau, 25 m W of US 51

Twin Lakes, Chequamegon NF   BTC
17 P sites, boating, fishing   715-762-2461
Park Falls   45.95240, -90.07188
80 m N of Wausau, 15 m W of US 51

Birch Grove, Chequamegon NF   BTC
16 P sites, boating, fishing   715-373-2667
Washburn   46.68655, -91.06144
50 m E of Superior, 12 m N of US 2

Perch Lake, Chequamegon NF   BTC
16 P sites, boating, fishing,   715-373-2667
      North Country Trail   46.40446, -91.27233
Drummond
25 m E of Superior, 5 m S of US 2

Moose Lake, Chequamegon NF   715-634-4821
15 P sites, beach, fishing, boating   46.01720, -91.01677
Hayward
40 m SE of Superior, 15 m E of US 63

Westpoint, Chequamegon NF   715-748-4875
15 sites, showers, beach, boating,   45.32657, -90.45314
      fishing
Westboro
60 m NE of Eau Claire, 15 m S of US 8

Horseshoe Lake Camp,   715-373-2667
      Chequamegon NF   46.73274, -91.08189
11 P sites, equestrian trails, wildlife
      viewing
Ion
50 m E of Superior, 15 m N of US 2

East Twin, Chequamegon NF   715-634-4821
11 P sites, beach, boating, wildlife   46.19376, -90.85397
      viewing
CR GG, Clam Lake
70 m E of Superior, 15 m W of SR 13

Mineral Lake, Chequamegon NF   715-634-4821
11 P sites, fishing, eagle watching   46.28850, -90.82427
Mellen
70 m SE of Superior, 10 m W of SR 13

Smith Rapids, Chequamegon NF   715-762-2461
11 P sites, fishing, equestrian trails,   45.92718, -90.16483
    mosquitoes
Park Falls
70 m N of Wausau, 25 m W of US 51

Emily Lake, Chequamegon NF   715-762-2461
11 P sites, beach, fishing, boating   45.96406, -90.00987
Park Falls
70 m N of Wausau, 25 m W of US 51

Kathryn Lake, Chequamegon NF   715-748-4875
10 P sites, beach, fishing, boating   45.19962, -90.61635
Perkinstown
45 m NE of Eau Claire, 21 m N of
    SR 29

Beaver Lake, Chequamegon NF   BTC
10 remote P sites, hiking   715-634-4821
Mellen   46.30087, -90.89474
70 m SE of Superior, 10 m W of SR 13

County and Municipal Campgrounds

Petenwell Park, Adams CP   608-564-7513
500 sites, showers, beach, fishing   44.11919, -89.95742
2004 Bighorn Dr, Arkdale
40 m SW of Stevens Point, 20 m W of
    US 51

Russell Memorial Park, Clark CP   44.42592, -90.72417
230 sites, showers, fishing, boating
W8189 CR J, Merrillan715-743-5140
50 m SE of Eau Claire, 10 m NE of I-94

Rock Dam CG, Clark CP   715-743-5140
150 sites, showers, fishing   44.73319, -90.85535
W 10666 Camp Globe Rd, Willard
35 m E of Eau Claire, 15 m S of SR 29

Pine View Recreation Area,   608-388-3517
    US Army Park   44.00750, -90.60729
127 sites, showers, laundry, boating,
    miniature golf
Park Rd, Sparta
23 m E of La Crosse, 10 m N of I-90

Big Eau Pleine Park, Marathon CP   715-261-1566
106 P sites, two campgrounds, beach,   44.76327, -89.86905
  disc golf
3301 Eau Pleine Park Rd, Mosinee
20 m S of Wausau, 10 m W of US 51

North Wood Park, Wood CP   715-421-8422
99 sites, showers, beach, fishing,   44.54167, -90.03502
  hiking, disc golf
7500 Park Lane, Arpin
20 m SW of Stevens Point, 18 m W of
  I-39

Dexter Park, Wood CP   15-421-8422
95 sites, showers, beach, fishing,   44.38502, -90.12488
  boating
8200 SR 54, Pittsville7
35 m W of Stevens Point, 35 m E of
  I-94

Coon Fork Lake, Eau Claire CP   715-286-5536
88 sites plus an RV loop, showers,   44.69480, -91.00954
  beach
25501 CR CF, Augusta
20 m SE of Eau Claire, 10 m E of I-94

South Wood Park, Wood CP   715-421-8400
73 sites, showers, beach, disc golf   44.36589, -89.73229
6411 S Park Rd, Wisconsin Rapids
20 m SW of Stevens Point, 12 m W of
  I-39

North Mead Lake Park, Clark CP   715-743-5140
71 sites, showers, beach, fishing   44.79496, -90.75625
W 8771, N Lake Rd, Willard
40 m E of Eau Claire, 12 m S of SR 29

Totogatic Park, Washburn CP   715-635-4490
71 P sites, beach, fishing   46.13708, -91.94095
Minong
40 m S of Superior, 10 m W of US 53

Lac du Flambeau Tribal CG   715-588-4211
70 sites, showers, laundry, fishing   45.97146, -89.91067
Lac du Flambeau
75 m N of Wausau, 12 m W of US 151

Solberg Lake CG, Price CP   715-339-6371
60 sites, showers, fishing   45.76446, -90.36847
N10750 County Park Road, Phillips
65 m NW of Wausau, 15 m N of US 8

Nugget Lake County Park, Pierce CP   715-639-5611
55 sites, showers, nature movies, boat   44.69415, -92.22401
   rental, fishing
N4351 CR HH, Plum City
45 m SE of St Paul, MN, 2 m S of
   US 10

Memorial Park, Washburn MP   715-373-6160
51 sites, showers, beach, scenic views   46.67621, -90.88134
Memorial Park Rd, Washburn
60 m E of Superior, 7 m N of US 2

Thompson's West End Park,   715-373-6160
   Washburn MP   46.66636, -90.90508
51 sites, showers, beach
S 8th Ave W, Washburn
60 m E of Superior, 7 m N of US 2

Trego Town Park, Trego MP   715-635-6075
50 sites, showers, beach   45.90982, -91.82353
Trego Park Road, Trego
60 m S of Superior, on US 53

Snyder CG, Clark CP   715-743-5140
49 sites, showers, beach   44.57386, -90.72073
W8046 Arndt Rd, Neillsville
50 m SE of Eau Claire, 30 m E of I-94

Pine Point Park, Chippewa CP   715-726-7880
48 sites, beach, fishing   45.24606, -91.15561
Birch Creek
30 m NE of Eau Claire, 23 m E of
   US 53

Twin Bear Campground, Bayfield CP   715-372-8610
43 sites, showers, beach, fishing   46.50636, -91.35938
CR H, Iron River
40 m SE of Superior, 7 m S of US 2

Shell Lake MP   715-468-7846
42 sites, showers, beach   45.74041, -91.92378
Shell Lake
70 m S of Superior, 10 m SW of US 53

Big Bay Town Park, La Pointe MP   715-747-3031
42 P sites, beach, Apostle Islands   46.81744, -90.70861
2305 Towne Park Circle, La Pointe
On Madeline Island, 75 m E of
    Superior

Doolittle City Park, Birchwood MP   715-354-3300
40 sites, showers, beach   45.66201, -91.55046
CR D Hinman Dr, Birchwood
35 m N of Eau Claire, 8 m E of US 53

James N McNally CG,   715-463-5832
    Grantsburg MP   45.77837, -92.68830
38 sites, showers, fishing, wildlife
    viewing
300 W Olson Dr, Grantsburg
70 m N of St Paul, MN, 45 m W of
    US 53

Waldo Carlson Park, Barron CP   715-537-6295
36 sites, showers, fishing   45.62329, -91.59668
2717 29th Ave, Birchwood
90 m S of Superior, 10 m E of US 53

Delta Lake CG, Bayfield CP   715-372-8610
34 sites, showers, beach, fishing   46.48492, -91.29694
CR H, Iron River
40 m SE of Superior, 13 m S of US 2

Gordon Dam Park, Douglas CP   BTC
33 P sites, fishing, beach   715-395-1341
7201 E CR Y, Gordon   46.25231, -91.92728
37 m S of Superior, 7 m W of US 53

Southworth Memorial Park,   45.29817, -91.61712
    Barron CP
32 sites, showers, fishing, boating
650 26½–27 St, Chetek
    715-924-1875
35 m N of Eau Claire, 1 mile E of
    US 53

DuBay Park, Portage CP   715-346-1433
31 sites, showers, beach, fishing,   44.67402, -89.69091
    boating
4501 CR E, Junction City
12 m N of Stevens Point, 8 m W of
    I-39

Sherwood CG, Clark CP
31 P sites, beach, fishing
W1251 Dyer Rd, Pittsville
60 m E of Eau Claire, 3 m N of SR 73

715-743-5140
44.42757, -90.3658

Smith Lake CG, Price CP
30 sites, showers, beach, fishing
N14763 Omaha Rd, Park Falls
100 m SE of Superior, 30 m N of US 8

715-339-6371
45.91454, -90.50084

Morris-Erickson CP, Chippewa CP
28 sites, showers, fishing
SR 40, New Auburn
30 m N of Eau Claire, 8 m E of US 53

715-726-7880
45.25524, -91.40899

Veterans Memorial Park, Barron CP
28 P sites, fishing
2126 13–12½ Ave, Cameron
45 m N of Eau Claire, 2 m E of US 53

715-458-4125
45.38813, -91.71631

Harstad Park, Eau Claire CP
28 P sites, fishing, paddling
Augusta
18 m SE of Eau Claire, 10 m E of I-94

BTC
715-286-5536
44.74039, -91.16769

Sawmill Lake, Washburn CP
25 P sites, fishing
Spooner
40 m N of Eau Claire, 16 m E of US 53

715-635-4490
45.75389, -91.55359

Lucius Woods Park, Douglas CP
24 sites, showers, beach, fishing,
 concerts
9231 E Marion Ave, Solon Springs
22 m S of Superior, 5 m E of US 53

715-395-1341
46.35107, -91.81715

Otter Lake, Chippewa CP
22 P sites, beach fishing
165th Ave, Stanley
30 m NE of Eau Claire, 12 m N of
 SR 29

715-726-7880
45.08133, -90.94250

Big Rock CG, Bayfield CP
13 P sites, fishing, wildlife viewing
Big Rock Rd (CR C), Washburn
70 m E of Superior, 15 m N of US 2

715-373-6114
46.70632, -90.92549

Mooney Dam Park, Douglas CP
11 P sites, fishing
14293 S Flowers Circle, Gordon
37 m S of Superior, 2 m W of US 53

715-395-1341
46.25646, -91.56876

Big Falls CG, Price CP
6 P sites, water recreation, fishing,
    hiking, playground
W11337 Big Falls Rd, Kennan
60 m NW of Wausau, 10 m S of US 8

715-339-6371
45.40507, -90.63763

Michigan's Lower Peninsula

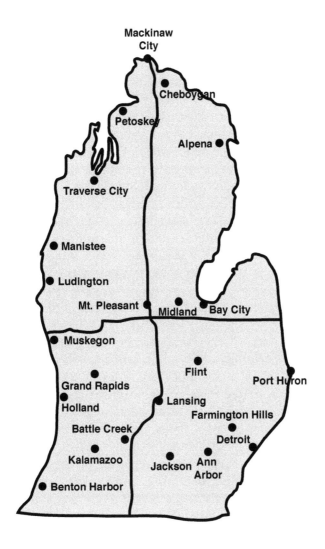

3

Michigan's Lower Peninsula

Michigan is the second state in our guide to family camping in the Lake Michigan states. The state of Michigan consists of two large peninsulas surrounded by four Great Lakes. The Lower Peninsula is bordered by Lake Michigan to the west, Lake Huron to the east, and Lake Erie on the southeast corner. The Upper Peninsula, or UP, is bordered by Lake Michigan to the south and Lake Superior to the north. All total, the state has 3,200 miles of shoreline on the four Great Lakes.

In addition to the 3,200 miles of Great Lakes shoreline, Michigan has almost 11,000 inland lakes carved by glaciers that covered the land many years ago. These smaller lakes offer many exciting tourist attractions that draw thousands of vacationers every summer. The largest of these inland lakes is Houghton Lake, located in the north central region of the state about 120 miles north of Lansing. Houghton Lake has 20,044 acres of water (31 square miles) with over 30 miles of shoreline. Other large inland lakes include Torch Lake (18,770 acres), located about forty miles northeast of Traverse City; Lake Charlevoix (17,260 acres), located near Lake Michigan in the northern Lower Peninsula; and Burt Lake (17,120 acres), located about forty miles south of Mackinaw City. Smaller lakes are scattered throughout the entire state.

Michigan also has over three hundred named rivers that extend over 51,000 miles. Sixteen of these rivers, having a combined total of 650 miles of waterway, have been designated by the federal government as national wild and scenic rivers. These rivers are protected by federal law from commercial pollution, damming, and exploitation. For the most part, these wild and scenic rivers are gentile rivers that meander through miles and miles of forest land and picturesque rock formations. One of the best-known rivers in the state is the Au Sable that flows through Grayling and Mio in the northeast corner of the Lower Peninsula out to Lake Huron. Other well-known rivers include the Kalamazoo that flows through the southwestern corner of the Lower Peninsula, the Muskegon and Manistee Rivers that flow through the northwestern corner of the Lower Peninsula, and the Tahquamenon River that flows through the Upper Peninsula.

These lakes and rivers offer hundreds of outstanding fishing destinations. Fishing enthusiasts can enjoy deep-water fishing in one of the Great Lakes, fly fishing in one of the colder northern rivers, or rod and reel fishing in one of the shallow lakes. Experienced sport fishermen seem to enjoy catching steelheads (or Great Lakes trout), but anglers also pursue salmon, northern pike, trout, walleye, perch, bass, and sunfish. Personally, I prefer the taste of walleye and trout and occasionally try to catch one or two of these fish. Visitors who are unfamiliar with the best fishing spots and state regulations may want to hire a licensed fishing guide to maximize their chances of success and minimize their risks of problems. Since catch-and-release policies are enforced in several areas, readers should also read tips for catching and releasing trout to maximize their survival. Readers who want to find more information about fishing in Michigan can visit the DNR website (www.michigandnr.gov) and click on "Fishing in Michigan," or read one of the many books that describe Michigan fishing destinations and strategies.

Michigan's rivers and lakes also offer many prime paddling destinations with dozens of put-in and take-out ramps plus miles of calm unspoiled waterway through beautiful countryside. These rivers also have numerous beaches and riverbanks where paddlers can moor their craft and rest, eat a picnic lunch, swim, or even camp overnight. Small towns along these rivers offer restaurants, grocery stores, taverns, and outfitter stores, where paddlers can stop for provisions or eat a nice meal. Campers who do not have their own canoes or equipment can still enjoy a paddling adventure on many of the rivers. Dozens of canoe liveries and paddling outfitters are scattered all around the state. In addition to providing rental equipment, these businesses will offer suggestions for both short and long trips, and will transport customers to and from the river or lake. Readers who want to learn more about good paddling destinations and trips should visit www.CanoeingMichiganRivers.com.

In addition to its water recreational opportunities, Michigan also offers 1,300 miles of smooth surface bicycle trails throughout the state. The longest of these, White Pine State Trail (93 miles), runs from Cadillac down to Grand Rapids. Other popular bike trails include the North Central State Trail (62 miles) from Gaylord north to Mackinaw City and the North Eastern State Trail (71 miles) from Cheboygan along the Lake Huron coast down to Alpena. We enjoyed watching hundreds of bicyclists riding on the Little Traverse Wheelway (26 miles) from Petoskey down to Charlevoix. For more information about state bike trails, visit www.michigan.org/biking/.

Michigan has over 330 public campgrounds plus many more private campgrounds. The vast majority of these campgrounds are located on the shores or banks of one of the state's rivers or lakes. Along the Great Lakes shoreline, campers will find one national park, two national lakeshores managed by the National Park Service, one National recreation area managed by the U.S. Forest Service, over forty state parks, and over a dozen county and municipal park campgrounds. In (or near) each of these public parks and campgrounds, visitors will find sandy beaches for swimming, scenic views of the lake, charter fishing services, canoe and kayak adventures for experienced paddlers, and many more recreational activities. Inland, visitors will find over two hundred public campgrounds offering great campsites nestled among virgin and second-growth forests providing outstanding swimming, paddling, and fishing opportunities near one of the many rivers and small lakes.

Michigan also has fifteen U.S. wilderness areas spread across the Lower and Upper Peninsulas for adventurous people who prefer more primitive camping. Isle Royale and Beaver Basin in the Pictured Rocks National Lakeshore are managed by the National Park Service. Michigan Islands, Huron Islands, and Seney are managed by the U.S. Fish and Wildlife Service. And ten wilderness areas, including McCormick, Big Island Lake, Delirium, Horseshoe Bay, and Mackinac, are managed by the U.S. Forest Service.

Considering the extensive number of rivers and lakes with great fishing and paddling opportunities, Michigan's official nicknames—"The Great Lakes State," "The Wolverine State," and a French expression that means "If you seek a pleasant peninsula, look about you"—all seem to understate the strong recreational ambiance of the state. Within the past few years, the Michigan Department of Natural Resources adopted a new slogan that seems to be more fitting—"Great Lakes, Great Times, Great Outdoors." Personally, I think Michigan should be called the camping, biking, fishing, and paddling paradise of the eastern United States. All sixteen state parks I have visited have offered outstanding camping facilities and numerous recreational opportunities. In fact, I consider all the parks I have visited as being among my favorite camping destinations.

The Michigan Department of Natural Resources (DNR) manages a total of seventy-four state parks and recreation areas plus 124 state forest campgrounds. The state of Michigan manages more public campgrounds than Wisconsin and Illinois combined. Most of these properties have large level well-shaded campsites ideally suited for tents and hammocks, exceptionally clean bathrooms, and educational programs for both children and adults. Unlike public campgrounds in other states, Michigan campgrounds are filled with families and children all week long throughout the summer, even in late August. Recreational opportunities in and near these state parks are extensive, and local liveries provide rental equipment for campers who are unable to bring their own.

The new DNR website (www.michigan.gov/dnr), launched in 2014, makes it very easy to find and reserve available campsites. Campground maps show overall campground layout with locations of bathrooms and shower buildings and include photos of individual sites. Before camping in a Michigan state property, campers must also purchase a recreation passport. In 2014, this passport cost Michigan residents $11 annually and non-residents $8.55 daily or $31.10 annually.

For people who have never camped before but would like to give it a try, Michigan's DNR, in conjunction with The North Face, offers a "Camping 101 Program." For a nominal fee ($20 in 2014), selected state parks will provide a campsite for two nights with a tent, a tarp, a lantern, a camp stove, and a camping coach who will show novice campers how to set up a campsite, start a campfire, and cook a good tasting meal. For more information about this program, go to www.michigan.gov/dnr and search for the Camping 101 program.

An interesting piece of state trivia is that two properties claim to be Michigan's first state park. Mackinac Island was originally established as America's second national park in 1875 and was managed for twenty years by soldiers stationed at Fort Mackinac. In 1895, the fort closed and the property was given to the state of Michigan to be preserved and operated as a state park for the people. The second property claiming to be Michigan's first state park is Interlochen State Park. This park, located south of Traverse City, was the first park to be established by the Michigan state legislature. It was created in 1917 to preserve one of the few remaining virgin forests areas in the state. After establishing Interlochen, the Michigan legislature combined several small agencies in 1921 to make a stronger Department of Conservation to develop and protect several newly created state parks. P.J. Hoffmaster, a long-time director of this department, is now regarded as father of Michigan state parks. In 1968, the Department of Conservation was renamed as the Department of Natural Resources.

Considering Michigan's large number of public camping destinations, I decided to divide the state into two chapters. Campgrounds located in the Lower Peninsula will be described in this chapter and campgrounds in the Upper Peninsula will be described in the following chapter.

Although Michigan's Lower Peninsula and Wisconsin are adjacent to each other, the two states are separated by the ninety-mile-wide Lake Michigan. People who want to travel from one state to the other have four possible routes. They can take the long scenic northern route through the Upper Peninsula, the shorter but more congested southern route through Chicago, or one of the two direct car ferry routes that cross the lake every day during the summer. The S.S. *Badger* travels between the northern cities of Ludington, Michigan, and Manitowoc, Wisconsin. It offers a relaxing and reasonably priced four-hour cruise with activities for both children and adults. The *Lake Express* is a small high-speed catamaran that runs between the southern cities of Muskegon, Michigan, and Milwaukee, Wisconsin. It crosses the lake in only two and a half hours, but a one-way trip for two adults and a car costs about a hundred dollars more than the *Badger*. Whenever we travel to Michigan or Wisconsin, we prefer to take one of the ferries rather than driving the two-hour or longer stress-filled trip on the Chicago toll roads.

The S.S. Badger *is a large coal steamer car ferry that crosses northern Lake Michigan in four hours. Photo by Eva Douglass.*

The Lake Express *is a small high-speed catamaran car ferry that crosses southern Lake Michigan in two and a half hours. Photo by Eva Douglass.*

The Michigan DNR manages fifty-seven state parks and recreation areas with campgrounds in the Lower Peninsula. These state park and recreation areas tend to have campgrounds that are designed like suburban neighborhoods. Typically, there are four or more loops neatly divided into adjacent lots—some small and some large. Several campgrounds have over one hundred campsites neatly arranged in a relatively small area. Boundary lines between adjacent campsites are frequently noted by painted lines on roads rather than by understory vegetation. With a few notable exceptions such as Charles Mears, Holland Beach, and Sterling, most campgrounds are located in wooded areas with scattered trees providing partial shade but little, if any, additional vegetation. In addition to offering swimming and other water recreational activities, these campgrounds typically have good over-night security, campground hosts, electricity, exceptionally clean bath and shower buildings, flush toilets, bike trails, and many educational and recreational programs. Most campgrounds also feature unique steel-clad concrete fire rings that reduce the risks of wildfires and personal injuries. Because of their features and amenities, Michigan state parks and recreation areas in the Lower Peninsula attract large numbers of RVers and fill quickly during the summer months—even during weekdays. To assure that a site will be available on the days of a planned trip, campers must reserve campsites several months ahead if possible.

Many Michigan campgrounds have these unique steel-clad concrete fire rings.

The Michigan DNR also lists seventy-three state forest campgrounds in the Lower Peninsula. These state forest campgrounds, in contrast with state park campgrounds, are smaller (five to fifty campsites) with more dispersed and private campsites. Some of these forests are managed by the DNR while others are managed by local county governments. They typically have few amenities other than an onsite host, hand-pumped potable water, vault or pit toilets, picnic tables, and fire rings. These state forest campgrounds are ideal for tent campers who prefer more solitude and want to get away from congestion and noisy RVs. These campgrounds typically are located on small rivers and lakes providing ample fishing opportunities. They usually are available for walk-up occupancy and a few may not have on-site overnight security.

Two federal agencies manage campgrounds in Michigan's Lower Peninsula. The National Park Service manages one national lakeshore with a total of two developed campgrounds and the U.S. Forest Service manages two national forests with a total of thirty-two separate campgrounds. No U.S. Army Corps of Engineers campgrounds are located in the Lower Peninsula. County and municipal governments manage sixty-three public campgrounds that might be suitable for tent camping. As mentioned previously, county and municipal parks should be investigated carefully before deciding to stay in them.

To organize these public campgrounds, the Lower Peninsula is divided into four geographic regions. Within each region, popular tourist attractions and public campgrounds are summarized and a few popular camping destinations are featured that should be considered when planning a camping vacation trip to the region.

Southwestern Region: Lake Michigan Sand Dunes

The southwestern region is defined as the area that is south of a line running from St. Louis, Michigan, west to Lake Michigan (along state roads M-46 and M-82 plus county road B-86), and west of US 127 and I-69 running south from St. Louis through Lansing to the Indiana line. The western border of this region is defined by Lake Michigan and the southern border is defined by the Indiana state line. Reference cities in this region are Benton Harbor and Muskegon on Lake Michigan, Grand Rapids located in the north central part, Kalamazoo and Battle Creek in the south central part, St. Louis in the northeastern corner, and Lansing on the eastern border. South Bend, Indiana, is just across the line in the southwestern corner.

Popular tourist attractions in this region include the beaches and sand dunes that run from Indiana northward two hundred miles along the Lake Michigan shore. Every summer, thousands of visitors flock to this area to enjoy the sandy beaches' moderate temperature and cool lake water. Some of these visitors will charter boats to fish the deep waters of Lake Michigan while others will enjoy relaxing on the warm sunny beaches or shopping in nearby towns. Holland is an especially popular tourist destination along the Lake Michigan shore because it offers an interesting assortment of Dutch treats, costumes, festivals, and cultural events.

The Michigan Department of Natural Resources manages nine state parks with campgrounds in this region and six of these parks are located along the shores of Lake Michigan. Tent campers planning vacations in this region may want to consider one of the following destinations.

Yankee Springs Recreational Area (320 sites), surrounding a cluster of nine small lakes about twenty-five miles north of Kalamazoo near the center of the region, is the largest of the state properties in the southwestern region. It has been named by both *Michigan's Best Campgrounds* and *Best Tent Camping: Michigan* as one of the best camping destinations in the state. It is also one of my favorite camping destinations. The park has a modern family campground with 200 sites, a rustic campground with 120 sites, and an equestrian campground with 25 sites. Gun Lake is the largest of the lakes. Popular activities in this park include swimming, fishing, paddling, mountain bike riding, wildlife viewing, and horseback riding. Anglers can try their luck finding bass, bluegill, and perch in the nine lakes. Hikers will enjoy exploring the Devil's Soup Bowl, Graves Hill Overlook, and The Pines.

Yankee Springs State Recreation Area's Campground is level, partly shady, and popular during late August. A nice beach is just a few feet away from the campground.

Holland State Park (309 sites), on the shore of Lake Michigan about twenty-eight miles south of Muskegon, was established in 1926 as one of Michigan's early state parks and is one of the most popular and crowded parks in southwestern Michigan. It is my favorite Michigan camping destination because of its beautiful beach, its proximity to a popular tourist area, and its proximity to the Muskegon car ferry dock. The park has two modern campgrounds: Beach Campground, located on Lake Michigan, has lots of asphalt, lots of wind, no trees, and many RVs, while Lake Macatawa campground, located away from the beach, has more shade and grass for tent campers. We mistakenly decided to camp on the asphalt of the Beach Campground and almost got blown away. Within the park, visitors can enjoy basking in the sun on the large lakefront beach, swimming in the cold Lake Michigan water, biking, visiting the Big Red lighthouse, attending one of the ranger-led nature programs, hiking to the top of Mount Pisgah on the Dune Climb Walkway, or watching beautiful sunsets. Outside the park, visitors can enjoy biking, strolling through the historic downtown area of Holland, eating at great restaurants, shopping, visiting museums and concerts, fishing in Lake Michigan's deep water, attending the Tulip Festival during the first week of May or another Dutch heritage event, and enjoying a dinner cruise aboard an old-fashioned paddleboat.

Holland State Park's Lake Macatawa Campground is my favorite Michigan campground, despite the fact that it is located almost a mile away from the Lake Michigan beaches.

Holland State Park's
Beach Campground
is poorly suited for
tent campers, as we
discovered first hand,
because it is hot and
windy with no place to
anchor tents.

Holland State Park,
like several other parks
along the Lake Michigan
shoreline, has impressive
sand dunes and beaches.

Holland State Park's beach
features several sand
volleyball courts, a nice
bathhouse, concession
stand, and the Big Red
lighthouse in the distance.

P.J. Hoffmaster State Park (293 sites), on the shore of Lake Michigan about seven miles south of Muskegon near the town of Norton Shores, was named after the father of Michigan's state parks and subsequently named by *National Geographic* as one of the most scenic and historically significant state parks in the United States. It is one of my favorite camping destinations because of its spectacular pine/ hemlock/oak forest and its proximity to the Muskegon car ferry dock. The dirt and sand campground has five loops with spacious shady sites nestled in a stand of tall trees. Unfortunately, the park has recently lost several trees to oak wilt, emerald ash borer, Hemlock woolly adelgid, and other destructive pests. Within the park, visitors will find the Gillette Visitor Center, three miles of beach along the Lake Michigan shore, ten miles of hiking trails through the sand dunes, and picturesque views of Lake Michigan.

P.J. Hoffmaster's campground is situated in a beautiful hemlock, pine, and oak forest.

P.J. Hoffmaster's campsites have plenty of trees for stringing clotheslines, hanging hammocks, and setting up kitchen flies. This site is in the center loop around #190.

Van Buren State Park (220 sites), on the shore of Lake Michigan about twenty miles north of Benton Harbor, is the fifth largest camping destination in the southeastern region and one of my favorite camping destinations because its campground is immaculately clean and its beach is refreshing. The park has one large heavily wooded campground divided into five loops located about a half mile east of the lakeshore. Most campsites are large and shady but are crowded together with little privacy. We enjoyed staying in site #49 because it was large, level, shady, and located across the road from the bathhouse. But we wished that our back door neighbors had walked on the designated pathways rather than through our site on the way to and from the bathhouse. Inside the park, swimming in Lake Michigan and sunning on the sandy beach are two popular activities. Hiking over the tall sand dunes is another popular park activity. Outside the park, bicyclists will enjoy riding on the Van Buren Bike Trail, driving up to Holland for the day, or visiting various Kalamazoo attractions such as the Kalamazoo Valley Museum, Nature Center, and Institute of Arts.

Van Buren State Park is neatly designed and very popular. Our site #49 was to the right of this road and the bathhouse was to the left.

Van Buren State Park has an impressive stone walkway out to the Lake Michigan beaches.

Warren Dunes State Park (211 sites), on the shores of Lake Michigan about ten miles north of the Indiana state line, was established in 1930 as one of Michigan's early state parks and has been named by both *Best Tent Camping: Michigan* and *Michigan's Best Campgrounds* as one of the best campgrounds in the state for tent camping. This park has two campground loops that are situated in a wooded area well away from the beach. Compared with the other state parks on Lake Michigan, Warren Dunes is less congested and offers a rustic campground for tent campers who prefer more solitude. Within the park, visitors can enjoy exploring six miles of trails that traverse the massive sand dunes and walking along three miles of sandy beaches along the lakeshore.

County and municipal governments in the southwestern region manage eleven additional public campgrounds. **Pioneer County Park** (235 sites), located on Lake Michigan ten miles north of Muskegon, is the largest of these county and municipal parks. **Angle Cove County Park Campground** (130 sites), located in Coldwater about ten miles north of the Indiana line just off of I-69, and **Shamrock Municipal Park** (112 sites), located in Berrien Springs twelve miles north of the Indiana line just off of US 31 are two other large and comfortable campgrounds. **Ed Henning County Park** (60 sites), located in Newaygo about thirty-five miles north of Grand Rapids, and **Cold Brook County Park** (44 sites), located in Coldwater about eleven miles east of Kalamazoo, were both named by *Michigan's Best Campgrounds* as two of the best public campgrounds in the state.

Southeastern Region: Detroit Attractions

The southeastern region is defined as the area of the state that is south of a line running from St. Louis east to Lake Huron (along State Road M-46), and east of US Highway 27 and I-69 from St. Louis south through Lansing to the Indiana state line. The eastern border of this region is defined by Lake Huron to the north, the St. Clair River and Lake St. Clair in the center, and Lake Erie to the south. Reference cities in this region include the Detroit metropolitan area on Lake St. Clair, Ann Arbor located about thirty miles west of Detroit, Port Huron located at the mouth of the St. Clair River, Flint located in the north central area, Lansing located on the western edge, Jackson located in the south central area, and Toledo, Ohio, located in the south eastern corner.

Popular tourist attractions in and around the Detroit area include the Detroit Zoo, Ford Rouge Factory Tour, Henry Ford Museum, Motown Museum, Detroit Institute of Arts, Comerica Park (home of the

Detroit Tigers), Fox Theatre, Detroit Historical Society Museums, Riverfront Walk, Wright Museum of African American History, Dossin Great Lakes Museum, and Holocaust Memorial Center. Tourists who want to explore some Detroit attractions should consider parking their cars in one of the suburban parking lots and taking one of the Detroit City busses into the city and the Detroit People Mover. For more information about the system, go to www.ci.detroit.mi.us and www.thepeopleMover. com. A few miles to the west of Detroit, the University of Michigan in Ann Arbor offers many concerts, lectures, plays, cultural activities, and sporting events plus the Gerald R. Ford Presidential Museum. Similar attractions and the Abrams Planetarium can be found on the campus of Michigan State University in East Lansing. About twenty miles north of Flint, the Bavarian-styled village of Frankenmuth attracts many tourists every year. Here visitors can enjoy German music, festivals, shops, and restaurants. A long-standing tradition in the Bavarian village is to eat a chicken dinner at Zehnder's.

The Michigan State Department of Natural Resources manages sixteen state parks and recreation areas in this region and eight of these properties are located within forty miles of Detroit. Tent campers planning vacations in this region may want to consider one of the following destinations.

Waterloo State Recreation Area (350 sites), about fifty-five miles west of Detroit, has been named by both *Michigan's Best Campgrounds* and *Best Tent Camping: Michigan* as one of the best camping destinations in the state. Before becoming a state recreation area, the property was privately owned as infertile farmland and subsequently sold to the U.S. Department of Agriculture during the great Depression. Subsequently, the federal government established a CCC camp there, then a prison, and then a national park. Eventually, the federal government gave the property to the state of Michigan with stipulations that it be used as a public park and as a sanctuary for sandhill cranes. Today the recreation area is the largest state managed property in the Lower Peninsula with sixteen fishing lakes, two large swimming beaches, many miles of hiking, biking, and horse riding trails, and four campgrounds. Tent campers who want to have showers and modern conveniences should try to get sites in the Big Portage Lake campground while those who prefer more rustic accommodations may want to consider the Sugarloaf or Green Lake Campgrounds. While visiting in the park, campers should plan to spend an hour or two viewing and interacting with exhibits in the Gerald E. Eddy Discovery Center.

Algonac State Park (296 sites), on the shores of the St. Clair River about fifty miles northeast of Detroit, is the second largest state property in the southeastern region. The park has two developed campgrounds: Riverfront is a large, crowded, and partly shaded campground located directly on the St. Clair River. Campers staying in this campground spend many hours a day watching huge Great Lakes freighter ships and smaller pleasure yachts passing up and down the river only a few feet away from their campsites. Wagon Wheel Campground, located farther away from the river, offers more shady and private sites. Within the park, visitors can also enjoy fishing, wildlife viewing, and hiking.

Sterling State Park (256 sites), on the shore of Lake Erie about thirty miles south of Detroit, was established in 1920 as one of Michigan's early state parks and is the only state property located on Lake Erie. The park was originally created to help protect the lake coastline and its ecosystem from industrial pollution. Today, the campground has one of the largest campgrounds in the region that is organized into a large figure eight pattern with three nested loops at the top and bottom of the eight. Unfortunately, the campground has very little shade to protect tent campers on hot summer days. Inside the park, visitors can enjoy scenic views of the lake, fishing for walleye, swimming, hiking, and biking on the paved trail. Birders and wildlife enthusiasts will enjoy watching the many species that inhabit this waterbound area.

Campers who prefer more rustic campgrounds with privacy and solitude in the southeastern region may want to consider **Pinckney Recreation Area** (255 sites), **Metamora-Hadley Recreation Area** (214 sites), and **Proud Lake Recreation Area** (130 sites). Each of these three properties was named by *Michigan's Best Campgrounds* as one of the best in the region. **Lake Hudson Recreation Area** (50 sites) was named by *Best Tent Camping: Michigan* as one of the most private campgrounds in the state for tent camping.

County and municipal governments in the southeastern region manage five additional public campgrounds that may be suited for tent campers. **Wolverine County Park Campground** (194 sites), located in Columbiaville about eighteen miles northeast of Flint, is the largest of these parks. **Addison Oaks County Park Campground** (174 sites), located in Leonard about twenty-five miles north of Detroit, is another large campground and was named by *Michigan's Best Campgrounds* as one of the best in the state.

Northwestern Region: Traverse City Area

The northwestern region is defined as the area that is north of the line running from St. Louis west to Lake Michigan and west of a line running from St. Louis north through Grayling to Mackinaw City (along US 27 and I-75). Lake Michigan defines the western border of this region. Also in this region are several islands including Beaver and North Manitou Islands in Lake Michigan. More than a dozen large lakes can be found in the northern tip of this region and several pristine rivers flow through the southwestern corner of the area out to Lake Michigan. Reference cities in this region include Traverse City in the northwestern area, Ludington and Manistee on the southwestern edge, Cadillac in the center, Mount Pleasant, Grayling, and Gaylord on the eastern edge, Petoskey in the north, and Mackinaw City at the far northern tip. The Sleeping Bear Dunes National Lakeshore is located about twenty miles to the west of Traverse City and the Manistee National Forest is a few miles to the south. The Leelanau Peninsula extends northward from the Sleeping Bear Dunes and Traverse City.

This northwestern region of Michigan is arguably the most popular tourist and camping region in the state and Traverse City is perhaps the center of activities in the region. The Traverse City area is surrounded by acres of cherry and apple orchards plus dozens of vineyards, blueberry farms, and strawberry farms. Popular tourist activities in the area include live theatre, concerts, unique shops, wineries, and great restaurants. A few miles to the west, the Sleeping Bear Dunes National Lakeshore draws thousands of tourists every summer to enjoy scenic views from atop towering sand dunes and unique lakeshore ecology. A few miles to the south, the Interlochen Center for the Arts hosts many famous performers every summer. Fishing and boating enthusiasts enjoy outstanding marinas and waterways in this region both on Lake Michigan and on several large inland lakes in the area. Elsewhere in the region, tourists can enjoy exploring protected sand dunes stretching along Lake Michigan down to Ludington, fishing and paddling on the numerous rivers in the region, and exploring various tourist attractions in the Mackinaw City and Straits area.

The Michigan Department of Natural Resources manages fifteen state parks, one recreation area, and thirty-eight state forests in this northwestern region. State park campgrounds typically attract large numbers of RVers while state forest campgrounds tend to attract experienced and hardy tent campers. Many of these state properties are clustered along the shore of Lake Michigan, in the Traverse City area, and along several scenic rivers. Tent campers planning vacations in this region may want to consider one of the following destinations.

Interlochen State Park (490 sites), between Duck Lake and Green Lake about fifteen miles south of Traverse City, was established by the state legislature in 1917 as Michigan's first state park to preserve an area of virgin forest land. Today, the park is one of Michigan's most popular parks and has the largest camping area in the state. The park offers three separate campgrounds. The North Campground and the South Campground are two large, shady, compact, and congested camping areas located along the shores of Duck Lake. They are separated by a concession building and a large sandy beach swimming area. Our campsite (#373) in the South Campground was large and located on a bluff above Duck Lake. We set up our hammocks in the shade at the edge of the bluff and watched boaters and skiers riding across the lake all afternoon. Sites 371 through 390 in the South Campground and sites 11 through 43 in the North Campground offer similar views. A smaller, more-rustic camping area is located across the state highway on Green Lake. Unless tent campers want to be near the beach area, they might enjoy the more private sites on the bluff above Green Lake.

Within the park, visitors enjoy walking through a virgin forest of towering white pines, swimming, fishing, and paddling. Outside the park, visitors flock to the Interlochen Center of the Arts where they can enjoy concerts and live theater almost every evening. Some of the entertainers appearing during the 2013 summer season included Josh Groban, Trace Adkins, The Avett Brothers, Steve Miller Band, Melissa Etheridge, and ZZ Top. We just enjoyed touring the campus, seeing hundreds of gifted young people, and soaking up the artistically stimulating environment. Other popular activities include day trips up to Traverse City and over to Sleeping Bear Dunes National Lakeshore.

Interlochen State Park's Duck Lake Campground has several sites along the lakeshore. During the day, campers can swim, boat, fish, ride up to Traverse City, or ride over to Sleeping Bear Dunes National Lakeshore. At night, many campers attend programs at the Interlochen Center for the Arts.

Ludington State Park (373 sites), on the shore of Lake Michigan about eight miles north of Ludington, was established in 1936 as one of Michigan's early state parks and is currently the second largest property in the northwestern region. It has been named by *National Geographic* and several other authorities as one of the best state parks and campgrounds in Michigan and is one of my favorites. The park, along with its beautiful beach and three family campgrounds, is located on a narrow isthmus that stretches between Lake Michigan and Hamlin Lake. Pines Campground (sites 1 to 97) is located in a wooded area close to Lake Michigan and has many shaded sites. Cedars Campground (sites 101 to 205) is farther away from the beach and has both shaded and open sites. Beechwood Campground (sites 210 to 354) is on Hamlin Lake and has mostly shady sites with a few water view sites. In addition, the park has ten walk-in sites. Recreational activities inside the park include, swimming, tubing, paddling, fishing, hiking, and visiting the Great Lakes Visitor Center. Just outside the park, visitors frequently enjoy touring the historic Point Sable Lighthouse and walking through the historic town of Ludington. This park is a perfect overnight camp destination for travelers who plan to cross the lake on the S.S. *Badger* but, as we learned the hard way, all summer weekend campsites are reserved over five months ahead.

Traverse City State Park (343 sites), on the shore of East Grand Traverse Bay about two miles east of Traverse City, has the third largest campground in the region and obviously is one of the more popular camping destinations in the state. Although the park is small, congested, and noisy due to exuberant camping groups and U.S. Highway 31, it is located in the center of tourist attractions in the northeastern region. The park's beautiful beach area is accessible to campers via a pedestrian crosswalk over the busy highway. Other popular activities include hiking through the Reffitt Nature Preserve and riding bicycles three miles into the main tourist area. Just outside the park, campers will find quaint shops, vineyards, fruit stands, a museum, a zoo, scenic drives, and a wide variety of tourist attractions. About twenty miles to the west, campers can visit the Sleeping Bear Dunes National Lakeshore.

Charles Mears State Park (175 sites), on the shore of Lake Michigan about eleven miles south of Ludington, was established in 1923 as one of Michigan's early state parks. The park was named for a wealthy businessman who built a lumber and ship building empire and established towns along the Lake Michigan shore for shipping his products. The park has a large, crowded, sandy campground with a few sparsely spread shade trees that is located a few hundred feet from the beach and about three blocks from the Pentwater business district. Primary activities in this laid-back park are swimming in Lake Michigan, hanging out at the beach, and walking into town. Groups of adults can be seen milling around under their RV awnings in the campgrounds while groups of children and teenagers can be seen hanging out on the beach and in the parking lot. Eva and I enjoyed camping in this park two years ago before boarding the S.S. *Badger* ferry over to Wisconsin. After setting up our tent in the sand under a tree, we swam in Lake Michigan for an hour or so and then drove about ten miles north of the park to pick up two take-out fried walleye fish dinners from Bortell's. After finishing our supper, we strolled into the Pentwater business district and enjoyed an ice cream and music performed by one of the three musical groups giving free concerts along the main street.

Charles Mears State Park's campground is not much more than an RV park, but it is conveniently located near beautiful Lake Michigan beaches and the quaint tourist town of Pentwater.

Bortells's is a great fried fish take-out restaurant located between Charles Mears State Park and Ludington.

The Michigan State DNR also manages several state forests in this region with a total of thirty-eight small rustic campgrounds. The largest of these state forest campgrounds is **Goose Lake** (54 primitive sites), located about ten miles north of Cadillac. Several other state forest campgrounds in this area have been named by other authorities as some of the best campgrounds in the state. Some of these campgrounds are **Arbutus Lake** (36 primitive sites) about eight miles east of Traverse City, **Tubbs Lake** (33 primitive sites) about fifty-five miles north of Grand Rapids, **Platte River** (26 primitive sites) about twenty miles southwest of Traverse City, and **Long Lake** (20 primitive sites) located in Missaukee County about ten miles northeast of Cadillac.

Two federal agencies manage public campgrounds in this northwestern region. The U.S. Forest Service manages eighteen small, rustic campgrounds in the Manistee National Forest. **Lake Michigan Campground** (99 primitive sites), located on Lake Michigan about twelve miles south of Manistee, is the largest of these national forest campgrounds. **Sand Lake** (47 primitive sites) located about twenty-three miles east of Manistee, **Pines Point** (32 primitive sites) located about twenty-five miles northeast of Muskegon, and **Peterson Bridge** (30 primitive sites) about twenty-three miles east of Manistee are three of the campgrounds in this forest that have been named by other authorities as among the best in the state. The National Park Service manages the **Sleeping Bear Dunes National Lakeshore** (262 sites). This large federal property, stretching along the shore of Lake Michigan about twenty miles west of Traverse City, has three distinct geographical areas and four campgrounds. Two of the campgrounds—D.H. Day (20 sites) and the South Manitou Island Weather Station (20 sites)—have been named by other camping authorities as among the most secluded tent campgrounds in the state.

County and municipal governments in the northwestern region manage thirty-two additional public campgrounds that may be suited for tent campers. **Brower County Park** (230 sites), located in Stanwood about forty miles north of Grand Rapids, is the largest of these properties. **School Section Lake Veteran's County Park** (167 sites) located in Mecosta, **Merrill Lake County Park** (147 sites) located in Sears, and **White Cloud Municipal Park Campground** (104 sites) located about forty-five miles north of Grand Rapids are three more large county and municipal parks that were named by *Michigan's Best Campgrounds* as some of the best public campgrounds in the state. **Camp Pet-O-Se-Ga** (90 sites), **Barnes Park** (76 sites), **Paris Park** (68 sites), **Whitewater Township** (53 sites), **Buttersville Town-**

ship Park (50 sites), **Bill Wagner** (22 primitive sites), and **Power Island** (5 primitive sites) were all named by *Michigan's Best Campgrounds* while **St. James Township Park** (12 primitive sites) was named by *Best in Tent Camping: Michigan.*

Northeastern Region: Au Sable River

The northeastern region is defined as the area north of the line running from St. Louis east to Lake Huron and east of the line running from St. Louis north to Mackinaw City. Lake Huron, Saginaw Bay, and the "thumb" area define the eastern border of this region and the Au Sable plus several other scenic rivers flow through the center of the region out to Lake Huron. Reference cities in this region include Cheboygan at the far northern tip, Gaylord, Grayling, and Mount Pleasant down the western edge, Bay City on Saginaw Bay, and Alpena to the north on Lake Huron. The Huron National Forest is located in the Grayling and Mio area.

Popular tourist destinations in this region include the Au Sable, Rifle, Indian, Pigeon, and other scenic rivers that offer outstanding fishing and paddling opportunities. Visitors who do not have their own equipment will find dozens of liveries, outfitters, tackle shops, and guide services that will help to assure successful and enjoyable trips. Near Grayling and the Au Sable River, many tourists visit the Michigan Forest Visitor Center and Lumberman's Monument Visitor Center. Other popular tourist spots in this region are Houghton Lake, Higgins Lake, Mullett Lake, and other smaller lakes scattered across the region. These lakes also offer outstanding fishing and paddling adventures. Along the shores of Lake Huron, tourists will find several towns and state parks offering beautiful sand beaches, scenic lake views, and excellent fishing opportunities.

The Michigan Department of Natural Resources manages fourteen state parks and two recreation areas in this region—and nine of these state properties are located on the shores of Lake Huron. Tent campers planning vacations in this region may want to consider one of the following destinations.

South Higgins Lake State Park (400 sites), about eighteen miles south of Grayling, was established as one of Michigan's early state parks in 1927 and is clearly the most popular park in the region. The large, mostly shady campground is arranged in the shape of ten long finger-shaped loops pointing toward the lakeshore and swimming area. Most of the sites are reserved months ahead of time. Inside the park, visitors will enjoy swimming on the nearly mile-long beach, fishing for perch in the crystal-clear, spring-fed lake water, and hiking along ten miles of trails.

Aloha State Park (283 sites), on Mullett Lake about twenty-five miles south of Mackinaw City, is the second largest state camping destination in the northeastern region. The mainly sunny campground, organized into five loops spread along the lakeshore, typically fills to capacity every summer weekend. As one might guess, fishing and boating are the most popular activities in the park. Some say the lake is one of the best walleye fishing areas in the state. Outside the park, campers frequently ride up to shop in Cheboygan and visit tourist attractions in the Mackinaw City area.

Albert E. Sleeper State Park (226 sites), near the tip of Michigan's thumb in Saginaw Bay, was first established in 1925 as a county park, then transferred to the state in 1927 and named Huron State Park, and finally renamed Albert E. Sleeper State Park in 1944 in memory of Michigan's early governor who created the state park system. The park was named by *Best Tent Camping: Michigan* as having one of the best campgrounds for tent camping in the state. The heavily shaded campground is divided onto two large blocks that are located across the road from the lakeshore. Inside the park, visitors enjoy swimming, hiking, attending ranger-led nature programs, and watching sunrises and sunsets. Outside the park, visitors can charter fishing boats at one of several local marinas in the area or enjoy typical tourist activities in the resort village of Caseville.

Hartwick Pines State Park (100 sites), about nine miles north of Grayling, was established in 1927 as one of Michigan's first state parks and was named by *National Geographic* as one of the most scenic and historically significant state parks in the United States. The primary activities in this park are hiking through the 49-acre stand of old-growth pines and visiting the logging museum. Outside the park, visitors can fish or paddle in the Au Sable River or one of the small rivers in the area.

In addition to the state parks, the Michigan DNR also manages thirty-five rustic state forest campgrounds in this region. The largest of these state forest campgrounds is **Houghton Lake** (50 primitive sites), located about eighteen miles south of Grayling. **Ossineke** (42 primitive sites), located on Lake Huron about fifteen miles south of Alpena, was named by *TripleBlaze, Michigan's Best Campgrounds*, and *Best in Tent Camping: Michigan* as one of the best campgrounds in the state. **Tomahawk Creek Flooding** (47 primitive sites), **Big Bear Lake** (30 primitive sites), **Shupac Lake** (29 primitive sites), **Ess Lake** (27 primitive sites), and **Keystone Landing** (18 primitive sites) were all named by *Michigan's Best Campgrounds* while **Tomahawk Lake** (25 primitive sites) was named by *Best Tent Camping: Michigan.*

The U.S. Forest Service manages fourteen small, rustic campgrounds in the Huron National Forest. Many of these campgrounds are located near the Au Sable River that flows from Grayling east to Lake Huron. **Mack Lake** (42 primitive sites), located about thirty miles east of Grayling, is the largest of these state forest campgrounds. **Jewell Lake** (32 sites), about thirty miles south of Alpena, **Kneff Campground** (26 primitive sites), about ten miles east of Grayling, **Monument Campground** (19 primitive sites), on the Au Sable River about thirteen miles west of Lake Huron, **Rollways Campground** (19 primitive sites), about fifty miles southeast of Grayling, and **Island Lake** (17 primitive sites), about sixteen miles southeast of Grayling, were all named by *Michigan's Best Campgrounds* as among the best public campgrounds in the state. **Sawmill Point** (15 canoe-in primitive sites) was named by *Best in Tent Camping: Michigan.*

County and municipal governments in the northeastern region manage sixteen additional public campgrounds that may be suited for tent campers. **Alcona County Park** (502 sites), located about fifty miles east of Grayling on the Pine River, is the largest of these county and municipal parks. **Wagener County Park** (96 sites), located on Lake Huron about sixty miles north of Port Huron, **Herrick Recreation Area** (73 sites), located about forty miles northwest of Saginaw, **Gladwin City Park** (60 sites), located about sixty miles northwest of Saginaw, and **Pinconning Park** (42 sites), located on Saginaw Bay about thirty miles north of Saginaw, were all named by *Michigan's Best Campgrounds* as some of the best camping destinations in the state.

Useful Resources

After reading this chapter, readers should consult additional resources to determine specific destinations and campgrounds that best fit their family's particular interests and expectations. Some helpful resources are listed below.

- The Michigan Department of Natural Resources website (www. michigan.gov/dnr) contains information about all state-managed properties.
- The official Michigan state highway map, available from the Michigan Department of Transportation (www.michigan.gov/mdot) and at highway rest areas, shows approximate geographic locations of each state and most federal properties. The map also

provides a table that summarizes driving directions and amenities for each state property.

- *Michigan State Parks & Recreation Areas: Park Visitor Welcome Map 2012–2013* (brochure), available in highway rest areas, provides an overview of all state properties and provides brief descriptions of each one.
- *Michigan Campground 2012 Directory* (brochure), available in most highway rest areas, describes a few private campgrounds in the state.
- *Michigan State and National Parks: A Complete Guide* (book) provides detailed descriptions of state properties and National Park Service properties.
- *Michigan's Best Campgrounds* (book) briefly describes 150 state, federal, and local campgrounds in the state.
- *Best Tent Camping: Michigan* (book) provides detailed descriptions of fifty secluded campgrounds, including a few county and municipal parks.
- The Michigan state DNR (www.midnrreservations.com/, 800-447-2757) accepts reservations for state properties. First-time users will have to register a user name and password.
- Recreation.Gov (www.Recreation.gov, 877-444-6777) is a private organization that makes reservations for all federal properties.

Michigan, Lower Peninsula Public Campgrounds

Campgrounds are listed by number of campsites available from most numerous to least. The following abbreviations are used to note public campgrounds that have been named by various authorities as among the best in the state:

FD   This property is one of my favorite camping destinations.

YS   This property was named by *Yahoo Sports* as being one of Michigan's five best state parks for summer tent camping.

TB   This property was named by the *TripleBlaze* website as having one of the best fifteen campgrounds in the state.

MBC This property was named and described by *Michigan's Best Campgrounds* as being one of the best 150 campgrounds in the state.

BTC This property was named and described by *Best in Tent Camping: Michigan* as having one of the 50 most quiet and most private campgrounds in the state.

NG   This property was named and described by *National Geographic's Guide to State Parks in the United States* as one of America's most historic and scenic state parks.

(P = primitive)

Southwestern Region: Lake Michigan Sand Dunes

State Parks and Recreation Areas

Yankee Springs SP
345 sites, showers, beach, fishing,
    sailing, bridle trails, bike trails
2104 S Briggs Rd, Middleville
30 m N of Kalamazoo, 5 m E of
    US 131

FD, MBC, BTC
269-795-9081
42.61756, -85.51775

Holland SP
309 sites, showers, beach, fishing,
    boat rental, Wi-Fi, Dutch culture
    & cuisine
2215 Ottawa Beach Rd, Holland
On Lake Michigan, 28 m S of
    Muskegon

FD
616-399-9390
42.77734, -86.20012

P.J. Hoffmaster SP
293 sites, showers, beach, nature
    center, observation area
6585 Lake Harbor Rd, Muskegon
On Lake Michigan, 7 m S of
    Muskegon

FD, TB, MBC, NG
231-7983711
43.13291, -86.26545

Muskegon SP
244 sites, showers, beach, fishing,
    winter activities
3560 Memorial Dr, North Muskegon
On Lake Michigan, 10 m N of
    Muskegon

MBC
331-744-3480
43.24849, -86.33386

Van Buren SP
220 sites showers, beach, bike trail,
    hiking
23960 Ruggles Rd, South Haven
On Lake Michigan, 15 m N of I-94

FD
269-637-2788
42.33179, -86.30393

Fort Custer SP   269-731-4200
219 sites, showers, beach, fishing,   42.32308, -85.35329
   boat rental, bike trail, bridle trails
5163 Fort Custer Dr, Augusta
18 m E of Kalamazoo, 2 m N of I-94

Warren Dunes SP   MBC, BTC
211 sites, showers, beach   269-426-4013
12032 Red Arrow Hwy, Sawyer   41.91083, -86.58857
On Lake Michigan, 10 m N of
   Indiana line

Grand Haven SP   MBC
174 sites, showers, beach, fishing,   616-847-1309
   concerts   43.05580, -86.24696
1001 Harbor Ave, Grand Haven
On Lake Michigan 10 m S of
   Muskegon

Ionia SP   616-527-3750
147 sites, showers, beach, bridle trails,   42.95108, -85.09692
   fishing, hunting, dog field-trial area
2880 W David Hwy, Ionia
25 m E of Grand Rapids, 8 m N of I-96

County and Municipal Campgrounds

Pioneer Park, Muskegon CP   MBC
235 sites, showers, beach   231-744-3480
1563 N Scenic Dr, Muskegon   43.28528, -86.36935
On Lake Michigan, 10 m N of
   Muskegon

Angle Cove CG, Branch CP   517-278-8541
130 sites, showers, fishing, boat rental   42.00684, -85.03998
851 River Rd, Coldwater
1 m W of I-69, 10 m N of Indiana

Shamrock Park, Berrien Springs MP   269-473-5691
112 sites, showers, Wi-Fi, fishing,   41.99359, -86.39741
   boat rental
9385 Old US 31 S, Berrien Springs
2 m E of US 31, 12 m N of Indiana line

Meinert Park Pines CG,   231-894-4881
  Muskegon CP   43.45854, -86.45605
67 sites, showers, beach
8390 Meinert Rd, Montague
On Lake Michigan, 20 m N of
  Muskegon

Covert Park Beach & CG, Covert MP   269-764-1421
62 sites, showers, beach, shopping,   42.30086, -86.31468
  trail, dinner cruises, concerts,
  lighthouses
80559 32nd Ave, Covert
On Lake Michigan, 18 m N of
  Benton Harbor

Ed Henning Park, Newaygo CP   MBC
60 sites, showers, fishing, beach,   231-652-1202
  paddling   43.24368, -85.78989
500 Croton Rd, Newaygo
35 m N of Grand Rapids, on M-82

Kalamazoo Expo Center,   269-383-87761
  Kalamazoo CP   42.27925, -85.54401
60 sites, showers
2900 Lake St, Kalamazoo
In Kalamazoo

Memorial Park, Branch CP   517-279-2254
50 P sites, beach, fishing   41.92728, -85.00438
175 Memorial Park Dr, Coldwater
1 m W of I-69, 10 m N of Indiana

Cold Brook Park, Kalamazoo CP   MBC
44 sites, showers, beach   269-746-4270
14467 E MN Ave, Climax   42.25690, -85.35367
11 m E of Kalamazoo

Markin Glenn Park, Kalamazoo CP 269-381-7570
38 sites, showers, beach   42.33789, -85.58983
5300 N Westnedge Ave, Kalamazoo
21 m N of I-94, 3 m E of US 131

Blue Lake Park, Muskegon CP   231,894-5574
25 sites, showers, beach, fishing   43.44832, -86.19411
10701 Nichols Rd, Holton
18 m NE of Muskegon, on M-120

Southeastern Region: Detroit Attractions

State Parks and Recreation Areas

Waterloo RA
350 sites, showers, beach, fishing, nature center, birding, Detroit attractions
16345 McClure Rd, Chelsea
50 m W of Detroit, 2 m N of I-94

MBC, BTC
734-475-8307
42.33343, -84.10603

Algonac SP
296 sites, showers, fishing, nature programs, ship watching
8732 River Rd, Marine City
On St. Clair River, 40 m NE of Detroit

810-765-5605
42.65214, -82.52964

Sterling SP
256 sites, showers, beach, fishing, bike trail, birding, Detroit attractions
2800 State Park Rd, Monroe
On Lake Erie, 20 m S of Detroit

MBC
734-289-2715
41.92134, -83.34213

Lakeport SP
250 sites, showers, beach
7605 Lakeshore Dr, Lakeport
On Lake Huron, 10 m N of I-69

810-327-6224
43.12447, -84.49736

Pinckney RA
220 sites, showers, beach, paddling, bike trail, bridle trail, Detroit attractions
8555 Silver Hills Rd, Pinckney
35 m W of Detroit, 8 m N of I-94

MBC, BTC
734-426-4913
43.41198, -83.96558

Metamora-Hadley RA
214 sites, showers, beach, fishing, canoe rental, Detroit attractions
3871 Hurd Rd, Metamora
40 m N of Detroit, 5 m S of I-69

MBC
810-797-4439
42.94505, -83.35890

Brighton RA
213 sites, showers, beach, fishing, bike trail, horse rental, Detroit attractions
6360 Chilson Rd, Howell
30 m W of Detroit, 4 m S of I-96

810-229-6566
42.51751, -83.85534

Pontiac Lake RA   248-666-1020
206 sites, showers, beach, fishing,   42.67365, -83.43960
  nature center, bridle trails,
  Detroit attractions
7800 Gale Rd, Waterford
15 m NW of Detroit, 8 m S of I-75

Walter J Hayes SP   517-467-7401
185 sites, showers, beach, fishing,   42.05996, -84.14079
  Detroit attractions
1220 Wampler's Lake Rd, Onsted
50 m SW of Detroit, 40 m W of I-275

Sleepy Hollow SP   YS
181 sites, showers, beach, fishing,   517-651-6217
  bike & bridle trails   42.94128, -84.40109
7835 East Price Rd, Laingsburg
15 m N of Lansing, 5 m E of US 127

Holly RA   248-634-8811
159 sites, showers, beach, fishing,   42.81070, -83.54956
  bird watching, bike trail, Detroit
  attractions
8100 Grange Hall Rd, Holly
30 m NW of Detroit, 2 m E of I-75

Proud Lake RA   MBC
130 sites, showers, beach, fishing,   248-685-2433
  canoe rental, bike & bridle trail,   42.56970, -83.55943
  Detroit attractions
3500 Wixom Rd, Milford
20 m W of Detroit, 5 m N of I-96

Seven Lakes SP   248-634-7271
70 sites, showers, beach, fishing, boat 42.81669, -83.64810
  rental, Detroit attractions
14390 Fish Lake Rd, Holly
35 m NW of Detroit, 8 m W of I-75

Lake Hudson SP   BTC
50 P sites, beach, fishing, astronomy 517-445-2265
5505 Morey Hwy, Clayton   41.83538, -84.23569
10 m N of Ohio border, 38 m E of I-69

Highland RA

248-889-3750

25 P equestrian sites, beach, fishing,   42.63837, -83.57334
   bridle trail, horse rental, Detroit
   attractions
5200 East Highland Rd, White Lake
20 m NW of Detroit, 10 m N of I-96

Ortonville RA

810-797-4439

25 P sites, beach, fishing, bike & bridle   42.88470, -83.40410
   trails, hunting, trap range, Detroit
   attractions
5779 Hadley Rd, Ortonville
30 m NW of Detroit, 10 m E of I-75

County and Municipal Campgrounds

Wolverine CG, Genesee CP

800-648-7275

194 sites, showers, paddling   43.15669, -83.41050
7698 N Baxter Rd, Columbiaville
18 m NE of Flint, 6 m E of M-15

Addison Oaks, Oakland CP

MBC

174 sites, showers, beach, trails,   248-693-2432
   disc golf, Detroit attractions   42.79907, -83.16763
1480 W Romeo Rd, Leonard
25 m N of Detroit, 8 m W of M-53

Wayne County Fairgrounds,

734-697-7002

   Wayne CP   42.22450, -83.49205

110 sites, showers, laundry, Detroit
   attractions
10871 Quirk Rd, Belleville
Near I-94 & 275 intersection

Quincy-Marble Lake, Branch CP

517-639-4414

100 P sites, beach, fishing, boating   41.93936, -84.89600
301 Lake Blvd, Quincy
1 m E of I-69, 10 m N of Indiana

Water Tower Travel Trailer Park,

810-664-4296

   Lapeer MP   43.06142, -83.31928

30 sites, showers, fishing, tennis
1552 N Main St M-24, Lapeer
40 m N of Detroit, 20 m E of Flint

Northwestern Region: Traverse City Area

State Parks, Recreation Areas, and Forests

Interlochen SP
490 sites, showers, beach, fishing,
    paddling, concerts, Traverse City
    attractions
M-137, Interlochen
15 m S of Traverse City, 5 m W of
    US 31

FD, MBC
231-276-9511
44.62810, -85.76365

Ludington SP
373 sites, showers, beach, fishing,
    paddling, tubing, bike trail,
    lighthouse
8800 West M-166, Ludington
On Lake Michigan, 4 m N of
    Ludington

TB, MBC, BTC
231-843-2423
44.00324, -86.48239

Traverse City SP
343 sites, showers, beach, bike trail,
    shopping, Traverse City attractions
1132 US Highway 31 N, Traverse City
2 m E of Traverse City, on US 31

FD
231-922-5270
44.74594, -85.55027

Burt Lake SP
306 sites, showers, beach, fishing,
    paddling
6635 State Park Dr, Indian River
25 m S of Mackinaw City, 2 m W
    of I-75

231-238-9392
45.39611, -84.63444

Wilderness SP
250 sites, showers, beach, boating,
    trails, Straits attractions
Carp Lake
On Lake Michigan, 10 m W of
    Mackinaw City

MBC, BTC
231-436-5381
45.75058, -84.86277

Young SP
240 sites, showers, beach, fishing,
    boating, Ernest Hemingway history
02280 Boyne City Rd, Boyne
40 m S of Mackinaw City, 20 m W of
    I-75

231-582-7523
45.23687, -85.04299

William Mitchell SP
221 sites, showers, beach, fishing,
    paddling, boating, bike rental,
    nature programs
6093 East M-115, Cadillac
In Cadillac, 4 m W of US 131

FD
231-775-7911
44.24765, -85.45157

Silver Lake SP
200 sites, showers, beach, fishing,
    off-road vehicle area
9679 West State Park Rd, Mears
On Lake Michigan, 35 m N of
    Muskegon

YS
231-873-3083
43.67271, -86.51476

Petoskey SP
180 sites, showers, beach, scenic
    views, bike trail, shopping
2475 Harbor Petoskey Rd, Petoskey
On Lake Michigan, 30 m SW of
    Mackinaw City

MBC
231-347-2311
45.40155, -84.90948

Charles Mears SP
175 sites, showers, beach, fishing,
    shopping, concerts, Wi-Fi
400 West Lowell St, Pentwater
On Lake Michigan, 11 m S of
    Ludington

FD, MBC
231-869-2051
43.79620, -86.43011

Orchard Beach SP
166 sites, showers, beach, fishing,
    scenic views
2064 Lakeshore Rd, Manistee
On Lake Michigan, 15 m N of
    Ludington

231-723-7422
44.27880, -86.31443

Otsego Lake SP
155 sites, showers, beach, fishing
7136 Old US Hwy 21 S, Gaylord
35 m S of Mackinaw City, 2 m W
    of I-75

989-732-5485
44.93101, -84.68956

Newaygo SP
99 P sites, beach, fishing, paddling
2793 Beech St, Newaygo
43 m N of Grand Rapids, 5 m W of
    US 131

TB, MBC
231-856-4452
43.49901, -85.58959

Fisherman's Island SP
80 P sites, beach, solitude, shopping
Bells Bay Rd, Charlevoix
On Lake Michigan, 50 m N of
    Traverse City

MBC, BTC
231-547-6641
45.26594, -85.34145

Goose Lake SF CG
54 P sites, fishing, boating
Cadillac
10 m NE of Cadillac, 8 m E of US 131

MBC
231-775-7911
44.35208, -85.24446

Leelanau SP
51 P sites, beach, scenic views,
    lighthouse
15310 N Lighthouse Point Rd,
    Northport
On Lake Michigan, 18 m N of
    Traverse City

MBC
231-386-5422
45.20980, -85.54576

Lake Dubonnet SF CG
50 P sites, fishing, bike trail
Traverse City
8 m W of Traverse City, 2 m N of
    US 31

MBC
231-276-9511
44.67817, -85.78382

Reedsburg Dam SF CG
47 P sites, fishing paddling
Houghton Lake
50 m N of Mount Pleasant, 2 m W of
    US 127

989-422-5192
44.35721, -84.85479

Tippy Dam RA
40 P sites, boating, fishing
1500 Dilling Rd, Brethren
30 m W of Cadillac, 23 m N of US 10

231-848-4880
44.28134, -85.98123

Lake Margrethe SF CG
37 P sites, fishing, paddling
M-72, Grayling
8 m W of Grayling, 3 m S of SR 72

MBC
989-348-7068
44.65732, -84.81771

Maple Bay SF CG
38 P sites, beach, fishing, paddling
1700 Maple Bay Rd, Brutus
22 m S of Mackinaw City, 4 m E of
    US 31

MBC
231-238-9313
45.48835, -84.70682

Guernsey Lake SF CG
36 P sites, fishing, bike trail
Campground Rd, Kalkaska
18 m E of Traverse City, 5 m S of SR 72

MBC
231-922-5270
44.71481, -85.32038

Arbutus Lake SF CG
30 P sites, fishing
Garfield Rd, Traverse City
8 m E of Traverse City, 8 m S of SR 72

MBC, BTC
231-922-5270
44.66529, -85.52066

Tubbs Lake SF CG
33 P sites, some canoe-in, fishing,
    paddling
17005 Main Island Dr, Mecosta
60 m NE of Muskegon, 15 m E of
    US 131

TB, BTC
231-775-9727
43.70619, -85.18944

CCC Bridge SF CG
32 P sites, fishing, paddling
Sunset Trail Rd, Kalkaska
30 m E of Traverse City, 8 m S of SR 72

BTC
231-922-5270
44.57921, -85.07400

Spring Lake SF CG
32 P sites, fishing paddling
US 131, Fife Lake
20 m SE of Traverse City, 15 m S of
    SR 72

231-922-5270
44.56411, -85.35922

Carrieville SF CG
31 P sites, fishing, paddling
Old M-63 & Kings Hwy, Baldwin
35 m E of Ludington, 10 m N of US 10

TB
231-745-9465
44.01565, -85.73215

Scheck's Place SF CG
30 P sites, fishing, paddling
Williamsburg Rd, Kalkaska
13 m SE of Traverse City, 8 m S of
    SR 72

231-922-5270
44.67475, -85.39655

Lake Ann SF CG
30 P sites, fishing, paddling, bike trail
Almira & Reynolds Rd, Lake Ann
12 m W of Traverse City, 5 m N of
    US 31

231-276-9511
44.72499, -85.85909

Upper Manistee River SF CG
30 P sites, fishing, paddling
CR 612, Grayling
10 m NW of Grayling, 5 m N of SR 72

MBC
989-348-7068
44.75831, -84.85977

Platte River SF CG
26 P sites, fishing, paddling, bike trail
5685 Lake Michigan Rd, Beulah
20 m W of Traverse City, 3 m S of
  US 31

TB, MBC
231-276-9511
44.63189, -86.07891

Silver Creek SF CG
26 P sites, fishing, paddling, bike trail
N State Rd, Baldwin
20 m SW of Cadillac, 12 m W of
  US 131

MBC
231-745-9465
44.10305, -85.68288

Baxter Bridge SF CG
25 P sites, fishing, paddling
M-42 & 31, Manton
20 m S of Traverse City, 8 m W of
  US 131

231-775-7911
44.49662, -85.48157

Old US 131 SF CG
25 P sites, fishing, paddling
Old US 131, Manton
20 m S of Traverse City, 1 m W of
  US 131

231-775-7911
44.48928, -85.41647

Veterans Memorial SF CG
24 P sites, fishing, paddling
US 31, Beulah
15 m W of Traverse City, 3 m S of
  US 31

231-276-9511
44.62077, -85.93540

Healey Lake SF CG
24 P sites, fishing, paddling
Healey Lake Rd, Manistee, Springdale
  Township
25 m SW of Traverse City, 8 m E of
  US 31

231-864-2531
44.43978, -86.00239

Manistee River Bridge SF CG
23 P sites, fishing, paddling
M-72, Grayling
8 m W of Grayling, 2 m S of SR 72

989-348-7068
44.69062, -84.84638

Tubbs Island SF CG
21 P sites, fishing, paddling
17018 65th Ave, Mecosta
60 m NE of Muskegon, 15 m E of
  US 131

MBC
989-382-7158
43.70803, -85.21442

Long Lake SF CG (Missaukee Co)
20 P sites, fishing
Green Rd N, Cadillac
10 m NE of Cadillac, 5 m E of US 131

TB, MBC
231-775-7911
44.32,317, -85.36269

Leverentz Lake SF CG
18 P sites, fishing, bike trail
US 10 & Forest Dr, Baldwin
33 m E of Ludington, 1 m N of US 10

TB, MBC
231-745-9465
43.90852, -85.81944

Weber Lake SF CG
18 P sites, bike trail, fishing, paddling
Prue Rd, Indian River
35 m S of Mackinaw City, 4 m W of
    I-75

231-238-9313
45.29608, -84.72029

Haakwood SF CG
18 P sites, fishing
11000 S Straits Hwy, Indian River
33 m S of Mackinaw City, 3 m W of
    I-75

231-238-9313
45.30024, -84.61455

Sunrise Lake SF CG
17 P sites, fishing, bike trail
Sunrise lake Rd, Reed City
20 m S of Cadillac, 10 m E of US 131

989-386-4067
44.03022, -85.33531

Long Lake SF CG (Wexford Co)
16 P sites, fishing
Campground Rd, Cadillac
10 m N of Cadillac, 1 m E of US 131

231-775-7911
44.32, -85.37715

Hopkins Creek Equestrian SF CG
16 P sites, fishing, bridle trail
Lucas Rd, Cadillac
15 m N of Cadillac, 1 m E of US 131

231-775-7911
44.48205, -85.39072

Grass Lake SF CG
15 P sites, fishing, paddling
CR 669, Thompsonville
10 m W of Traverse City, 4 m S of
    US 31

231-378-4462
44.60819, -85.86437

Pinney Bridge SF CG
15 P sites, fishing, bike trail
620 & Cascade Rd, East Jordan
15 m W of Gaylord, 4 m S of SR 32

231-582-7523
45.03955, -85.03566

Pickerel Lake (Kalkaska) SF CG   MBC
13 P sites, fishing   989-348-7068
Sunset Trail Rd, Kalkaska   44.79342, -84.97435
35 m W of Traverse City, 8 m N of
    SR 72

Goose Creek SF CG   989-348-6371
12 P sites, fishing   44.69925, -84.83979
CR 612, Fredric
10 m NW of Grayling, 8 m W of I-75

Graves Crossing SF CG   BTC
10 P sites, fishing, paddling, bike trail   231-582-7523
Graves Crossing, East Jordan   45.03225, -85.05954
18 m W of Gaylord, 7 m W of US 131

Bray Creek SF CG   231-745-9465
9 P sites, fishing, bike trail   43.92947, -85.83171
Merriville Rd, Baldwin
33 m E of Ludington, 3 m N of US 10

Lincoln Bridge SF CG   BTC
9 P sites, fishing, paddling, bike trail   231-745-9465
10 Mile Rd, Baldwin   44.11717, -85.68323
18 m SE of Cadillac, 12 m W of
    US 131

Mud Lake SF CG   989-386-4067
8 P sites, boating, fishing   43.90720, -85.07739
7 Mile Rd, Clare
30 m SE of Cadillac, 2 m N of US 10

Hopkins Creek SF CG   231-775-7911
7 P sites, fishing   44.44787, -85.33235
Lucas Rd, Manton
15 m N of Cadillac, 5 m E of US 131

National Lakeshore and National Forest Campgrounds

Sleeping Bear Dunes NLS   TB, MBC, BTC
262 sites, beach, showers,   231-326-5134
9922 Front Street, Empire   44.71278, -86.11778
On Lake Michigan, 24 m W of
    Traverse City

Lake Michigan CG, Manistee NF
99 P sites, beach, sand dunes, sunsets
Manistee
On Lake Michigan, 12 m S of
    Manistee

MBC
231-723-2211
44.11735, -86.41442

Hungerford CG, Manistee NF
50 P sites, bridle trail
Big Rapids
45 m NE of Muskegon, 1 m W of
    US 131

231-745-4631
43.71667, -85.62444

Sand Lake CG, Manistee NF
47 sites, showers, beach, fishing,
    paddling
Wellston
23 m E of Manistee, 5 m S of M-55

MBC, BTC
231-723-2211
44.16806, -85.92944

Pines Point CG, Manistee NF
32 P sites, paddling, fishing
Hesperia
25 m NE of Muskegon, 2 m S of M-20

MBC, BTC
231-745-4631
43.52778, -86.11944

Peterson Bridge CG, Manistee NF
30 P sites, paddling, fishing
Baldwin
23 m E of Manistee, 20 m N of US 10

MBC
231-723-2211
44.20417, -85.79611

Nichols Lake CG, Manistee NF
29 P sites, fishing, hiking
Brohman
30 m SE of Ludington, 16 m S of
    US 10

MBC
231-745-4631
43.72285, -85.89986

Benton Lake CG, Manistee NF
25 P sites, fishing
Brohman
35 m SE of Ludington, 18 m S of
    US 10

MBC
231-745-4631
45.87689, -87.90384

Marzinski Horse CG, Manistee NF
21 P sites, bridle trail
Wellston
5 m E of Manistee, 1 m S of M-55

231-723-2211
44.22518, -86.16336

Old Grade CG, Manistee NF
20 P sites, fishing, wildlife, mosquitoes
Baldwin
35 m E of Ludington, 13 m N of US 10

MBC
231-745-4631
44.05983, -85.84287

Bowman Bridge CG, Manistee NF   MBC
20 P sites, canoeing, fishing, bike trail   231-745-4631
Baldwin   43.88833, -85.94222
23 m W of Ludington, 3 m S of US 10

Bear Track CG, Manistee NF   231-723-2211
20 P sites, paddling, fishing   44.14375, -85.97205
Wellston
28 m NE of Ludington, 10 m N of
    US 10

Driftwood Valley CG, Manistee NF   MBC
19 P sites, paddling, fishing, hiking   231-723-2211
Wellston   44.1319, -85.9967
30 m NE of Ludington, on M-55

Hemlock CG, Manistee NF   MBC
18 P sites, wildlife, mosquitoes   231-723-2211
Cadillac   44.23013, -85.50341
10 m W of Cadillac, 1 m N of M-55

Seaton Creek CG, Manistee NF   MBC
17 P sites, solitude, trail nearby   231-723-2211
Mesick   44.34973, -85.80142
20 m NW of Cadillac, 6 m N of M-56

Pine Lake CG, Manistee NF   231-723-2211
12 P sites, beach, fishing, paddling   44.19931, -86.00689
Wellston
30 m W of Cadillac, 5 m S of M-55

Minnie Pond CG, Manistee NF   231-745-4631
11 P dispersed sites, fishing, paddling   43.60435, -85.91003
White Cloud
35 m NE of Muskegon, 5 m N of
    M-20

Shelley Lake CG, Manistee NF   MBC
9 P sites, fishing   231-745-4631
Brohman   43.71117, -85.81777
45 m NE of Muskegon, on M-37

Highbank Lake CG, Manistee NF   MBC, BTC
9 P sites, beach, fishing, paddling   231-745-4631
Bitely   43.77747, -85.88313
45 m NE of Muskegon, 1 m W of
    M-37

County and Municipal Campgrounds

Brower Park, Mecosta CP
230 sites, showers, beach, fishing,
paddling, disc golf, tennis
23056 Polk Rd, Stanwood
40 m N of Grand Rapids, 4 m E of
US 131

231-823-2561
43.56271, -85.54673

Rose Lake Park, Osceola CP
172 sites, showers, beach, miniature
golf, fishing
17726 Youth Dr, LeRoy
15 m S of Cadillac, 5 m E of US 131

231-768-4923
44.07133, -85.38278

**School Section Lake Veteran's Park,
Mecosta CP**
167 sites, showers, beach, volleyball,
disc golf, boat rental, fishing,
paddling
9003 90th Ave, Mecosta
50 m NE of Grand Rapids, 15 m E of
US 131

MBC
231-972-7450
43.59787, -85.26517

Merrill Lake Park, Mecosta CP
147 sites, showers, beach, fishing,
boating
3275 Evergreen Rd, Sears
60 m NE of Grand Rapids, 20 m E of
US 131

MBC
989-382-7158
43.80518, -85.15342

Missaukee Lake Park, Missaukee CP
117 sites, showers, shopping, laundry,
boating
Lake City
10 m NE of Cadillac, on M-55

231-839-4945
44.33895, -85.21948

White Cloud CG, White Cloud MP
104 sites, showers, fishing, walking
680 E Wilcox, White Cloud
45 m N of Grand Rapids, on M-37

MBC
231-689-2021
43.54775, -85.78679

**Coldwater Lake Family Park,
Isabella CP**
95 sites, showers, beach, fishing
1703 N Littlefield Rd, Weidman
13 m NW of Mount Pleasant, 11 m W
of US 127

989-644-2388
43.66459, -84.94875

Camp Pet-O-Se-Ga Park, Emmet CP
90 sites, beach, fishing
11000 Camp PetOSeGa Dr, Alanson
25 m S of Mackinaw City, on US 31

MBC
231-347-6536
45.38690, -84.73008

John Gurney Park, Ludington MP
85 sites, showers, beach, bike trail,
    tennis, near Lake Michigan
300 N Griswold, Hart
20 m S of Ludington, 3 m E of US 31

231-873-4959
43.70275, -86.35790

**Lake Billings RV Park & CG,
    Manton MP**
85 sites, showers, fishing
232 E Elmore St, Manton
10 m N of Cadillac, 1 m W of US 131

231-824-3572
44.41857, -85.39504

Otsego Lake CG, Otsego CP
80 sites, showers, beach, volleyball
1657 County Park Rd, Otsego Lake
20 m N of Grayling, 3 m W of I-75

989-731-6448
44.96653, -84.70300

Barnes Park, Antrim CP
76 sites, showers, beach, bike trail,
    Traverse City attractions
12298 Barnes Park Rd, Eastport
On Grand Traverse Bay, 30 m NE of
    Traverse City

MBC
231-599-2712
45.11098, -85.36069

Mangus Park, Petoskey MP
72 sites, showers, scenic views,
    bike trail, Wi-Fi
901 West Lake St, Petoskey
On Lake Michigan, 30 m S of
    Mackinaw City

231-347-1027
45.37323, -84.97442

Paris Park, Mecosta CP
68 sites, showers, bike rentals, trails,
    fishing, paddling
22090 Northland Dr, Paris
55 m N of Grand Rapids, 4 m E of
    US 131

MBC
231-796-3420
43.78709, -85.50282

Whiting Park, Charlevoix CP
58 sites, showers, beach, fishing,
    paddling
05820 Lake Shore Rd, Boyne City
40 m S of Mackinaw City, 20 m W of
    I-75

231-582-7040
45.23247, -85.09220

Mason County CG & Picnic Area   231-845-7609
56 sites, showers, Wi-Fi, golf, disc golf   43.90777, -86.42923
5906 W Chauvez Rd, Ludington
Near Lake Michigan, in Ludington

Whitewater Township MP   MBC
53 sites, showers, beach, fishing,   231-267-5091
  paddling   44.81628, -85.38824
9500 Park Rd, Williamsburg
18 m E of Traverse City, on M-72

Crooked Lake Park, Missaukee CP   231-839-4945
52 P sites, beach, boating, fishing   44.32843, -85.28476
Lake City
10 m NE of Cadillac, 4 m W of M-55

Buttersville CG, Pere Marquette   MBC
  Township   231-843-2114
50 sites, showers, beach   43.93872, -86.45257
991 S Lakeshore Dr, Ludington
On Lake Michigan, 2 m S of
  Ludington

Craven Park, Antrim CP   231-533-8931
50 sites, showers, fishing   44.97700, -85.18763
3737 S Derenzy Rd, Bellaire
25 m NE of Traverse City, 10 m E of
  US 31

Wooden Shoe Park, Antrim CP   231-588-6382
40 sites, showers, beach, boating   45.16403, -85.24088
6625 Bridge St, Elsworth
35 m NE of Traverse City, 5 m E of
  US 31

Log Lake CG, Kalkaska CP   231-258-2940
40 sites, golf, disc golf, swimming,   44.74636, -85.14872
  fishing, paddling, casino, bike trail
2475 East Log Lake Rd, Kalkaska
20 m E of Traverse City, on US 131

Thurston Park, Antrim CP   231-544-6854
36 sites, showers, beach, boating   45.06887, -85.25966
Old State East at Lake St, Central Lake
30 m NE of Traverse City, 5 m E of
  US 31

Maple Grove CG, Lake City MP   231-839-4429
33 sites, showers   44.32998, -85.20784
5547 W Davis Rd, Lake City
10 m NE of Cadillac, on M-55

Bill Wagner Memorial MP CG   MBC
22 P sites, beach, fishing, scenic views 231-448-2505
East Side Road, Beaver Island   45.65766, -85.49946
In Lake Michigan, 40 m W of
    Mackinaw City

Crittenden Park, Osceola CP   231-734-2588
19 sites, showers, beach, fishing,   43.86721, -85.18818
    paddling
3641 S 50th Ave, Sears
25 m SE of Cadillac, 18 m E of US 131

Ben D Jeffs River Park, Missaukee CP 231-839-4945
17 P sites, paddling   44.33474, -84.88912
CR M-55, Lake City
10 m NE of Cadillac, on M-55

Rambadt Park, Reed City MP   231-832-2884
17 sites, showers, bike trails, concerts 43.88476, -85.51455
Reed City
30 m S of Cadillac, 2 m E of US 131

Black Lake CG, Oceana CP   231-638-3365
15 P sites, beach, fishing   43.74558, -86.11817
5601 N 176th Ave, Walkersville
20 m SE of Ludington, 12 m E of
    US 31

St James Township MP CG   BTC
12 P sites, secluded sites   231-448-2505
Beaver Island   45.79894, -85.52856
In Lake Michigan, 40 m W of
    Mackinaw City

Power Island CG, Grand Traverse CP   MBC
5 P sites, fishing boating, boat access   231-922-4818
    only   44.86888, -85.57583
Traverse City
In Lake Michigan, 9 m N of
    Traverse City

Northeastern Region: Au Sable River

State Parks, Recreation Areas, and Forests

South Higgins Lake SP
400 sites, showers, beach, fishing,
    boat rental
106 State Park Rd, Roscommon
18 m S of Grayling, 2 m W of I-75

989-821-6374
44.42299, -84.67811

Aloha SP
283 sites, showers, beach, fishing, bike
    trail, Straits attractions
4347 Third St, Cheboygan
25 m S of Mackinaw City, 10 m E of
    I-75

231-625-2522
45.52013, -84.46432

Albert E. Sleeper SP
226 sites, showers, beach, bike trails
6573 State Park Rd, Caseville
On Saginaw Bay (Lake Huron), 55 m
    NE of Saginaw

BTC
989-856-4411
43.96934, -83.20521

Clear Lake SP
200 sites, showers, beach, fishing,
    boat rental, wild life viewing
20500 M-33, North Atlanta
25 m NE of Gaylord, on SR 33

989-785-4388
45.13383, -84.17690

Harrisville SP
195 sites, showers, fishing, paddling,
    bike trail
248 state Park Rd, Harrisville
On Lake Huron, 30 m S of Alpena

MBC
989-724-5126
44.64751, -83.29764

Bay City RA
184 sites, showers, beach, fishing,
    boat rental, bike & bridle trail,
    nature center
3582 State Park Dr, Bay City
On Lake Huron, 18 m N of Saginaw

989-684-3020
43.66714, -83.91170

Tawas Point SP
193 sites, showers, beach, fishing, bike
    trail, birding, lighthouse
686 Tawas Beach Rd, East Tawas
On Lake Huron, 5 m N of SR 55

MBC
989-362-5041
44.25363, -83.44893

Rifle River RA   BTC
174 sites, showers, fishing, bike trail 989-4732258
Lupton   44.41738, -84.02116
65 m N of Saginaw, 20 m E of I-75

North Higgins Lake SP   989-821-6125
174 sites, showers, beach, fishing, bike 44.51462, -84.74952
    trail, CCC museum
11747 North Higgins Lake Dr,
    Roscommon
10 m S of Grayling, between I-75 &
    US 127

Wilson SP   989-539-3021
159 sites, showers, beach, fishing   44.03098, -84.80713
Harrison
55 m NW of Saginaw, 2 m E of US 127

P.F. Hoeft SP   MBC
144 sites, showers, beach, bike trail   989-734-2543
5001 US 23 N, Rogers City   45.46816, -83.89024
On Lake Huron, 55 m SE of
    Mackinaw City

Port Cresent SP   MBC
137 sites, showers, beach, fishing,   989-738-8663
    paddling, boat rental, bridle trail 44.01079, -83.05027
1775 Port Austin Rd, Port Austin
On Saginaw Bay (Lake Huron), 65 m
    NE of Saginaw

Hartwick Pines SP   FD, MBC, NG
100 sites, showers, fishing, bike trail, 989-348-7068
    forestry museum   44.74317, -84.65023
4216 Ranger Rd, Grayling
10 m N of Grayling, 2 m E of I-75

Onaway SP   MBC
82 sites, showers, small beach, fishing 989-733-8279
3622 N M-211, Onaway   45.43216, -84.22898
35 m SE of Mackinaw City, 20 m E of
    I-75

Cheboygan SP   231-627-2811
75 sites, showers, beach, fishing, boat 45.64458, -84.40074
    rental, bike trail, lighthouse
4490 Beach Rd, Cheboygan
On Lake Huron, 20 m SE of
    Mackinaw City

Houghton Lake SF CG
50 P sites, fishing, paddling
Roscommon
18 m S of Grayling, 4 m E of US 127

989-821-6125
44.40122, -84.78492

Tomahawk Creek Flooding SF CG
47 P sites, bike trail, fishing, paddling
Onaway
25 m SE of Cheboygan, 21 m E of I-75

MBC
989-785-4388
45.21309, -84.18527

Canoe Harbor SF CG
44 P sites, paddling, fishing
Roscommon
15 m E of Grayling, 2 m S of M-72

989-275-5151
44.60510, -84.46821

Ossineke SF CG
42 P sites, beach, fishing
Ossineke
On Lake Huron, 15 m S of Alpena

TB, MBC, BTC
989-724-5126
44.91923, -83.42021

Jones Lake SF CG
42 P sites, fishing, paddling
Grayling
15 m N of Grayling, 5 m E of I-75

989-348-7068
44.78232, -84.58721

House Lake SF CG
41 P sites, fishing, paddling, bike trail
Meredith
55 m NW of Saginaw, 12 m E of
    US 127

989-386-4067
44.14076, -84.57382

Black Lake SF CG
52 P sites, bike and bridle trail, fishing,
    paddling
Cheboygan
18 m SE of Cheboygan, 15 m E of I-75

231-627-2811
45.48908, -84.26213

Pickerel Lake (Otsego) SF CG
41 P sites, fishing, paddling, bike trail
Vanderbilt
13 m NE of Gaylord, 8 m E of I-75

989-983-4101
45.17644, -84.51752

Trout Lake SF CG
35 P sites, fishing, bike trail
Meredith
55 m NW of Saginaw, 14 m E of
    US 127

989-386-4067
44.13414, -84.56563

Big Bear Lake SF CG   MBC
30 P sites, beach, fishing, paddling,   989-732-5485
  bike trail   44.94508, -84.37997
Vienna
15 m E of Gaylord, 2 m S of M-32

Shupac Lake SF CG   MBC
30 P sites, fishing, paddling   989-348-7068
Lovells   44.81521, -84.48100
18 m NE of Grayling, 12 m E of I-75

Shoepac Lake SF CG   989-785-4388
29 P sites, bike trail, fishing, paddling   45.25174, -84.16608
Onaway
30 m NE of Gaylord, 3 m E of M-33

Ess Lake SF CG   MBC
27 P sites, fishing   989-785-4388
Atlanta   45.10672, -83.97970
45 m SE of Cheboygan, 30 m W of
  Alpena

Tomahawk Lake SF CG   BTC
25 P sites, fishing, paddling, bike trail   989-785-4388
Onaway   45.21986, -84.16505
40 m NW of Alpena, 22 m E of I-75

Ambrose Lake SF CG   989-345-0472
25 P sites, fishing, paddling   44.40677, -84.24809
Rose City
30 m SE of Grayling, 10 m NE of I-75

Mio Pond SF CG   989-826-3211
24 P sites, fishing, paddling   44.66541, -84.14656
Mio
25 m E of I-75, on M-72

Little Wolf Lake SF CG   989-785-4251
24 P sites, fishing   44.85684, -84.27878
Lewiston
25 m NE of Grayling, 20 m E of I-75

Black Creek SF CG   989-386-4067
23 P sites, fishing   43.71205, -84.39335
Midland
30 m NW of Saginaw, 2 m N of US 10

McCollum Lake SF CG   989-848-5045
20 P sites, fishing   44.76599, -83.89924
Fairview
38 m E of I-75, 4 m N of M-72

Pigeon River SF CG   MBC, BTC
19 P sites, fishing, paddling   989-983-4101
Vanderbilt   45.17663, -84.42779
18 m NE of Gaylord, 10 m E of I-75

Keystone Landing SF CG   MBC
18 P sites, fishing, paddling   989-348-6371
Grayling   44.66309, -84.62725
3 m E of I-75, 2 m N of M-72

Jackson Lake SF CG   989-785-4388
18 P sites, bike trail, fishing, paddling   45.08876, -84.16788
Atlanta
25 m E of Gaylord, 25 m N of M-72

Avery Lake SF CG   989-785-4251
16 P sites, fishing paddling   44.93345, -84.18042
Atlanta
22 m E of I-75, 15 m N of M-72

AuSable River SF CG   BTC
15 P sites, fishing, paddling   989-348-6371
Grayling   44.66013, -84.64768
3 m E of I-75, 2 m N of M-72

Ocqueoc Falls SF CG   MBC, BTC
14 P sites, waterfalls, bike trail, fishing   989-734-2543
Ocqueoc   45.39525, -84.05742
42 m SE of Mackinac City, 5 m SW of
  US 23

Big Bear Point SF CG   989-732-5485
14 P sites, fishing, paddling, bike trail   44.94511, -84.37993
Vienna
16 m SE of Gaylord, 15 m E of I-75

Town Corner Lake SF CG   MBC
12 P sites, fishing, hiking   989-785-4251
Gaylord   45.11548, -84.36837
15 m E of Gaylord, 10 m N of M-32

Burton's Landing SF CG   989-348-6371
12 P sites, paddling, fishing   44.66227, -84.64751
Grayling
2 m E of I-75, 2 m N of M-72

Round Lake SF CG   989-983-4101
10 P sites, bike trail, fishing, paddling   45.13634, -84.45336
Vanderbilt
14 m NE of Gaylord, 12 m E of I-75

Pigeon Bridge SF CG   989-983-4101
10 P sites, fishing, hiking   45.15628, -84.46800
Vanderbilt
12 m NE of Gaylord, 10 m E of I-75

Elk Hill SF Equestrian CG   989-983-4101
10 P sites, fishing, paddling, bridle trail   45.17607, -84.51687
Vanderbilt
18 m NE of Gaylord, 13 m E of I-75

Walsh Road SF Equestrian CG   989-348-7068
9 P sites, bridle trail, fishing   44.78354, -84.37096
Lovells
18 m NE of Grayling, 10 m N of M-72

Parmalee Bridge SF CG   989-826-3211
7 P sites, paddling, fishing   44.67616, -84.29221
Luzerne
18 m E of Grayling, 5 m N of M-72

Rainbow Bend SF CG   989-348-6371
7 P sites, paddling, fishing   44.66938, -84.41765
Grayling
15 m E of Grayling, 4 m N of M-72

Pine Grove SF CG   989-983-4101
6 P sites, bike trail, fishing, paddling   45.27742, -84.51460
Wolverine
18 m N of Gaylord, 5 m E of I-75

Negwegon SP   989-724-5126
4 P sites, beach, hunting   44.86216, -83.33700
248 State Park Rd, Harrisville
On Lake Huron, 18 m S of Alpena

National Forest Campgrounds

Mack Lake CG, Huron NF   989-826-3252
42 P sites, off-road area, bird watching   44.58013, -84.06437
Mio
30 m E of Grayling, 5 m S of M-72

Round Lake CG, Huron NF
33 P sites, beach, paddling, fishing
Tawas City
15 m W of Lake Huron, 5 m N of
   M-55

989-739-0728
44.33456, -83.66488

Jewell Lake CG, Huron NF
32 P sites, beach, fishing, paddling
Barton City
30 m S of Alpena, 15 m W of US 23

MBC
989-739-0728
44.68052, -83.59394

Kneff CG, Huron NF
26 P sites, beach, fishing, paddling
Grayling
10 m E of Grayling, 2 m S of M-72

MBC
989-826-3252
44.64041, -84.57605

Monument CG, Huron NF
19 P sites, Lumberman's Monument
   Visitor Center
Tawas City
13 m W of Lake Huron, 16 m S of
   M-72

MBC
989-739-0728
44.43418, -83.62025

Rollways CG, Huron NF
19 P sites, paddling, fishing
Hale
25 m W of Lake Huron, 22 m S of
   M-72

MBC
989-739-0728
44.45949, -83.77406

Island Lake CG, Huron NF
17 P sites, beach, fishing, paddling
Mio
40 m SE of Grayling, 5 m N of M-55

MBC
989-826-3252
44.37788, -84.11585

Meadows CG, Huron NF
16 P sites, off road vehicle area
Luzerne
25 m E of Grayling, 5 m N of M-72

989-826-3252
44.56081, -84.31247

South Branch Trail CG, Huron NF
16 P sites, bridle trail dispersed
   campsites
Hale
25 m W of Lake Huron, 22 m S of
   M-72

989-739-0728
44.48514, -83.80072

Sawmill Point CG, Huron NF   BTC
15 P canoe-in sites on Au Sable River   989-3628961
Oscoda   44.43528, -83.62289
15 m W of Lake Huron, 15 m S of
  M-72

Wagner Lake CG, Huron NF   MBC
12 P sites, beach, paddling, fishing   989-826-3252
Mio   44.55549, -84.14913
30 m E of Grayling, 7 m S of M-72

Pine River CG, Huron NF   989-826-3252
11 P sites, fishing, bird watching   44.50376, -83.64522
Glennie
15 m W of Lake Huron, 8 m S of M-72

Gabions CG, Huron NF   989-826-3252
10 P sites, fishing, solitude   44.62175, -83.83396
Glennie
45 m E of Grayling, 5 m W of M-65

Horseshoe Lake CG, Huron NF   MBC
11 P sites, solitude   989-735-3580
Glennie   44.60064, -83.76088
50 m E of Grayling, 9 m S of M-72

County and Municipal *Campgrounds*

Alcona CP   989-735-3881
502 sites, showers, laundry, paddling   44.58044, -83.81310
2550 AuSable Rd, Glennie
50 m E of Grayling, 8 m S of M-72

North Park CG, Harbor Beach MP   989-479-9554
184 sites,showers, bike trail, Lake   43.85600, -82.65701
  Huron fishing
766 State St, Harbor Beach
On Lake Huron, 68 m N of Port Huron

East Tawas City Park MP   989-362-5562
170 sites, showers, cable TV, beach,   44.27858, -83.49410
  boating, fishing
Newman St, East Tawas
On Lake Huron, 60 m N of Saginaw

Oscoda Park, Oscoda CP   989-826-5114
153 sites, showers, beach, paddling,   44.65360, -84.1408
   trails, Wi-Fi
1110 Jay Smith Dr, Mio
30 m E of Grayling, on M-72

Caseville Park, Huron CP   989-856-2080
125 sites, showers, beach, fishing,   43.94753, -83.27334
   boating, Wi-Fi
6400 Main St, Caseville
On Lake Huron, 50 m NE of Saginaw

Lighthouse Park, Huron CP   888-265-2583
110 sites, beach, bike trail, lighthouse   44.01855, -82.79839
7320 Lighthouse Rd, Port Hope
On Lake Huron, 68 m N of Port Huron

Au Gres City Park CG   989-876-8310
109 sites, boating, fishing   44.04981, -83.68597
522 Park St, Au Gres
45 m N of Saginaw, 3 m W of
   Lake Huron

Wagener Park, Huron CP   MBC
96 sites, showers, fishing, boating,   888-265-2583
   bike trail, lighthouse, theatre   43.77240, -82.62368
2671 S Lakeshore Rd, Harbor Beach
On Lake Huron, 58 m N of Port Huron

Herrick RA, Isabella CP   MBC
73 sites, showers, beach, fishing   989-386-2010
6320 E Herrick Rd, Clare   43.80024, -84.7118
40 m NW of Saginaw, 5 m S of US 10

Stafford Park, Huron CP   888-265-2583
73 sites, beach, bike trail, fishing   43.94325, -82.70959
4451 W Huron St, Port Hope
On Lake Huron, 68 m N of Port Huron

River Park CG, Grayling MP   906-863-5101
69 sites, showers, laundry, bike trail,   44.71993, -84.64120
   paddling, fishing
Peters Rd, Grayling
On I-75, in Grayling

Sebewaing Park, Huron CP   888-265-2583
64 sites, fishing, walking, wildlife   43.73713, -83.45925
   viewing
759 Union St, Sebewaing
On Lake Huron, 30 m NE of Saginaw

**Gladwin City Park & CG,
 Gladwin MP**
60 sites, showers, beach
1000 W Cedar Ave, Gladwin
60 m NW of Saginaw, 15 m E of
 US 127

MBC
989-426-8126
43.98068, -84.49188

**Finn Rd Park CG, Hampton
 Township Park**
56 sites, showers, fishing, trail, golf
2300 N Finn Rd, Essexville
On Lake Huron, 20 m N of Saginaw

989-894-0055
43.62632, -83.77942

Oak Beach Park, Huron CP
55 sites, beach, miniature golf
3356 Port Austin Rd, Port Austin
On Lake Huron, 65 m NE of Saginaw

888-265-2583
43.99597, -83.12633

Pinconning Park, Bay CP
42 sites, showers, fishing, boating,
 casino
3041 E Pinconning Rd, Pinconning
On Saginaw Bay, 30 m N of Saginaw

MBC
989-879-5050
43.85319, -83.92442

Michigan's Upper Peninsula

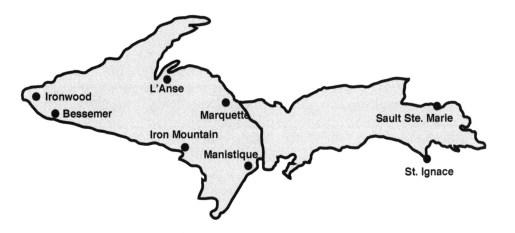

4

Michigan's Upper Peninsula

Although the Upper Peninsula (UP) is a part of Michigan, it could easily be viewed as a separate state for several reasons. For example, it has 16,452 square miles of land area—more than Connecticut, Vermont, and four other states. It can only be accessed from Michigan's Lower Peninsula by one highway—I-75—that crosses over the Straits of Mackinac on the Mackinac Bridge, while it can be accessed from Wisconsin on six major highways and dozens of smaller roads along the two-hundred-mile-long common border. People who have lived in the UP for a few years proudly call themselves Yoopers, rather than Michiganders. And finally, a serious effort was launched during the 1970s to establish the UP, along with part of Wisconsin, as the 51st state—called Superior—and this effort continues to receive some support from local residents.

During the winter, Yoopers must endure average daily high temperatures of 20 degrees and average nighttime lows of 3 degrees, plus about 200 inches of snow a year. On colder winter days, the daily high may only reach -10 degrees and the nighttime low may drop down to -30 degrees. In the winter of 2000–01, some parts of the UP recorded over three hundred inches of snow and the brutal winter of 2013–14 matched that record. All year long, Yoopers must learn to live without many conveniences enjoyed by people living in the Lower Peninsula and the rest of the United States because of the small population base and the cost of transporting goods to this remote region. In the summer, people living in the UP are blessed with pleasant weather but must deal with biting black flies, aggressive mosquitoes, and ticks. Much of the Upper Peninsula is rural and sparsely populated. In fact, a third of the land area is forest land owned by federal, state, and county governments. Along major highways in the western UP, drivers will see numerous old and deserted buildings but very few other travelers on the road. On rural roads, drivers may occasionally see black bear and moose. Many tourists who venture into this region come to fish and hunt in its unspoiled lakes and forests.

This is the land of Gitche Gumee that was introduced to the American public by Henry Wadsworth Longfellow in his story titled "Song of

Hiawatha." Gitche Gumee was derived from the Ojibwe word (gichi-gami) for Lake Superior. The story describes the life of an Ojibwe (or Chippewa) child named Hiawatha who was born in a wigwam on the shores of the Big Sea Waters, in a dark pine and fir forest. After its publication in 1855, the story attracted national attention and became the topic of literary discussions for several years. In 1976, Gitche Gumee again received national attention when Gordon Lightfoot wrote and sang a song dedicated to the twenty-nine men who lost their lives in the 1975 wreck of the SS *Edmund Fitzgerald* on Lake Superior.

Eva and I had the pleasure of driving and camping in the UP for five days during the summer of 2013 and consider that experience to be one of the highlights of our camping life. We drove up from Wisconsin, camped two nights at the Porcupine Mountains State Wilderness Park, one night at Tahquamenon Falls State Park, and two nights at Straits State Park. During the trip, we enjoyed spending an afternoon at Pictured Rocks National Lakeshore and a day on Mackinac Island. Along the way we also stopped at several establishments and visited six

Mackinaw Island State Park does not permit motor-driven vehicles. Visitors must walk, ride bicycles, or charter horse-drawn taxis. No campgrounds are located on the island, but several hotels are available for those who want to spend the night. While on the island, visitors should visit the historic fort.

other campgrounds. We especially enjoyed eating breakfast at a small local café in Bergland, touring Pictured Rocks by boat, seeing the lower Tahquamenon Falls, and touring Fort Mackinac. As a retired psychologist, I also enjoyed observing the people who live in the UP. Although five days is a short observation period, I would describe Yoopers as very stoic people. In contrast with jovial Wisconsinites and excessively tactful southerners, Yoopers seem to be blunt and to-the-point. One morning I walked into a convenience store and cheerfully said, "Good morning, it sure is a beautiful day," and the clerk responded, "How can I help you?" In general, I found that Yoopers will answer direct questions but engage in little idle conservation with tourists.

Today, the Michigan DNR manages seventeen state parks and recreation areas with campgrounds in the Upper Peninsula. It also manages fifty-one state forests. Two federal agencies manage campgrounds in Michigan's Upper Peninsula. The U.S. Forest Service manages two national forests with a total of thirty-six separate campgrounds, and one national recreation area on Grand Island with a dispersed camping area. The National Park Service manages one national park on Isle Royale with thirty-six small primitive campgrounds, and one national lakeshore with a total of three developed campgrounds. No U.S. Army Corps of Engineers campgrounds are located in the UP. County and municipal governments manage a total of nineteen public campgrounds.

Eastern Upper Peninsula: Pictured Rocks

The eastern Upper Peninsula (UP) is defined as the area that is east of US 41 running from Escanaba north to Marquette. The northern edge of this region is defined by Lake Superior and the southern edge is defined by Lake Michigan. Included in this region is Mackinac Island in the Straits of Mackinac between the Lower Peninsula and Upper Peninsula. Reference towns in this region include St. Ignace near the Straits of Mackinac in the southeastern corner, Sault Ste. Marie on the Canadian border in the northeast corner, Munising located on Lake Superior near the center of the region, Marquette in the northwestern corner, Escanaba on Lake Michigan in the southwest corner, and Manistique on Lake Michigan in the center of the region. The Hiawatha National Forest occupies a large amount of land area in this region.

Several popular tourist destinations can be found in this region. Perhaps the most spectacular tourist attraction in the eastern UP is the massive cliff wall in the Pictured Rocks National Lakeshore near Grand Maris on Lake Superior. Thousands of tourists come every summer to

Pictured Rocks National Lakeshore is a popular tourist destination in the Upper Peninsula. Although a few visitors drive through the park to observation areas, most charter tour boats in Munising to get the best views.

view the beautiful multi-colored sandstone wall that stretches fifteen miles along the lakeshore. Visitors can view some of the walls from landside observation areas but they can only appreciate the full effect of the rock wall from a boat in the lake. Consequently, hundreds of tourists take chartered tours out of Munising every day. As we discovered, these boats fill quickly and passengers line up well before scheduled boarding times to secure one of the upper deck seats.

Another popular tourist destination in the eastern UP is Mackinac Island. Although the island does not permit motorized vehicles and does not have a campground, tourists come by the thousands to walk through the old Victorian-style town and tour the restored Fort Mackinac. These visitors take a passenger ferry from St. Ignace or Mackinaw City and either return at the end of the day or spend the night in one of the hotels on the island. The Grand Hotel is one of the best-known hotels in the United States. After arriving on the island, most tourists walk to the fort and local attractions; a few bring or rent bicycles while others ride in horse-drawn carriages.   A third popular tourist destination in this region is Tahquamenon Falls State Park. Hundreds of visitors come every summer season to hike the trails and view the upper and lower waterfalls. The lower falls seem to be the more popular camping destination. Finally, hundreds of tourists come to the eastern UP every summer to paddle and fish in dozens of small remote lakes and rivers scattered throughout the area.

The Michigan DNR manages seven state parks, one state recreation area, and thirty-eight state forests in the eastern UP. Tent campers planning vacations in this region may want to consider one of the following destinations.

Tahquamenon Falls State Park (296 sites), on the Tahquamenon River near Lake Superior about thirty-five miles west of Sault Ste. Marie, is said to be one of the places described in Longfellow's Song of Hiawatha. The park has three family campgrounds and has been named by both *Michigan's Best Campgrounds* and *Best Tent Camping: Michigan* as one of the best tent camping destinations in the state. It is also one of my favorite camping destinations because of its beautiful campground and family-friendly atmosphere. Overlook Loop Campground and Riverbend Loop Campground are located near the lower falls, while the Rivermouth Campground is located near the upper falls on the opposite side of the park. Of the three campgrounds, Riverbend seems to be the most popular. Although the sites are small and crowded, we found that the campground was packed with families and their children. We camped in site #20 during the middle of a July week and found it to be one of the most popular campgrounds we have ever visited. Within the park, attending naturalist programs and walking the boardwalk to the "root beer" colored waterfalls are the primary activities. The upper falls plunge over fifty feet and are said to be the second largest waterfall in the eastern United States. The lower falls are a series of small waterfalls or rapids that have been described as a noisy cascade. Hiking, paddling, fishing, and wildlife watching (bear, moose, coyotes, and porcupines) are other popular activities in the park. As a note of caution, mosquitoes and flies can be so aggressive that visitors must sometimes wear head nets, long-sleeved shirts, and long pants.

Tahquamenon Falls State Park in the Upper Peninsula offers two waterfall areas, three campgrounds, and a soothing north country forest atmosphere. This photo was taken at the lower falls.

Straits State Park (270 sites), on the northern side of the Mackinac Bridge and Straits of Mackinac, was established in 1924 as one of Michigan's early state parks and is one of my favorite camping destinations. The park has three family camping areas. The lower campground, located down the hill on the shore of Lake Huron, has two sections (east and west) with nice views of the Mackinac Bridge. The upper campground on the top of the hill has 136 sites and these sites are generally larger with more shade. Inside the park, campers can enjoy swimming and hiking. Outside the park, many visitors drive a few blocks down into St. Ignace and take one of the three passenger ferries over to Mackinac Island. Hundreds of tourists make day trips over to the island and enjoy strolling through the unique tourist district and walking up the hill to the historic fort. Other tourists take time to visit the Father Marquette Memorial and unique shops and restaurants in St. Ignace. We spent a beautiful July weekend in site #10 near the lakeshore. The site was large and level but very hot during the day because of limited shade trees. We avoided the heat by spending most of the daylight hours touring St. Ignace and Mackinac Island. In the evening, we ate s'mores with the campground host and enjoyed refreshing showers in one of the exceptionally nice family shower units.

Straits State Park, in St. Ignace, is conveniently located only a few blocks away from three passenger ferries that take tourists over to Mackinac Island several times a day. This is site #10 in the Lower Campground. Sites 8A and 9A in the background are extremely nice.

The state DNR also manages thirty-eight small state forest campgrounds in this region. **Munuscong River** (50 primitive sites), located on the Canadian border about thirty-five miles northeast of St. Ignace, is the largest of these state forest campgrounds. **Big Knob** (23 primitive sites), located on Lake Michigan about fifty miles west of St. Ignace, and **Portage Bay** (23 primitive sites), located on Lake Michigan about twenty-three miles southwest of Manistique, were named by both *Michigan's Best Campgrounds* and *Best in Tent Camping: Michigan* as among the best in the region. **Mouth of Two Hearted River** (40 primitive sites), **Perch Lake** (35 primitive sites), and eight more campgrounds were named by *Michigan's Best Campgrounds*.

Two Federal agencies manage campgrounds in this area. The U.S. Forest Service manages twenty small, rustic campgrounds in the Hiawatha National Forest and seventeen dispersed campsites in the Grand Island National Recreation Area. Within the Hiawatha National Forest, **Brevoot Lake** (70 sites), located eighteen miles northeast of St. Ignace, is the largest campground and was named by both *Michigan's Best Campgrounds* and *Best Tent Camping: Michigan* as among the best camping destinations in the state. **Pete's Lake** (47 primitive sites), located eighteen miles south of Munising, and **Monocle Lake** (39 primitive sites), located on Lake Superior about ten miles west of Sault Ste. Marie, were also named by *Michigan's Best Campgrounds* and *Best Tent Camping: Michigan*. We visited **Bay Furnace** (50 primitive sites) on Lake Superior and found it to have an onsite manager and campground host. Site #10 offers a great view of the lake. The **Grand Island National Recreation Area** is located on a large island in Lake Superior near Munising. To get to the island, visitors must take a passenger ferry. Campers who do not

Bay Furnace Campground in the Hiawatha National Forest is conveniently located in the Upper Peninsula near Munising. Site #10 is located on Lake Superior and provides a picturesque view of the Grand Island National Recreation Area.

have their own camping gear may rent gear from local camping outfitters. The National Park Service manages **Pictured Rocks National Lakeshore**. This federal property has three campgrounds and fifty-five sites available on a first-come basis. Many of these sites are located directly on Lake Superior.

Municipal governments in the eastern UP manage six public campgrounds that may be suited for tent camping. **Woodland County Park** (132 sites), located on Lake Superior in Grand Marais, has nice bathrooms with hot showers and is located only a few miles east of the Pictured Rocks National Lakeshore. Consequently, it serves as a popular alternative to the primitive campgrounds in the lakeshore. Three municipal parks in the tourist-centered eastern edge of this region are called RV parks but will accept tent campers.

Western Upper Peninsula: Wilderness Country

The western UP is defined as the area that is west of US 41 running from Escanaba north to Marquette. The southern border of this region is defined by the Wisconsin state line and Green Bay of Lake Michigan. The northern border is defined by Lake Superior. In the north central part of this region, the Keweenaw Peninsula juts out about seventy miles into Lake Superior. Also included in this region is Isle Royale and its surrounding small islands located in Lake Superior about fifty-six miles northwest of the Keweenaw Peninsula. Although the island is only fifteen miles from the shorelines of Minnesota and Ontario, Canada, it is politically aligned with Keweenaw County Michigan. Reference towns in this region include Bessemer in the far western corner, Iron Mountain on the Wisconsin state line, Escanaba on Lake Michigan in the southeastern corner, Marquette on Lake Superior in the northeastern corner, and L'Anse on Lake Superior at the base of the Keweenaw Peninsula. The Ottawa National Forest is located in the western part of this region.

This region, also known as big snow country and copper country, once supported a profitable mining industry, but by 1930, those mines had played out. Today the region features miles and miles of rural two-lane highways and snowmobile trails cut through expansive pine and hardwood forest land with numerous old and abandoned buildings. Popular tourist destinations in the western UP are Lake Gogebic, Lake Superior shoreline, Lake of the Clouds in the Porcupine Mountains State Park (Porkies), and the Ottawa National Forest. Adventurous campers may want to take a ferry out of Houghton or Copper Harbor (or a sea plane from Houghton) up to Isle Royale National Park. Visitors come to the western UP to enjoy fishing, hunting, paddling, hiking, observing bear, moose and other wildlife, and enjoying the beauty of God's creation undefiled by civilization. Many of those who have ventured into this region have fallen in love with its unique beauty and return as often as possible, despite pesky biting black flies, mosquitoes, ticks, and chilly nights.

The Michigan Department of Natural Resources manages nine state parks and thirteen state forest campgrounds in this region. Tent campers planning vacations in this region may want to consider one of the following destinations.

Van Riper State Park (187 sites), just off of US Highway 2 about thirty-five miles west of Marquette, is the largest camping destination in the western UP and has been named by *Yahoo Sports* as one of the best parks in the state. It is also a very popular campground and one of my favorite camping destinations. The park has a large modern campground with very nice bathrooms, plenty of shade trees, and Wi-Fi, plus a smaller, more rustic campground. Inside the park, visitors enjoy swimming and other recreational activities at the beautiful beach, fishing, hiking, ranger-guided programs, and wildlife viewing. The snack bar offers burgers, ice cream, and other snack foods. Moose, bear, wolves, fishers, and other animals can occasionally be seen in the park. Canoe and kayaks can also be rented in the park.

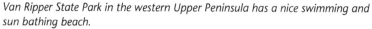

Van Ripper State Park in the western Upper Peninsula has a nice swimming and sun bathing beach.

Van Ripper State Park's concession offers snacks, drinks, hamburgers, and ice cream. Photo by Eva Douglass.

Porcupine Mountains State Park (169 sites), on the far western shore of Lake Superior, protects one of the few remaining tracts of virgin timberland in the state. The park was named by *National Geographic* as one of the most historically significant and scenic state parks in the United States and is one of my favorite camping destinations. Campers who prefer modern amenities will appreciate the Union Bay campground located on the eastern edge of the park, while campers who prefer more rustic settings may enjoy the Presque Isle Rustic Campground on the western edge, back-country camping area, or one of the more remote outpost areas. The Union Bay Campground is one of my favorite camping destinations because its campsites offer spectacular views of Lake Superior, its bathrooms are very clean, and it has nice laundry facilities. We spent two nights there and, although annoying flies bit our ankles and our small lakeside campsite was jammed next to our neighbors, we enjoyed listening to the waves lapping on the rocky shore as we drifted off to sleep. During the day, we drove a few miles east to beautiful sandy beaches and swam in Lake Superior. Visitors to the park enjoy touring the nature center, hiking through miles of virgin forest land, viewing Lake of the Clouds, fishing for brook trout, and climbing the observation tower for panoramic views of Michigan, Wisconsin, and Lake Superior. Birding and wildlife viewing are also popular activities in the park.

Porcupine Mountain Wilderness State Park's Union Bay campground is located on the shore of Lake Superior but the lakeside sites are very crowded. Our site #27 was a small spot beside the second vehicle.

Porcupine Mountains Wilderness State Park's Lake of the Clouds is a popular tourist attraction.

Fort Wilkins State Park (160 sites), on the northern tip of the Keweenaw Peninsula, was dedicated as a state park in 1923 and recently named by *National Geographic* as one of the most historically significant and scenic state parks in the United States. The park, situated on a small isthmus between Lake Superior and Lake Fanny Hooe, was originally built as an Army outpost in 1844 to maintain peace between the local Ojibwes and miners who migrated into the area to work in copper mines. The fort was abandoned by the Army forty-seven years later and was privately owned for the next one hundred years. In 1923, the property was acquired by the state of Michigan and was added to the National Register of Historic places in 1970. The modern, heavily shaded campground is divided into two areas located on either side of the fort and Fanny Hooe Creek. In addition to touring the fort, visitors enjoy relaxing at the beach, touring a restored historic lighthouse, fishing, hiking, and bicycling.

Lake Gogebic State Park (127 sites), located on M-64 about twenty-five miles east of Bessemer, was named by *Michigan's Best Campgrounds* as one of the best campgrounds in the state and is my favorite campground in the western U.P. Although the park is small and campsites are small, fishermen are drawn to the park because of excellent fishing opportunities. Most grassy and partly shaded campsites are spread along the lakeshore allowing fishermen to moor their boats near their sites. The primary drawback of this campground is the voracious mosquitoes that were present all day long.

Lake Gogebic State Park's campground stretches along the shore of Lake Gogebic in the western Upper Peninsula. Campers can moor their boats right at their campsites. These are sites #38, 40, and 42.

Baraga State Park (115 sites), about five miles west of L'Anse, is a small park located on U.S. Highway 41 running along the edge of Keweenaw Bay of Lake Superior. Although most sites have a water view, the view is frequently interrupted by cars and trucks traveling along U.S. Highway 41. And, since no vegetation or noise barriers have been placed between the campsites and the highway, campers must adjust to traffic noise during the night. Nevertheless, I could easily spend a week camping here and enjoying area activities. Outside the park, Lake Superior fishing and boating seem to be the primary activities.

The state DNR also manages thirteen small state forest campgrounds in this region. **Little Lake** (26 primitive sites), located twenty miles south of Marquette, is the largest of these state forest campgrounds. **Carney Lake** (16 primitive sites), located eight miles northeast of Iron Mountain, and **Squaw Lake** (15 primitive sites), located thirty-five miles southwest of Marquette, were named by both *Michigan's Best Campgrounds* and *Best Tent Camping: Michigan* as two of the best camping destinations in the state. Several other small state forest campgrounds in the region were named by one of these two authorities as good camping destinations.

Two federal agencies manage camping areas within the western UP area. The National Park Service manages the **Isle Royale National Park**, located on an island in Lake Superior about fifty-six miles northwest of the Keweenaw Peninsula. The park can only be accessed by passenger ferry (departing from Houghton and Copper Harbor), by sea plane, or by private boat. While a few adventurous people will camp in one of the primitive sites in the park, most visitors come for a few hours during the day and return to the mainland by the end of the day. The U.S. Forest Service manages the Ottawa National Forest and its sixteen small campgrounds. **Clark Lake** (47 primitive sites), located about forty miles east of Bessemer, is the largest of these campgrounds and was named by both *Michigan's Best Campgrounds* and *Best Tent Camping: Michigan* as among the best in the state. Other campgrounds praised by various camping authorities include **Black River Harbor** (39 primitive sites), located on Lake Superior about fifteen miles north of Bessemer, **Lake Sainte Katherine** (23 Primitive sites), located about thirty miles south of L'Anse, and **Henry Lake** (11 primitive sites), located about twenty-five miles east of Bessemer.

County and municipal governments in the western UP manage thirteen public campgrounds that may be suited for tent camping. The largest of these campgrounds is **Pioneer Trail County Park** (213 sites), located in Gladstone about three miles north of Escanaba. **Tourist City**

Park (110 sites) in Marquette, **Pentoga County Park** (100 sites) in Crystal Falls, about twenty-five miles north of Iron Mountain, **Perkins Park** (83 sites), **Little Girl's Point** (30 primitive sites), and **Fox Park** (20 primitive sites) were all named by *Michigan's Best Campgrounds.* **Bond Falls Flowage** (48 primitive sites), managed by the Upper Peninsula Power Company (UPPCO) and located about fifty miles east of Bessemer, was named by both *Michigan's Best Campgrounds* and *Best Tent Camping: Michigan.* **Lake Gogebic County Park** (52 primitive sites) and **Ontonagon County Park** (44 primitive sites) offer secure campground alternatives on Lake Gogebic for campers who prefer less congestion than found at the nearby state park.

Useful Resources

After reading this chapter, readers should consult additional resources to determine specific destinations and campgrounds that best fit their family's particular interests and expectations. Some helpful resources are listed below.

- The Michigan Department of Natural Resources website (www.michigan.gov/dnr) contains information about all state managed properties.
- The official Michigan state highway map, available from the Michigan Department of Transportation (www.michigan.gov/mdot) and at highway rest areas, shows approximate geographic locations of each state and most federal properties. The map also provides a table that summarizes driving directions and amenities for each state property.
- *Michigan State Parks & Recreation Areas: Park Visitor Welcome Map 2012–2013* (brochure), available in highway rest areas, provides an overview of all state properties and provides brief descriptions of each one.
- *Michigan Campground 2012 Directory* (brochure), available in most highway rest areas, describes a few private campgrounds in the state.
- *Michigan State and National Parks: A Complete Guide* (book) provides detailed descriptions of state properties and National Park Service properties.
- *Michigan's Best Campgrounds* (book) briefly describes 150 state, federal, and local campgrounds in the state.
- *Best Tent Camping: Michigan* (book) provides detailed descriptions

of twenty secluded campgrounds in the UP, including a few
county and municipal parks.

- The Michigan state DNR (www.midnrreservations.com/, 800-
447-2757) accepts reservations for state properties. First time users will have to register a user name and password. Recreation.
Gov (www.Recreation.gov, 877-444-6777) is a private organization that makes reservations for all federal properties.

Upper Peninsula Public Campgrounds

Campgrounds are listed by number of campsites available from most
numerous to least. The following abbreviations are used to note public
campgrounds that have been named by various authorities as among
the best in the state:

FD   This property is one of my favorite camping destinations.

YS   This property was named by *Yahoo Sports* as being one of Michigan's five best state parks for summer tent camping.

TB   This property was named by the *TripleBlaze* website as having one
of the best fifteen campgrounds in the state.

MBC This property was named and described by *Michigan's Best Campgrounds* as being one of the best 150 campgrounds in the state.

BTC This property was named and described by *Best in Tent Camping:
Michigan* as having one of the 50 quietest and most private campgrounds in the state.

NG   This property was named and described by *National Geographic's
Guide to State Parks in the United States* as one of America's most
historic and scenic state parks.

(P = primitive)

Eastern Upper Peninsula: Pictured Rocks

State Parks, Recreation Areas, and Forests

Tahquamenon Falls SP
296 sites, showers, fishing, paddling,
  waterfalls
41382 West M-123, Paradise
On Lake Superior, 35 m W of
  Sault Ste. Marie

FD, MBC, BTC
906-492-3415
46.61044, -85.20631

Straits SP
270 sites, showers, beach, Straits
  attractions
720 Church St, St. Ignace
On Straits of Mackinac

FD
906-643-8620
45.85507, -84.71949

Brimley SP
237 sites, showers, beach, fishing
9200 West Six Mile Rd, Brimley
On Lake Superior, 10 m W of
  Sault Ste. Marie

906-248-3422
46.41291, -84.55504

Indian Lake SP
217 sites, showers, beach, fishing,
  boat rental
8970 W CR 442, Manistique
45 m E of Escanaba, 3 m N of US 2

TB
906-341-2355
45.93981, -86.33348

Muskallonge Lake SP
159 sites, showers, beach, fishing,
  Pictured Rocks NLS
30042 CR 407, Newberry
On Lake Superior, 60 m W of
  Sault Ste. Marie

MBC
906-658-3338
46.67693, -85.62746

J.W. Wells SP
153 sites, showers, beach, fishing,
  walking trail
7670 M-35, Cedar River
On Lake Michigan, 28 m N of
  Menominee

906-863-9747
45.39495, -87.36714

Fayette SP
61 P sites, beach, fishing, historic iron
    mill & town
13700 13.25 Lane, Garden
On Lake Michigan, 20 m E of
    Escanaba

YS, MBC
906-644-2603
45.72553, -86.64218

Munuscong River SF CG
50 P sites, fishing, paddling
Munuscong
On Canadian Border, 35 m NE of
    St. Ignace

906-248-3422
46.20288, -84.27981

Hog Island Point SF CG
50 P sites, beach, fishing
Naubinway
On Lake Michigan, 30 m NW of
    St Ignance

MBC
906-447-6048
46.09365, -85.37527

Mouth of Two Hearted River SF CG
40 P sites, fishing, paddling
Deer Park
On Lake Superior, 26 m E of
    Grand Marais

MBC
906-492-3415
46.69662, -85.41883

Perch Lake SF CG
35 P sites, fishing, paddling
Deer Park
20 m E of Grand Marais, 3 m S of
    Lake Superior

MBC
906-658-3338
46.62816, -85.60267

Milakokia Lake SF CG
35 P sites, fishing, paddling
Naubinway
25 m E of Manistique, 7 m N of
    Lake Michigan

906-293-5131
46.08454, -85.79258

South Manistique Lake, SF CG
30 P sites, fishing, paddling
Curtis
55 m NW of St. Ignace, 4 m N of US 2

906-293-5131
46.17584, -85.79150

Blind Sucker No. 2 SF CG
31 P sites, fishing, paddling, bike trail
Grand Marais
12 m E of Grand Marais, 5 m S of
    Lake Superior

906-658-3338
46.65868, -85.74470

Andrus Lake SF CG
28 P sites, fishing, paddling
Paradise
35 m NW of Sault Ste. Marie, 1 m W
  of Lake Superior

MBC
906-492-3415
46.70313, -85.03562

Forest Lake SF CG
26 P sites, fishing, paddling
Limestone
15 m SW of Munising, 28 m N of US 2

906-341-2355
46.33211, -86.85482

Pike Lake SF CG
23 P sites, fishing, paddling
Deer Park
28 m E of Grand Marais, 5 m S of
  Lake Superior

906-492-3415
46.63647, -85.42659

Portage Bay SF CG
23 P sites, fishing, bike trail
Garden
On Lake Michigan, 23 m SW of
  Manistique

MBC, BTC
906-644-2603
45.72111, -86.53441

Big Knob SF CG
23 P sites, beach, fishing, bike trail
Engadine
On Lake Michigan, 50 m W of
  St. Ignace

MBC, BTC
906-293-5131
46.05515, -85.57954

Pretty Lake SF CG
23 P sites, fishing, paddling
Deer Park
15 m SE of Grand Marais, 5 m S of
  Lake Superior

BTC
906-658-3338
45.60363, -85.65756

Culhane Lake SF CG
22 P sites, fishing, paddling
Paradise
28 m E of Grand Marais, 2 m S of
  Lake Superior

906-492-3415
46.69669, -85.35673

**Little Brevort Lake –North Unit
  SF CG**
20 P sites, fishing, paddling
Naubinway
20 m NW of St. Ignace, 1 m N of
  Lake Michigan

MBC
906-477-6048
46.02754, -85.0177

Bodi Lake SF CG   MBC
20 P sites, fishing, paddling   906-492-3415
Paradise   46.70701, -85.33529
30 m E of Grand Marais, 4 m S of
    Lake Superior

DeTour SF CG   MBC
20 P sites, fishing, paddling   906-297-5947
De Tour Village   45.95741, -84.00584
On Lake Huron, 40 m E of St. Ignace

East Branch of Fox River SF CG   906-293-5131
19 P sites, fishing, paddling   46.42292, -85.93870
Seney
34 m E of Munising, 6 m N of M-28

Bass Lake SF CG   MBC
18 P sites, fishing, paddling,   906-293-5131
Newberry   46.46163, -85.70855
20 m SE of Grand Marais, 10 m N of
    M-28

Lake Superior SF CG   MBC
18 P sites, fishing, paddling   906-658-3338
Grand Marais   46.67794, -85.81592
1 m S of Lake Superior, 10 m E of
    Grand Marais

Blind Sucker No. 1 SF CG   906-658-3338
17 P sites, fishing, paddling, bike trail   46.66758, -85.75335
Grand Marais
2 m S of Lake Superior, 10 m E of
    M-77

N Gemini Lake SF CG   906-341-2355
17 P sites, fishing, paddling, bike trail   46.49112, -86.30331
Melstrand
15 m NE of Munising, 10 m N of
    M-28

Kingston Lake SF CG   MBC
16 P sites, fishing, Pictured Rocks NLS   906-341-2356
Grand Marais   46.58570, -86.22714
23 m NE of Munising, 15 m N of
    M-28

Holland Lake SF CG   906-658-3338
15 P sites, fishing, paddling   46.61513, -85.65629
Deer Park
5 m S of Lake Superior, 18 m E of
    Grand Marais

Black River SF CG   906-477-6048
12 P sites, fishing, bike trail   46.11660, -85.36555
Naubinway
3 m N of Lake Michigan, 32 m W of
    St. Ignace

Natalie SF CG   TB
12 P sites, bike trail, fishing, paddling   906-293-5131
Newberry   46.34992, -85.58135
60 m W of Sault Ste. Marie, 2 m N of
    M-28

Lime Island SF CG   906-643-8620
12 P sites, fishing paddling   46.08792, -84.01182
Raber
On Canadian Border, 40 m NE of
    St. Ignace

Garnet Lake SF CG   906-595-7202
10 P sites, fishing   46.15456, -85.29922
Rexton
35 m NW of St. Ignace, 4 m N of US 2

Ross Lake SF CG   906-341-2355
10 P sites, fishing, paddling   46.47868, -86.26246
North Gemini Lake
18 m E of Munising, 10 m N of M-28

Merwin Creek SF CG   906-341-3618
10 P sites, fishing, paddling   46.03344, -86.12092
Gulliver
8 m E of Manistique, 2 m N of US 2

Mead Creek SF CG   906-341-2355
9 P sites, fishing, paddling   46.18003, -85.98616
Blaney Park
20 m NE of Manistique, 3 m W of
    M-77

S Gemini Lake SF CG   906-341-2355
8 P sites, fishing, paddling, bike trail   46.48045, -86.30378
Shingleton
13 m W of Munising, 4 m N of M-28

Reed & Green Bridge SF CG   906-492-3415
7 P sites, fishing, paddling   46.66113, -85.52272
Deer Park
2 m S of Lake Superior, 10 m NW of
    M-123

High Bridge SF CG   906-658-3338
7 P sites, fishing, paddling   46.60487, -85.60306
Deer Park
3 m S of Lake Michigan, 20 m N of
    Newberry

Fox River SF CG   906-341-2355
7 P sites, bike trail, fishing, paddling   46.39315, -86.01342
Seney
30 m E of Munising, 5 m N of M-28

Cusino Lake SF CG   MBC
6 P sites, fishing, paddling   906-341-2355
Melstrand   46.45007, -86.26042
18 m E of Munising, 8 m N of M-28

Canoe Lake SF CG   906-341-2355
4 P sites, fishing, paddling   46.4601, -86.29805
Melstrand
16 m E of Munising, 8 m N of M-28

National Lakeshore, Recreation Area, and Forest Campgrounds

Pictured Rocks NLS   MBC, BTC
65 P sites, beach, scenic views, fishing,   906-387-3700
    paddling   46.64849, -86.19615
Munising
On Lake Superior, between Munising
    and Grand Marais

Grand Island NRA   906-387-2512
17 P sites, dispersed camping,   46.45027, -86.67182
    accessed by passenger ferry, beach,
    fishing, paddling
Munising
On Lake Superior, 25 m NE of US 41

Brevort Lake CG, Hiawatha NF   MBC, BTC
70 P sites, beach, fishing, Mackinac   906-643-7900
    straits attractions   46.00722, -84.9722
St. Ignace
18 m NW of St. Ignace, 1 m N of US 2

Foley Creek CG, Hiawatha NF
54 P sites, beach, Mackinac straits
   attractions
St. Ignace
On Lake Huron, 3 m N of St. Ignace

MBC
906-643-7900
45.93278, -84.7500

Bay Furnace CG, Hiawatha NF
50 P sites, scenic views, black flies
Munising
On Lake Superior, 2 m N of Munising

FD, MBC
906-387-2512
46.43833, -86.70833

Pete's Lake CG, Hiawatha NF
47 P sites, beach, paddling, fishing,
   bike trail
Wetmore
18 m S of Munising, 7 m W of M-94

MBC, BTC
906-387-2512
46.22819, -86.5970

Island Lake CG, Hiawatha NF
45 P sites, fishing, lighthouse tour,
   waterfalls, Pictured Rocks NLS
Wetmore
12 m S of Munising, 9 m W of M-94

906-387-2512
46.27462, -86.61505

Soldier Lake CG, Hiawatha NF
44 P sites, beach, paddling, fishing,
   North Country Trail
Strongs
30 m W of Sault Ste. Marie, 2 m S of
   M-28

MBC
906-635-5311
46.35056, -84.86833

Camp 7 Lake CG, Hiawatha NF
41 P sites, beach, boating, fishing
Garden Corners
18 m NW of Manistique, 12 m N of
   US 2

906-341-5666
46.05778, -86.54972

Monocle Lake CG, Hiawatha NF
39 P sites, beach, lighthouse
Brimley
On Lake Superior, 10 m W of
   Sault Ste. Marie

MBC, BTC
906-635-5311
46.47250, -84.63917

Carp River CG, Hiawatha NF
38 P sites, fishing, paddling, Mackinac
   straits attractions
St. Ignace
14 m N of St. Ignace, 3 m W of I-75

906-643-7900
46.03306, -84.71917

Little Bay de Noc CG, Hiawatha NF
38 P sites, beach, paddling, fishing
Rapid River
5 m E (across the bay) from Escanaba,
    8 m S of US 2

MBC
906-474-6442
45.84167, -86.98306

AuTrain Lake CG, Hiawatha NF
36 P sites, paddling, beach, fishing,
    songbird trail
Au Train
8 m W of Munising, 18 m NW of
    US 41

MBC
906-387-2512
46.39167, -86.83806

Lake Michigan CG, Hiawatha NF
35 P sites, beach, fishing, Mackinac
    straits attractions
St. Ignace
On Lake Michigan, 15 m NW of
    St. Ignace

MBC
906-643-7900
45.98583, -84.97167

Widewaters CG, Hiawatha NF
34 P sites, paddling, fishing, trail
Wetmore
13 m S of Munising, 9 m W of M-94

MBC
906-387-2512
46.21944, -86.62833

Colwell Lake CG, Hiawatha NF
34 P sites, beach, fishing, paddling,
    Pictured Rocks attractions
Shingleton
25 m N of Manistique, 2 m E of M-94

MBC, BTC
906-341-5666
46.22167, -86.4375

Three Lakes CG, Hiawatha NF
28 P sites, fishing
Strongs
30 m SW of Sault Ste. Marie, 4 m S of
    M-28

MBC
906-635-5311
46.31917, -84.97889

Bay View CG, Hiawatha NF
24 P sites, beach, scenic view
Brimley
On Lake Superior, 20 m W of
    Sault Ste. Marie

MBC, BTC
906-635-5311
46.46, -84.77944

Little Bass Lake CG, Hiawatha NF
12 P sites, fishing
Manistique
20 m N of Manistique, 5 m W of M-94

MBC
906-428-5800
46.16384, -86.44952

Indian River CG, Hiawatha NF
11 P sites, paddling, fishing
Shingleton
15 m N of Manistique, on M-94

906-341-5666
46.15444, -86.40199

Flowing Well CG, Hiawatha NF
10 P sites, paddling, fishing
Garden Corners
20 m W of Manistique, 6 m N of US 2

MBC
906-474-6442
45.93747, -86.70709

Council Lake CG, Hiawatha NF
4 P dispersed sites, fishing, paddling
Wetmore
15 m S of Munising, 10 m S of M-94

MBC
877-444-6777
46.40917, -86.64917

County and Municipal Campgrounds

Woodland Park, Burt Township MP
132 sites, showers, beach, fishing,
    Pictured Rocks NLS
Millen St, Grand Marais
On Lake Superior, 40 m NE of
    Munising

MBC
906-494-2381
46.67323, -85.98990

**Aune-Osborn RV Park, Sault Ste
    Marie MP**
100 sites, showers, Wi-Fi, boating,
    fishing, golf
1225 Riverside Dr, Sault Ste. Marie
In Sault Ste. Marie, just off I-75

906-632-3268
46.48759, -84.30792

Kinross RV Park East, Kinross MP
64 sites, some tent sites, showers,
    beach, bridle trails, golf
Tone Rd, Kinross
35 m N of Mackinaw City, 2 m E of
    I-75

906-495-3023
46.26055, -84.46218

Kinross Park West, Kinross MP
52 sites, rustic tent sites, showers, golf,
    beach
Exit 378, Kinross
35 m N of Mackinaw City, just off I-75

906-495-3023
46.26823, -84.48849

Luce County Park   906-586-6460
45 sites, showers, beach, boating   46.27422, -85.72646
CR 98, McMillan
55 m W of Sault Ste. Marie, 4 m N of
   M-28

Seney Township CG   906-499-3332
25 sites, showers, hiking, fishing,   46.35338, -85.96286
   Ernest Hemingway sites
7264 W Osborn Rd, Seney
23 m S of Grand Marais, on M-28

Western Upper Peninsula: Wilderness Country

State Parks, Recreation Areas, and Forests

Van Riper SP   FD, YS
187 sites, showers, beach, fishing,   906-339-4461
   bike trail, Wi-Fi   46.52113, -87.98435
851 CR AKE, Champion
30 m W of Marquette, on US 41

Porcupine Mountains SP   FD, YS, TB, MBC, BTC, NG
169 sites, showers, beach, fishing,   906-885-5275
   bike trail, visitor center, waterfalls, 46.81970, -89.62060
   solitude
33303 Headquarters Rd, Ontonagon
On Lake Superior, 40 m NE of
   Bessemer

Fort Wilkins SP   MBC, NG
160 sites, showers, fishing, bike trail, 906-289-4215
   lighthouse, tour boats, historic fort, 47.46715, -87.86749
   waterfalls
Copper Harbor
On Lake Superior, on Keweenaw
   Peninsula

Bewabic SP   MBC, BTC
137 sites, showers, beach, fishing,   906-875-3324
   paddling, boat rental, tennis,   46.09415, -88.42556
   solitude
720 Idlewild Rd, Crystal Falls
25 m NW of Iron Mountain, on US 2

Lake Gogebic SP
127 sites, showers, beach, fishing,
    boat rental, solitude
9995 M-64
30 m E of Bessemer, 8 m N of US 2

FD, MBC
906-842-3341
46.45633, -89.56930

Baraga SP
115 sites, showers, beach, fishing,
    Wi-Fi
1300 US 41 S, Baraga
On Keweenaw Bay (Lake Superior)

FD
906-353-6558
46.76043, -88.50111

F.J. McLain SP
97 sites, showers, beach, fishing
18350 Hwy M 203, Hancock
On Lake Superior, on Keweenaw
    Peninsula

MBC
906-482-0278
47.23583, -88.60812

Twin Lakes SP
62 sites, showers, beach, fishing,
    bike trail
6204 East Poyhonen Rd, Toivola
On Keweenaw Peninsula, 1 m E of
    M-26

906-288-3321
46.89083, -88.8575

Little Lake SF CG
26 P sites, fishing, paddling
Little Lake
20 m S of Marquette, 2 m W of M-35

906-339-4461
46.28091, -87.33251

Glidden Lake SF CG
23 P sites, bike trail, paddling, fishing
Crystal Falls
15 m NW of Iron Mountain, 5 m SE
    of US 2

MBC
906-875-3324
46.07143, -88.23747

Bass Lake SF CG
22 P sites, fishing, paddling
Gwinn
20 m S of Marquette, 3 m E of M-35

906-339-4461
46.26273, -87.58433

Big Eric's Bridge SF CG
19 P sites, paddling, near Lake
    Superior
Skanee
20 m NE of L'Anse, 3 m S of Lake
    Superior

MBC
906-353-6558
46.86412, -88.08361

Anderson Lake SF CG   906-339-4461
19 P sites, fishing, paddling, bike trail   46.22426, -87.48696
Gwinn
22 m S of Marquette, 5 m SW of
   Gwinn

Cedar River North SF CG   MBC
18 P sites, paddling, fishing, hiking 906-863-9747
Cedar River   54.49957, -87.38225
30 m NE of Menominee, 5 m W of
   M-35

Craig Lake SP   906-339-4461
17 sites, showers, fishing, solitude   46.58467, -88.17433
Champion
40 m W of Marquette, 5 m N of US 41

Carney Lake SF CG   MBC, BTC
16 P sites, fishing, paddling   906-875-3324
Merriman   45.89466, -87.94263
8 m NE of Iron Mountain, 5 m E of
   M-95

Big Lake SF CG   906-353-6558
15 P sites, fishing   46.60353, -88.56935
Covington
14 m S of L'Anse, 5 m W of US 141

Squaw Lake SF CG   MBC, BTC
15 P sites, fishing, paddling   906-339-4461
Republic   46.29108, -88.06099
35 m SW of Marquette, 2 m W of
   M-95

Gene's Pond SF CG   MBC
14 P sites, fishing, paddling, bike trail   906-875-3324
Channing   46.07326, -87.86599
22 m N of Iron Mountain, 11 m E of
   M-95

Deer Lake SF CG   906-875-3324
12 P sites, fishing, paddling   46.31874, -88.33035
Amasa
35 m NW of Iron Mountain, 6 m E of
   US 141

Emily Lake SF CG   906-288-3321
9 P sites, swimming, fishing, paddling 46.85602, -88.86313
Twin Lakes
20 m NW of L'Anse, 8 m N of M-38

Beaufort Lake SF CG   906-339-4461
7 P sites, fishing, paddling   46.54590, -88.18365
Three Lakes
35 m W of Marquette, 4 m S of US 41

King Lake SF CG   TB
6 P sites, fishing, boating, hiking,   906-353-6558
    wildlife viewing   46.53040, -88.40127
Three Lakes
48 m W of Marquette, 5 m S of US 41

NPS and National Forest Campgrounds

Isle Royale NP   TB
112 P sites, 36 walk-in or canoe-in   906-482-0984
    camping areas, accessed by ferry   47.12255, -88.56453
Houghton
In Lake Superior, North of Keweenaw
    Peninsula

Clark Lake CG, Ottawa NF   MBC, BTC
47 P sites, Sylvania Wilderness Area   906-358-4551
Watersmeet   46.24463, -89.31003
40 m E of Bessemer, 3 m S of US 2

Black River Harbor CG, Ottawa NF   MBC, BTC
39 P sites, beach, fishing, charter   906-932-1330
    boats, Apostle Islands attractions 46.66280, -90.05192
Bessemer
On Lake Superior, 15 m N of Bessemer

Marion Lake CG, Ottawa NF   906-358-4551
38 P sites, fishing, beach, paddling   46.26938, -89.08652
Watersmeet
55 m E of Bessemer, 1 m N of US 2

Lake Ottawa CG, Ottawa NF   MBC
31 P sites, beach, fishing, paddling,   906-358-4551
    trail   46.07504, -88.76588
Iron River
35 m NW of Iron Mountain, 2 m S of
    US 2

Norway Lake CG, Ottawa NF   MBC
28 P sites, beach, towering red pines 906-852-3500
Sidnaw   46.41577, -88.68219
28 m S of L'Anse, 10 m W of US 141

Lake Ste Katherine CG, Ottawa NF   MBC, BTC
23 P sites, fishing, beach, paddling   906-852-3500
Sidnaw   46.39312, -88.72276
30 m S of L'Anse, 14 m W of US 141

Imp Lake CG, Ottawa NF   906-358-4551
22 P sites, loons, beach, paddling,   46.21776, -89.07046
   fishing
Watersmeet
54 m E of Bessemer, on US 2

Golden Lake CG, Ottawa NF   906-358-4551
22 P sites, fishing, paddling   46.17155, -88.88289
Iron River
45 m NW of Iron Mountain, on US 2

Courtney Lake CG, Ottawa NF   BTC
20 P sites, beach, fishing, paddling   906-884-2411
Nisula   46.75235, -88.94044
22 m W of L'Anse, 1 m S of M-38

Perch Lake CG, Ottawa NF   906-852-3500
20 P sites, fishing, paddling   46.36406, -88.67352
Sidnaw
30 m S of L'Anse, 10 W of US 141

Bob Lake CG, Ottawa NF   MBC
17 P sites, beach, fishing, paddling,   906-884-2411
   trail   46.66224, -88.91426
Nisula
20 m W of L'Anse, 7 m S of M-38

Pomeroy Lake CG, Ottawa NF   MBC
13 P sites, fishing, boating, scenic   906-932-1330
   views   46.28146, -89.57396
Watersmeet
30 m E of Bessemer, 8 m S of US 2

Moosehead Lake CG, Ottawa NF   MBC
13 P sites, fishing, paddling, isolation 906-932-1330
Watersmeet   46.24157, -89.60451
30 m E of Bessemer, on Wisconsin line

Langford Lake CG, Ottawa NF   906-932-1330
11 P sites, fishing, mosquitoes, black   46.27217, -89.49294
   flies
Watersmeet
34 m E of Bessemer, 5 m S of US 2

Henry Lake CG, Ottawa NF MBC, BTC
11 P sites, fishing, boating 906-932-1330
Marenisco 46.33093, -89.79116
25 m E of Bessemer, 8 m S of US 2

Bobcat Lake CG, Ottawa NF 906-932-1330
11 P sites, beach, fishing, paddling, 46.35924, -89.67294
  bike trail
Marenisco
28 m E of Bessemer, 2 m S of US 2

County and Municipal Campgrounds

Pioneer Trail Park, Delta CP 906-786-1020
213 sites, showers, fishing, near 45.79510, -87.07014
  Lake Michigan
Michigan 35, Gladstone
3 m N of Escanaba, 5 m W of US 41

Tourist Park, Marquette MP MBC
110 sites, beach, fishing 906-228-0465
2145 Sugarloaf Ave, Marquette 46.56839, -87.40607
On Lake Superior, in Marquette

Pentoga Park, Iron CP MBC
100 sites, showers, beach, fishing 906-265-3979
1630 CR 424, Crystal Falls 46.03861, -88.51076
25 m NW of Iron Mountain, on US 2

Perkins Park, Marquette CP MBC
83 sites, showers, trails, beach 906-345-9353
CR 550, Big Bay 46.80972, -87.82705
On Lake Superior, 30 m NW of
  Marquette

Hancock Recreation Area, 906-482-7413
  Hancock MP 47.13232, -88.61819
70 sites, beach, showers, laundry,
  fishing, Wi-Fi
Powder Dr, Hancock
On Keweenaw Peninsula, 2 m W of
  US 41

Gladstone Bay CG, Gladstone MP 906-4281211
62 sites, showers, beach, bike trail, 45.84717, -87.00642
  Wi-Fi
37 Michigan Ave, Gladstone
On Lake Michigan, 5 m N of Escanaba

Lake Gogebic, Gogebic CP   906-663-4428
52 P sites, beach, fishing   46.40786, -89.55539
M-64, Marenisco
28 m E of Bessemer, 5 m N of US 2

Bond Falls Flowage CG, UPPCO   MBC, BTC
   Property   not available
48 P sites, fishing, waterfalls   46.4088, -89.1329
Paulding
50 m E of Bessemer, 12 m N of US 2

Ontonagon CP   906-575-3952
44 P sites, fishing, boating   46.54897, -89.62579
M-64, Bergland
On Lake Gogebic, 28 m E of Bessemer

Iron River RV Park, Iron River MP   906-265-3822
32 sites, showers, paddling, fishing,   46.09145, -88.63840
   WiFi
50 E Genesee St, Iron River
75 m E of Bessemer, on US2

Little Girl's Point, Gogebic CP   MBC
30 P sites, beach, fishing, paddling   906-932-1913
Bessemer   46.60354, -90.32212
On Lake Superior, 15 m NW of
   Bessemer

Bergland Township MP   906-575-8733
28 sites, showers, beach, boating,   46.59052, -89.56807
   fishing
Bergland
On Lake Gogebic, 1 m S of M-28/64

Fox Park, Cedarville Township MP   MBC
20 P sites, beach, scenic views of   906-753-6911
   Green Bay   45.47353, -87.30802
Cedar River
On Lake Michigan, 28 m N of
   Menominee

Illinois

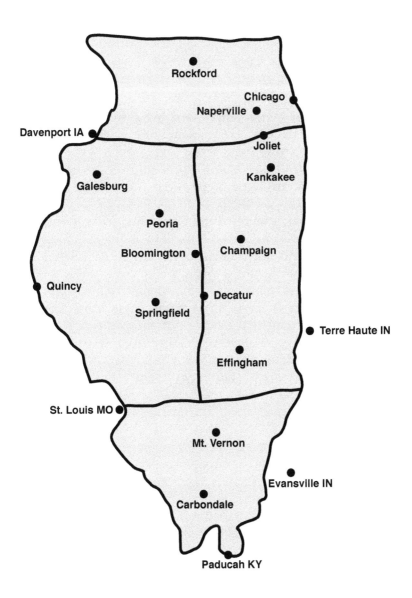

5

Illinois

The third stop on the tour of family camping destinations around Lake Michigan is Illinois—known as "The Land of Lincoln." This nickname was officially adopted in 1955 as a reminder that Illinois was the home of our nation's sixteenth president during his early adult years. He lived in New Salem and began his professional and political career in Springfield and surrounding areas. On the day of Lincoln's assassination, a group of Springfield citizens established the National Lincoln Monument Association to build President Lincoln's tomb in Springfield. After creating Lincoln's Tomb in Oak Ridge Cemetery, other historical preservation groups established several more Lincoln sites in and around Springfield. These Springfield sites include Lincoln's Home National Historic Site, Lincoln-Herndon Law Office, Old State Capitol, Lincoln Depot, and the Abraham Lincoln Presidential Library (formally known as the Illinois State Historical Library). A few miles away from Springfield, historic preservation groups established Lincoln's New Salem Site in Petersburg, Carl Sandburg's Birthplace in Galesburg, several Lincoln sculptures and markers in Decatur, the Lincoln Trail State Recreation Area in Marshall, Lincoln Log Cabin in Lerna, and Lincoln Trail Homestead State Park in Mount Zion.

In addition to being the Land of Lincoln, Illinois could easily be called the land of American history. Over five hundred museums and historic sites, spread across the state, celebrate the contributions of many historic people from the state. Historic forts reflecting life during the early French settlements and Indian wars include Fort Massac in the far southern tip of the state, Fort de Chartres about thirty-eight miles south of St. Louis on the Mississippi River, Fort Kaskaskia about forty-eight miles south of St. Louis near the Mississippi River, and Apple River Fort in the far northwestern corner of the state. The Black Hawk State Historical Site, located in Rock Island, preserves land that was used by prehistoric natives as well as the more recent Sauk nation. Cahokia Mounds, located about twelve miles east of St. Louis, is one of the largest and best-preserved mounds of the prehistoric Mississippian culture. Albany Mounds, located about twenty miles north of Moline on the Mississippi

River, preserves an archeological site that dates back to the Hopewell culture. Dickson Mounds, located on the Illinois River about forty miles northwest of Springfield, has four unique excavation sites and preserves artifacts from the Mississippian Culture. And Kincaid Mounds, located at the southern tip of the state, preserves another archeological site from the Mississippian Culture.

Major museums in the state include the Illinois State Museum in Springfield and other locations, the Chicago History Museum, the DuSable Museum of African American History in Chicago, and the Field Museum of Natural History in Chicago. Ronald Regan's birthplace and boyhood home sites can be found in the northwestern corner of the state and Ulysses S. Grant's home can be found in the extreme northwestern corner. Many more historic homes and mansions are scattered across the state. In 1985, the Illinois Historic Preservation Agency was established to manage most of the historic sites mentioned above plus many more including Jubilee College, Bishop Hill, Halfway Tavern, and the Lewis and Clark Historic Site near St. Louis. In total, this agency manages fifty-two historic sites across the state.

In addition to these historic sites, Illinois was the birthplace or home of Stephen A. Douglas (a popular politician who supported states rights and lost the presidential election to Abraham Lincoln), Wild Bill Hickok (a famous western scout, lawman, gunman, and gambler), Jane Addams (an early pioneer and sociologist), Wyatt Earp (an iconic gambler and lawman in the Old West), William Jennings Bryan (a liberal democrat who fought for the rights of common people and ran unsuccessfully for president three times), Walt Disney (a cartoon animator and producer), Betty Friedan (a feminist leader), Barack Obama (our forty-fourth president of the United States) and many more famous people. Indeed, the state of Illinois has nurtured a significant number of creative and progressive-minded people who have left an impact upon our nation's history.

Chicago in the northeastern corner and St. Louis on the southwestern edge offer many exciting tourist attractions and activities. Both cities offer a wide range of concerts, museums, festivals, fine restaurants, universities, sporting events, art shows, entertainment, and other attractions. In the Chicago area, families can tour the Museum of Science and Industry, the Art Institute, and Shedd Aquarium. A few miles north of the city, the Great America Amusement Park offers exciting rides and attractions that will please the whole family. In the St. Louis area, families can enjoy Six Flags amusement park, the St. Louis Zoo, Anheuser-Busch Brewery tours, and many more tourist attractions.

In 1903, Fort Massac State Park, located near the southern tip of the state, was established as the first Illinois state park. Starved Rock State Park, located in the northern part of the state, was established in 1911 as the second state park. As was true for most other midwestern states, establishing and maintaining these state parks was a difficult process during those early years. However, Governor Frank Lowden led a series of government reforms in 1917 to improve public land acquisition and management procedures that, in turn, led to the establishment of the state parks system. By 1925, the state parks system was operational and Black Hawk State Historic Site, Giant City State Park, and White Pines State Park were soon added to the growing list of state-managed properties.

Today, the Illinois Department of Natural Resources manages seventy-three state parks, recreation areas, wildlife areas, and forests with camping facilities. These campgrounds tend to be large, well-groomed open fields with scattered trees and little understory vegetation. In the northern half of the state, campgrounds are very popular and frequently fill to capacity on nice summer weekends until mid-August. In the southern half of the state, campgrounds seem to be considerably less popular and good campsites can usually be obtained without reservations. After mid-August, campgrounds are virtually empty. Campers who seek solitude and privacy will enjoy the state parks in southern Illinois. Budget problems have apparently taken their toll on Illinois state parks and, consequently, most contact staff are young temporary employees or volunteers. Furthermore, many old rustic bathroom buildings are in need of paint, repair, and remodeling. Fortunately, campers in Illinois state parks do not have to pay an extra park admission fee (as of 2013), making them the lowest priced camping destinations of the four Lake Michigan states.

The Illinois Department of Natural Resources website seems to be designed for hunters and fishermen rather than for campers. In fact, finding information about some state campgrounds can be challenging. After entering the home page, users should click the "Parks and Recreation" button at the top to open a drop-down box that includes "Camping." This camping page is a little cluttered but several links on the right side can be used to find state parks and other properties with campgrounds. Website visitors should know from the onset that many properties listed on the DNR website do not have campgrounds. When using the regional tabs on the right side of the page to find a property, users should immediately determine whether or not a listed property offers camping as a recreational option.

After identifying a property that offers camping, it is sometimes difficult to find the number of available campsites, campground maps, and other information. Individual park descriptions vary considerably in terms of their content. Some provide considerable information about campground fees and amenities—some do not. In general, campgrounds are classified into one of seventeen amenities/fee-schedule categories, rather than simply noting family campgrounds with showers and rustic campgrounds without. Class AA, A, B, and some C campgrounds have showers while other campground classifications usually do not have showers. A few property websites have campground maps but many do not. One important factor to consider when planning trips to Illinois state parks is that most have strict rules forbidding possession and consumption of alcoholic beverages. Anyone who plans to camp in an Illinois state park should check the park's web page to determine its alcohol policy before bringing alcoholic beverages into the park. Despite these peculiarities, future vacationers can still find great camping destinations in Illinois and sufficient information for planning enjoyable trips.

Three federal agencies manage campgrounds in the state of Illinois. The Army Corps of Engineers manage four areas with a total of twenty-five campgrounds. The Mississippi River Public Use Area, located in the northern region, has nine campgrounds; Carlyle Lake, located in the west central region, has six campgrounds; Lake Shelbyville, located in the east central region, has six family campgrounds; and Rend Lake, located in the southern region, has four family campgrounds. The National Fish and Wildlife Service manages the Crab Orchard National Wildlife Refuge with four campgrounds. And the U.S. Forest service manages nine campgrounds in the Shawnee National Forest.

County and municipal governments in the state manage twenty-six county parks, county forest preserves, and municipal park campgrounds. Compared with Wisconsin and Michigan, this number of locally managed properties is low but some of these campgrounds have amenities and activities that equal or exceed state parks in other states. As previously stated, campers should always assess safety at any county and municipal property before deciding to camp there.

Illinois also has eight U.S. Wilderness Areas suited for campers who prefer more primitive camping destinations. All eight of these wilderness areas are located in the southern part of the state in and around the Shawnee National Forest. Bald Knob, Clear Springs, Bay Creek, Burden Falls, Panther Den, Garden of the Gods, and Lusk Creek are all managed by the U.S. Forest Service while Crab Orchard is managed by the U.S. Fish and Wildlife Service.

In total, Illinois has 134 developed public campgrounds spread across the state. To summarize these campgrounds and their respective recreational activities, I divided the state into four geographic regions. Within each region, I summarized popular tourist attractions and featured a few popular camping destinations that readers may want to consider when planning camping vacations to the region. At the end of this chapter, I list all of Illinois' public campgrounds along with key details needed to evaluate their location, popularity, amenities, and activities.

Northern Region: Chicago Attractions

The northern region is defined as the area north of I-80 running from Moline on the Mississippi River east to Gary, Indiana. The Wisconsin state line defines the northern border of the region, the Mississippi River defines the western border, and Lake Michigan defines the eastern border. The Rock River flows through the center of the region. Reference cities in the region include Chicago located on the eastern edge, Rockford located in the center, Freeport located in the north central area, Dubuque, Iowa, located in the far northwestern corner, Moline located on the Mississippi River in the southwestern edge, and Peru/La Salle on the southern edge of the region near the center of the state.

Many tourist destinations in this region can be found in the Chicago metropolitan area. For example, the Shedd Aquarium, Museum of Science and Industry, Chicago Art Institute, Navy Pier, Adler Planetarium, Field Museum of Natural History, and two zoos, plus a wide range of theatre, concerts, shops, restaurants, and sporting events. Tourists who want to explore Chicago attractions should consider parking their cars in a suburban parking lot and riding the L into the city because parking in the city can be expensive. For more information about this system, go to the Chicago Transit Authority website (www.transitChicago.com).

Although the eastern side of this northern region is very urbanized with congested highways and high population density, the central and western parts of this region offer more rural experience, interesting historic sites, rustic camping destinations, and a much slower pace. Some of the interesting historic sites include Wild Bill Hickok Memorial just off of I-39 about ten miles north of Peru, President Ronald Regan Boyhood Home in Dixon between Rockford and Moline, Black Hawk Memorial, Saukenuk, and the Museum of Native American Life in Rock Island just a few miles west of Moline, Albany Mounds on the Mississippi River about twenty-five miles north of Moline, and Old Market

House, U.S. Grant's home, Apple River Fort, Galena, and the Washburne House—all in the extreme northwestern corner of the region.

The Illinois Department of Natural Resources manages twelve state parks plus one fish and wildlife area with campgrounds in this region. Four of the parks in this region (Rock Cut, Illinois Beach, Chain O'Lakes, and Shabbona Lake) have been designated by the DNR as "Premium Campgrounds"—defined as having a "preponderant history of consistently operating at capacity." To secure a campsite at any of these premium campgrounds, campers must make advance reservations. Tent campers planning vacations in this region may want to consider one of the following destinations.

Rock Cut State Park (268 sites), five miles north of Rockford, has the largest camping area in the northern region and is one of Illinois' premium campgrounds that fills to capacity almost every summer weekend. It is one of my favorite camping destinations because it is located along one of my travel routes to Wisconsin, it has a family-friendly atmosphere, and most of its campsites are large, level, and shady. Tent sites near the water are a little more crowded but offer nice views and a place to catch dinner right from the site. The park has a rich history

Rock Cut State Park has a large electric family campground at the top of the hill and a small rustic campground down by the lake. This site (#20) is on the lakeshore.

shaped by Miami and Winnebago Indians who lived in the area between 1740 and 1840, plus subsequent Scottish immigrants who moved into in the area after 1840. The campground, including two shower buildings, a separate tent camping area, twelve youth group campsites, and a camp store, is arranged as six loops spread along a winding park road. Most sites in the family campground have large level grassy areas suitable for tents, a gravel parking pad, several trees providing partial or full shade, and understory vegetation providing partial privacy. The park also offers an equestrian camp and the Plum Grove Nature Preserve. A major attraction of the park is the forty miles of trails suited for hiking, running, biking, and horseback riding. Two lakes provide opportunities for swimming, fishing, and paddling.

Mississippi Palisades State Park (241 sites), on the Mississippi River about forty miles south of Dubuque, has been designated as a national landmark and named by *National Geographic* as one of the most historically significant and scenic state parks in the United States. The park features towering bluffs that overlook the mighty Mississippi and 2,500 acres of ravines and heavily forested terrain. The campground, shaped like the capital letter Y, has three shower buildings and a camp store. Many sites cannot be reserved and are only available for walk-up campers. Most sites have partial shade but a few are open. Popular activities in the park include exploring Native American history, hiking along the nearly fifteen miles of trails, and exploring caves, sink holes, and rock formations in the park. Observation areas allow beautiful views of the Mississippi and Apple Rivers. Fishing, boating, and wildlife viewing are also popular activities. Outside the park, campers can ride about thirty miles to the north and find several historic sites, such as Apple River Fort and U.S. Grant's home in Jo Daviess County or fifty miles to the south and find the Black Hawk Memorial and the Museum of Native American History.

Shabbona Lake State Recreation Area (150 sites), about 40 miles south of Rockford, is another premium campground that was named by *TripleBlaze* as one of Illinois' best camping destinations. It is one of my favorite campgrounds because it is located along my travel route to Wisconsin, it offers a family-friendly atmosphere, it has large beautiful shaded campsites, and it has a well-stocked fishing lake where Eva can catch our supper in a few minutes. The campground is divided into three spurs with the shower building located at the junction of the spurs. Most sites are large and well shaded and these sites typically fill quickly on nice summer weekends. Throughout the campground, visitors will see large families relaxing and laughing, children riding bicycles, and teens enjoying each other's company. At the end of the Canvasback Cove spur, campers will find a small camp store, recreation area, lake, and teen hangout. A few years ago, Eva and I were lucky enough to secure a walk-up site for an overnight camp while traveling to Wisconsin. Since we did not have reservations and arrived late Saturday afternoon, we got one of the last and least desirable sites (#57) but our site was close to the shower building and had sufficient amenities to meet our needs for the night. After setting up our tent, we walked down to the lake area and mingled with several people fishing from the pier. After a few minutes, Eva decided to try her luck. She purchased a one-day license and some bait from the store and quickly caught three small perch and a crappie—which we took back to our campsite and boiled with potatoes and onions to make a great evening meal.

Shabbona Lake State Park's Class A family campground has three loops with several large, level, and shady sites. Site #57 was one of the last available but served us well as a safe and comfortable overnight camp.

Campers who prefer less congestion and more solitude can investigate parks and campgrounds located in the western side of this region. **Lake Le-Aqua-Na State Park** (171 sites) and **Apple River Canyon State Park** (47 primitive sites) have been named by *The Best in Tent*

Camping: Illinois as quiet and isolated places to camp. Other popular state parks in this region include **Lowden Memorial State Park** (130 sites) and **White Pines Forest State Park** (103 sites)—both of which are located southwest of Rockford. If you want to find an isolated canoe-in site, you may want to consider one of the few sites at **Castle Rock State Park**.

The Army Corps of Engineers manages a large public use area located along the Mississippi River near Moline with a total of nine different campgrounds. The largest of these campgrounds are **Thompson Causeway Recreation Area** (81 sites), forty miles north of Moline, **Fisherman's Corner Recreation Area** (56 sites), three miles north of Moline, and **Blanding Landing Recreation Area** (37 sites), 20 miles southeast of Dubuque.

County and municipal governments in the northern region manage a total of ten campgrounds. **Sugar River Forest Preserve** (92 sites) northwest of Rockford is the largest of these locally managed proper-

Sugar River Forest Preserve, located in Winnebago County a few miles northwest of Rockford, has a beautiful forest campground with campground hosts and a nice bathhouse.

ties and was named by the *Best in Tent Camping: Illinois* as having one of the most secluded campgrounds in the state. It is one of my favorite camping destinations because the campsites in the old towering pine forest are impressive. Although this campground is located several miles away from major highways, it is worth the effort to get here. It has two on-site hosts, clean bathrooms, and unusually nice level shady sites. Tent campers preferring more privacy will find a separate walk-in camping area. **Illiniwek Forest Preserve** (85 sites) near Moline is another property in this region with a large campground. **Marengo Ridge Forest Preserve** (46 primitive sites) located a few miles east of Rockford was named by the *Best in Tent Camping: Illinois*.

West-Central Region: Lincoln Land

The west-central region is defined as the area that is south of I-80, north of US Highway 50 connecting St Louis with Vincennes, Indiana, and west of US Highway 51 connecting Peru and Carbondale. The Mississippi River defines the western border of this region and the Illinois River flows through the center of the region. Carlyle Lake is located on the southern edge of this region. Reference cities in this area are Bloomington and Decatur located on the eastern edge of the region, Peoria and Springfield located in the center, Galesburg located in the northwestern corner, Quincy located on the far western edge, and St. Louis, Missouri, located in the southwestern corner.

Some of the more popular tourist areas in this region are the Lincoln sites located in and around Springfield. Hundreds of tourists visit this area to see the sites where the sixteenth president lived and practiced law. Among the popular Lincoln sites are the New Salem site, the presidential museum in Springfield, Sandburg Birthplace in Galesburg, and the Lincoln–Douglas Debate Museum in Charleston. Other popular historic sites in this region include Bishop Hill about twenty-five miles southeast of Moline, Jubilee College about fifteen miles northwest of Peoria, Historic Route 66 that follows the I-55 corridor from Bloomington to St Louis, Postville Courthouse about thirty miles southwest of Bloomington, and Cahokia Mounds about fifteen miles east of St. Louis. Popular camping destinations in this region include seven campgrounds located along the Illinois River and six campgrounds located on the shores of Carlyle Lake. Tourists also come to this west-central region to enjoy the many museums, concerts, sporting events, amusement parks, and other attractions scattered around the St. Louis metropolitan area.

The Illinois Department of Natural Resources manages twenty-two state parks, recreation areas, fish and wildlife areas, and forests in this west-central region. Tent campers planning vacations in this region may want to consider one of the following destinations.

Eldon Hazlet State Recreation Area (364 sites), on Carlyle Lake, is the largest camping destination in the west-central region. The campground is grouped into ten small spurs that extend down to the lakeshore along a one-and-a-half-mile park road that meanders along the lakeshore plus three larger loops. It also has three shower buildings that are located throughout the campground. Many sites have ample shade with nice lake views. Just behind the campground, campers have access to an Olympic-size swimming pool. Carlyle Lake, created by the Army Corps of Engineers by damming the Kaskaskia River, is well known for its sailing culture and events that are held many summer weekends. Other popular activities within the park include hiking, fishing, and wildlife viewing. Every summer weekend, naturalists offer a variety of educational programs. Visitors may be surprised to see that park rangers urge visitors to protect native snakes—especially the Eastern Massasauga rattlesnake—on trails and in the roadway.

Lincoln's New Salem State Historic Park (200 sites), located about twenty miles north of Springfield, displays the village of New Salem as it stood during the 1830s when young Abraham Lincoln lived there. The original village of New Salem was founded in 1828 but was abandoned a few years later after the county seat was moved to another location. In the 1930s, the Civilian Conservation Corps re-created the village by constructing twenty-three buildings as close to their original design as possible. Today the buildings have period furnishings and costumed interpreters who describe the life and times in the village during young Lincoln's residency. The campground has 200 shaded sites arranged in a square with back-to-back sites plus two shower buildings. In addition to touring the village and museum, visitors can hike the grounds and enjoy other activities. Near the park, visitors will find several more theatres, museums, and attractions commemorating Lincoln's life.

Campers who prefer more privacy and solitude may want to consider **Ramsey Lake State Recreation Area** (159 sites) about thirty miles west of Effingham, **Johnson Sauk Trail State Park** (95 sites) about thirty-five miles east of Moline, **Jim Edgar Panther Creek Fish and Wildlife Area** (82 sites) twenty-five miles northwest of Springfield, **Beaver Dam State Park** (77 sites) forty-five miles northeast of St Louis, **Spring Lake Fish and Wildlife Area** (70 primitive sites) twenty-five miles southwest of Peoria, **Delabar State Park** (56 sites) on the Mississippi River about thirty miles west of Galesburg, **Sand Ridge State Forest** (35 primitive sites) twenty-eight miles southwest of Peoria, and **Woodford County Fish and Wildlife Area** (25 primitive sites) on the Illinois River about forty miles northwest of Bloomington. Each of these campgrounds was named by *The Best in Tent Camping: Illinois* as one of the quietist and most private campgrounds in the state.

The Army Corps of Engineers manages two public use areas in this region (Carlyle Lake and Mississippi River) with a combined total of nine campgrounds. **Coles Creek Recreation Area** (119 sites) and **Dam West Recreation Area** (109 sites), both located on Carlyle Lake, have the two largest campgrounds.

County and municipal governments in the west-central region manage nine campgrounds that may be suited for tent camping. **Comlara Campground** (144 sites), located about ten miles north of Bloomington, is the largest county park campground in the region and was named by *The Best in Tent Camping: Illinois* as one of the more secluded campgrounds in Illinois. It is also one of my favorite camping destinations because of its proximity to my Wisconsin travel route and Bloomington. The campground is arranged around a large lake and over several gently rolling hills. Many sites have one or two trees offering partial shade but the small crowded sites offer no privacy. Tent sites in the back of the campground offer more space and privacy. The shower building is in the middle of the campground. Visitors can enjoy fishing in the park and driving down to Bloomington to shop and visit various attractions. **Loud Thunder Forest Preserve** (115 sites), located on the Mississippi River west of Moline is a second large county park named by *The Best in Tent Camping: Illinois* as a secluded campground. **Spring Lake Park** (120 sites), located in Macomb about sixty miles west of Peoria, is a third large municipal campground in this region. Campers who prefer very small, rustic, and remote campgrounds may want to consider the **McCully Heritage Project** (5 primitive sites) that was named by the *Best in Tent Camping: Illinois* as one of the most private campgrounds in the state.

East-Central Region: Lake Shelbyville

The east-central region is defined as the area that is south of I-80, north of US Highway 50 connecting St. Louis and Vincennes, Indiana, and east of US Highway 51 connecting Peru and Carbondale. Lake Shelbyville is located near the center of this region. Reference cities in this region are Kankakee located on the northern edge, Peru in the northwest corner,

Bloomington and Decatur located on the far western edge, and Champaign and Effingham located in the center.

One of the more popular camping destinations in this region is Lake Shelbyville with eight public campgrounds and loads of water recreational activities. A second popular destination is the LaSalle county area in the northwestern corner of the region. This tourist area includes four state parks along the Illinois River, picturesque canyons and rock formations, educational programs, unique shops, and other tourist attractions. Smaller lakes in this region with camping facilities and water recreational activities include Clinton Lake, Newton Lake, and Forbes Lake. Other popular tourist destinations in this region include Historic Route 66 that extends from Joliet down to Bloomington, Bryant Cottage about twenty miles southwest of Champaign, Amish Settlement about twenty-eight miles southeast of Decatur, Lincoln Trail Homestead about five miles west of Decatur, the Historic National Road that runs along I-70 from Terre Haute, Indiana, to St. Louis, and Vandalia State House about thirty miles southwest of Effingham.

The Illinois Department of Natural Resources manages fourteen state parks, recreation areas, and wildlife areas in this east-central region. Tent campers planning vacations in this region may want to consider one of the following destinations.

Wolf Creek State Park (382 sites), on Lake Shelbyville about twenty-eight miles north of Effingham, is the largest of the state camping properties in the east-central region and is one of eight public camping areas located on the shores of Lake Shelbyville. The campground has two sections. Sites in Sand Creek can be reserved while sites in Lick Creek are only available for walk-up occupancy. Both campgrounds are large level areas with scattered trees but we discovered that bathrooms in both areas are dark, damp, and dingy. On the day of our visit, no campers were in the Sand Creek campground and only a few were in the Lick Creek Campground. Despite its size, it is an under-used campground and was briefly closed in 2008 to balance the state budget. Inside the park, campers can enjoy swimming, fishing, and hiking on fifteen miles of trails. Outside the park, they can find paddling and boating outfitters, fishing supplies, and horse rentals.

Lincoln Trail State Park (242 sites), near the Indiana state line just south of I-70, was established to commemorate the 1,000-mile long trail followed by Abraham Lincoln's family as they migrated from Kentucky to the Springfield, Illinois, area. The campground is organized as a series of spurs and loops that follow the irregular lakeshore. Most sites have lush green grass and plenty of shade trees but no understory

Wolf Creek State Park, located a few miles north of Effingham, has two nice campgrounds, a beach, and recreation area.

Wolf Creek State Park's Sand Creek campground, only available for walk-up occupancy, seems to be the nicer of the two campgrounds but only a few people were camped there on the day of our visit.

vegetation. Inside the park, visitors can enjoy hiking, observing unique plant and wildlife species, fishing, and boating. The American Beech Woods Nature Preserve is a popular attraction within the park. Campers who would rather eat out than cook in their site will find a nice restaurant with scenic views of the lake located inside the park.

Moraine View State Recreation Area (199 sites), about fifteen miles east of Bloomington near the Bloomington Glacial Moraine, was named by *The Best in Tent Camping: Illinois* as one of the most private camping destinations in the state. The partially shaded campground is one of my favorite camping destinations because it is located along my travel route to Wisconsin and has nice bathrooms. The campground resembles a ladder with six rungs or roads across the side rails. Fishing is a primary activity at this park but hiking along various glacially created terrain features and horseback riding are also popular activities. This park holds special significance for me because I camped overnight in the park with two friends in 2005 on the way to Wisconsin. We set up our overnight camp in a site directly across the road from the shower house. Since I was tired from driving all day, I went to bed early that night. My friends stayed awake for several hours talking and snacking on food. When they finally went to bed, they neglected to properly secure their

Moraine View State Park, located near Bloomington and I-74, has nice level and partly shaded lots with many raccoons. Some friends and I camped in section D across from the shower building one night on the way to Wisconsin.

food and garbage. Although I slept through the whole affair, a dozen raccoons must have invaded our site and shredded food wrappers and containers into a million tiny pieces. When I awoke the next morning, our site looked like a garbage dump. One of my friends, who slept in the SUV with the windows open, reported that a raccoon actually got into the vehicle with her and she just pushed it back out. This experience gave me a personal reminder of the importance of packing all food items in a closed vehicle and disposing all garbage in appropriate receptacles. After this incident, subsequent camping companions will always get at least one mini-lecture on the importance of proper food storage.

Kickapoo State Recreation Area (184 sites), about twenty-five miles east of Champaign, was established in 1939 as one of Illinois' first state parks and was named by *The Best in Tent Camping: Illinois* as one of the best camping destinations in the state. It is also one of my favorite camping destinations. Located on the far eastern edge of the state, the park and surrounding areas feature scenic, winding roads through rolling hills and heavily forested areas. Within the park, campers will find several small lakes for fishing and canoeing. Bike trails are also available. Just a few miles to the north, visitors will find the Middle Fork Fish and Wildlife Area that offers more fishing and boating opportunities. In 2008, I camped overnight in this park on a motorcycle trip to Wisconsin. I selected a site near the bathrooms but was disappointed that it was a small RV site covered with large gravel. Farther away from the bathhouse several larger, grassier, and more shaded sites at the far end of the loop would have been better tent sites. Other motorcyclists arriving about the same time chose to stay in a separate tent camping area.

Starved Rock State Park (133 sites), on the Illinois River near Peru and LaSalle, was established in 1911 as one of the oldest state parks in Illinois and has been named by *National Geographic* as being one of the most historically significant and scenic state parks in the United States. It is also one of my favorite camping destinations because it is located along my travel route to Wisconsin and has a nice safe campground. The campground has two large loops with two shower houses and a camp store. Trees are scattered throughout the middle of the campground but many sites receive several hours of full sun on hot summer days. Visitors in the park especially enjoy hiking to magnificent glacial carved canyons, waterfalls, sandstone bluffs, river views, and rock formations located throughout the park. Park visitors can also enjoy viewing wildlife (especially bald eagles) and visiting the nature center to learn more about the park's geology, ecology, and social history. Other popular activities include fishing in the Illinois River, paddling in the Fox River, horseback riding, and attending one of the many concerts and special events held in the park. Outside the park, the LaSalle County area has dozens of popular tourist attractions.

Starved Rock State Park, located in a popular tourist area near the Illinois River, has a large, level, grassy, and partly shady campground with one bathhouse and several pit toilets. These are sites 2–11 and 36–41.

Starved Rock State Park's site #1 is not one of the best but was located near the bathhouse and water faucet.

Weldon Springs State Park (75 sites), about seventeen miles north of Decatur, was named by Yahoo Sports as one of Illinois' best state parks and is one of my favorite camping destinations because it is conveniently located just east of U.S. Highway 51 and features a very neat campground with nice bathrooms and interesting educational programs.

Weldon Springs State Park, located a few miles south of Bloomington, has a beautiful campground and a nice shower building but few campers. Photo by Eva Douglass.

Walnut Point State Park (60 sites), about thirty miles south of Champaign, is nested in a remote area of the state. The park has been named by *The Best in Tent Camping: Illinois* as one of the most peaceful and secluded tent destinations in the state and I would agree with this choice. It is one of my favorite camping destinations because of its proximity to my travel route and its scenic beauty. I made an overnight camp in the park on a trip up to Wisconsin in 1995 and remembered that the campground was a beautiful place with spacious sites, lots of shade trees and understory, giving a nice secluded feeling. My site was either #2 or #4 across from the host. Although I did not intend to fish in the lake, I noticed that many campers had boats parked near their sites and learned that the lake is famous for outstanding angling action. While packing up the next morning, I vowed to return to this park another time for a longer stay but never have.

Families who prefer smaller, more-secluded campgrounds may want to consider **Sam Parr Fish and Wildlife Area** (80 sites) about thirty-two miles southeast of Effingham, **Middle Fork Fish and Wildlife Area** (45 primitive sites) about ten miles west of Danville, **Channahon State Park** (25 primitive sites) about forty-five miles southwest of the Chicago loop, and **Gebhard Woods State Park** (25 primitive sites) about fifty-five miles southwest of the Chicago loop. All four of these campgrounds were named by *The Best in Tent Camping: Illinois* as among the best tent camping destinations in the state.

The Army Corps of Engineers manages one public use area located at Lake Shelbyville and this area has six separate campgrounds. **Coon Creek** (208 sites) is the largest of these campgrounds and it, along with **Opossum Creek** (78 sites), were named by *TripleBlaze* as two of the fifteen best campgrounds in Illinois.

County and municipal governments in this east-central region manage six campgrounds that may be suited for tent camping. **Mill Creek Park** (139 sites), located about eight miles west of the Indiana state line and two miles south of I-70, is the largest county campground in the region. **Prairie Pines Municipal Park Campground** (95 sites), located in Rantoul about fifteen miles north of Champaign, also has a large campground. **Forest Glen Preserve** (58 sites), located about five miles south of Danville, and **Lodge Park** (13 primitive sites), located about twenty miles west of Champaign, were named by the *Best in Tent Camping: Illinois* as among the most secluded campgrounds in the state. Campers traveling through the Bloomington area should also consider Comlara Park that was described in the west-central region.

Southern Region: Rend Lake

The southern region is defined as the area south of US Highway 50 running from St. Louis east to the Indiana State line. This region is arguably the best camping and outdoor recreation region in Illinois but most campgrounds have relatively few campers. The Mississippi River defines its western border; the Wabash and Ohio rivers define its eastern border; Rend Lake is located in the north-central area; and the Shawnee National Forest plus the Crab Orchard National Wildlife Refuge are located in the southern area. Reference cities in this region are St. Louis, Missouri, located in the northwestern corner, Vincennes, Indiana, located in the northeast corner, Mount Vernon located in the north-central half, Carbondale located in the south-central half, and Paducah, Kentucky, located just beyond the southern tip.

Visitors to this region can find the perfect vacation destination, regardless of their particular hobbies and interests. Two of the most popular camping and vacation destinations in the southern region are Rend Lake and the Shawnee National Forest. Another interesting destination in this region is **The World Shooting and Recreational Complex** (1,000 sites), located about fifty miles southeast of St. Louis. This complex hosts dozens of unique shooting ranges and competitions. Readers

Rend Lake features some of the most beautiful sunsets to be found anywhere.

who may be interested in this destination should visit the WSRC website, www.dnr.illinois.gov/recreation/WSRC, and check out the Cowboy Action Shooting video. A large open-field campground is available for RVers, but tent campers could set up their tents in one of these campsites if they needed a place to stay in the area. Three well-stocked lakes, as well as a nice restaurant, are located on the property.

Campers who enjoy concerts, museums, fine restaurants, festivals, and sporting events may want to ride over to the St. Louis metropolitan area. Popular attractions in the St. Louis area include the zoo, Six Flags St. Louis amusement park, and Anheuser Bush Brewery tours. Carbondale also offers a nice selection of concerts, museums, and sporting events. Other popular tourist destinations in this region include Fort Kaskaskia and the Pierre Menard Home on the Mississippi River about fifty miles south of East St. Louis; Illinois Caverns about thirty miles south of St. Louis; Fort de Chartres about forty miles south of St. Louis; and Cave-in-Rock, Garden of the Gods, Fort Defiance, and Fort Massac—all on the Ohio River near Paducah, Kentucky.

Garden of the Gods Recreation Area, located in the Shawnee National Forest, features several trails through picturesque rock formations and the Pharaoh Campground.

The Illinois Department of Natural Resources manages sixteen state parks, recreation areas, and wildlife areas in this southern region. Tent campers planning vacations in this region may want to consider one of the following destinations.

Wayne Fitzgerrell State Recreation Area (283 sites), located on Rend Lake, is the largest DNR-managed camping destination in the southern region and was named by *The Best in Tent Camping: Illinois* as one of the best camping destinations in the state. It is also one of my favorite camping destinations. The campground is designed as a large loop with five spurs that extend out to five points along the lakeshore. Sites in the first spur (Bay Area) can be reserved but these sites are not as nice as sites in the other four spurs, which are only available on a walk-up basis. Thus, reservations are unnecessary when planning a trip to this campground but mid-week arrival is advisable to get the best sites. Sites at the tip of the loops are the most popular, having the best water views. Regardless of the spur, most sites are large, level, well spaced, shady, and grassy—making them well suited for tent camping.

As we discovered, this park is a great destination for nature lovers. Deer, turkeys, and skunks roam the campground during the early evening. Raccoons prowl the campground at night looking for unattended food or garbage. Cicadas and owls are extremely loud during mid-August nights. Crows, turkeys, and a variety of songbirds will wake you up in the morning. Inside the park, campers can enjoy horseback riding, bike riding, hiking, birding, boating, fishing, and other water recreational activities. Outside the park, campers will find a nice beach for sun bathing and swimming at the south Sandusky area, an interesting visitor center

Wayne Fitzgerrell State Park's campground on Rend Lake is very spacious and clean with five spurs that extend out to points on the lake.

Wayne Fitzgerrell State Park's Bay Area sites can be reserved but are not as popular as sites on the other four spurs. This is site #15.

near the beach, and a nice golf course nearby. Despite its beauty and recreational opportunities, plus perfect camping weather, we discovered that very few campers come to this park after the middle of August.

Ferne Clyffe State Park (109 sites), about 40 miles southeast of Carbondale, was named by *The Best in Tent Camping: Illinois* as one of the more secluded camping destinations in the state and by *National Geographic* as one of the most historically significant and scenic state parks in the United States. The park has a small family campground with 66 sites, a shower building, a walk-in campground, a backpacking area, and an equistrian campground. Although campers who enjoy more rustic camp settings will probably enjoy the family or walk-in campground, these campgrounds are a little too isolated for my tastes. On the day we drove through the park, we saw only one camper. Park visitors typically enjoy hiking or horseback riding on scenic trails, exploring Hawk's Cave and unique rock formations, strolling through the Round Bluff Nature Preserve, relaxing by a seasonal waterfall, fishing in Ferne Clyffe Lake, browsing local shops, and eating in various restaurants.

Giant City State Park (99 sites), about ten miles south of Carbondale, was established in 1927 as one of Illinois' early state parks and has been named by several authorities as one of the best camping destinations in the state and by *National Geographic* as one of the most historically significant and scenic state parks in the United States. The main campground is grouped into five loops clustered around a central shower building and congregating area. The first loop past the campground entrance to the left has several pull-through sites for RVs but the other four loops are well suited for tent camping. One of the loops was

Ferne Clyffe State Park, conveniently located near the junction of I-24 and I-67, offers a rustic campground plus a very rustic, isolated, primitive campground. This is a site inside the rustic campground loop.

designed as a primitive area for tents. Horseback riders will find a separate equestrian campground on the opposite side of the park. Popular activities in the park include hiking, horseback riding, fishing, visiting the nature center, eating at the family-oriented park restaurant, rock climbing, and rappelling. Outside the park, visitors frequently enjoy playing golf at one of the nearby golf courses and touring the Southern Illinois Wine Trail.

Cave-in-Rock State Park (59 sites), on the Ohio River about forty miles northeast of Paducah, was established in 1929 as one of Illinois' early state parks and was named by *The Best in Tent Camping: Illinois* as one of the best camping destinations in the state. It is also one of my favorite camping destinations despite the fact that park staff did not stop a loud drunken party next to my site a few years ago. Most of the park's campsites are arranged around a large loop with a large level grassy field in the center. Sites located on the inside of the loop have plenty of open space behind them for soccer, Frisbee, softball, volleyball, badminton, croquet, and other activities requiring a large level playing area. In the early morning, campers may see a few wild turkeys grazing in the field. At the back of the loop, visitors will find a shower building and twenty-five tent sites with more trees and understory vegetation providing shade plus a little privacy.

The primary attraction of the park is the large cave located in the bluffs along the river. Years ago, this cave served as a hideout for river pirates and scoundrels preying upon settlers and traders passing by on the river. In fact, a scene in the movie *How the West was Won* features

Cave-in-Rock State Park, located on the Ohio River, has several campsites spread around a large loop. Inside sites such as this one are adjacent to a very large recreational field.

Cave-in-Rock State Park features a trail down to a famous cave on the Ohio River plus trails up to a bluff that provides more scenic views of the river.

the cave as the setting for such a robbery. While exploring the cave area, visitors should hike to the top of the bluffs and watch barges and river traffic passing below. For campers who do not want to cook meals at their campsites, a nice restaurant is located in the park just up the hill from the campground. Outside the park, campers will find the small town of Cave in Rock with a small ferry that transports cars and people across the river to Kentucky. Near the ferry dock, a few souvenir shops and a sandwich stand are available for travelers waiting for the ferry to return from the opposite side of the river. A few miles away from the park, visitors will find several more public campgrounds and attractions in the Shawnee National Forest. In particular, the Garden of the Gods hiking trail should be at the top of the list of things to do in the forest. Those who want to learn more about the Ohio River should book a boat tour in Golconda, located a few miles west of the park.

Fort Massac State Park (50 sites), on the Ohio River five miles north of Paducah, was established in 1908 as Illinois' first state park and has been named by *National Geographic* as one of the most histori-cally significant and scenic state parks in the United States. It is one of my favorite camping destinations because it is located along my travel route to Wisconsin and because the campground is exceptionally well maintained. The small campground is designed as an open loop with understory vegetation along the outside edges and several large trees in the center. A separate tent camping area to the side has many more trees providing almost full shade. Bathrooms are adequate but not the best. The central attraction of the park is a restored French fort located upon a bluff high above the Ohio River with interesting displays, historical re-enactments, and educational lectures. Unfortunately, the fort was closed indefinitely in 2013 until money becomes available to repair and restore the historic buildings. Park visitors will enjoy touring the visitor center, riding bicycles, and observing boats and barges traveling up and down the Ohio River. Outside the park, visitors can ride down to Paducah to shop or try their luck in the casino.

Fort Massac State Park, on the far southern tip of the state, features an educational visitor's center and a French fort built in 1760 on the Ohio River.

Fort Massac State Park has a large, level, partly shaded modern campground with 50 electric sites.

Fort Massac State Park's rustic tent camping area has many more trees and much more shade than the modern campground.

Families who prefer more remote and secluded campgrounds may want to consider **Washington County Fish and Wildlife Area** (150 sites) about twenty-two miles west of Mt. Vernon, **Randolph County State Recreation Area** (95 sites) about fifty-five miles southwest of Mt. Vernon, **Hamilton County Fish and Wildlife Area** (71 primitive sites) about thirty-five miles southeast of Mt. Vernon, and **Beall Woods State Park** (16 primitive sites) sixty miles east of Mt. Vernon. Each of these properties was named by *The Best in Tent Camping* as offering the quietest and most secluded campsites in the southern region.

Three federal agencies manage a total of seventeen more campgrounds in this southern region. The U.S. Forest Service manages nine campgrounds in the Shawnee National Forest. **Oak Point** (56 sites), located about twenty-five miles north of Paducah, is the largest of the seven. **Red Bud** (21 primitive sites), **Pine Hills** (13 primitive sites), **Camp Cadiz** (11 primitive sites), and **Pharaoh** (12 primitive sites) were named by *The Best in Tent Camping: Illinois* as among the fifty quietest and most secluded campgrounds in the state.

The Crab Orchard National Wildlife Refuge, located a few miles southeast of Carbondale, is a large federally protected wetland area with three lakes and four campgrounds. All campers in the refuge, regardless of their particular campground, must first stop at the visitor center on state highway 148 to obtain a pass. My pass was free since I am over age 65. **Crab Orchard Campground** (78 sites), located on Crab Orchard Lake near Carbondale, is managed by the U.S. Fish & Wildlife Service. The campground has three loops spread along the lakeshore: Loops A and B have electricity, showers, and partial shade provided by a few widely scattered towering pine trees. A beach is located in Loop B at the tip of the point. Loop E has primitive tent sites along the lakeshore. Boat ramps are located in both loops B and E. Campers who want to relax in their site most of the day and take occasional dips in the water will probably enjoy camping in Loop B.

Crab Orchard Lake Campground in the Crab Orchard National Wildlife Refuge has two electric loops nestled in a pine tree grove spread along the lakeshore.

Crab Orchard Lake Campground offers a nice beach area plus two boat-launch ramps.

Crab Orchard Lake Campground also has a primitive loop
for tenters who want to camp near the lakeshore.

Blue Heron Campground and Marina (40 sites), also located on Crab Orchard Lake, is managed by the City of Carterville as a small fishing camp. The campground has an RV section located in a grove of shade trees at the top of the hill and an open grassy tent section along the lakeshore. Campers who have their own boats can launch and moor them in the marina near their campsites. Those who do not have boats can rent them from the concession or fish from piers and platforms scattered along the lakeshore. Fishing licenses, bait, tackle, and ice can be purchased from the on-site store and fish can be cleaned at a nice cleaning station positioned a few yards away from the campground. Of the four campgrounds in the refuge, this is my favorite camping destination because it is close to Carbondale and because my wife can fish all day long along the shore and I do not have to leave my hammock. If we want to swim, we can easily ride over to the Crab Orchard Campground. **Little Grassy Lake Campground** and Marina (103 sites), located on Little Grassy Lake and managed by a private concessionaire, is the largest of the four campgrounds. This campground is beautiful! It was named by *The Best in Tent Camping* as one of the quietest and

Blue Herron Campground is a municipal park/fishing camp on Crab Orchard Lake that offers several tent camping sites near the water's edge plus boat rental and fishing platforms along the lakeshore.

most secluded campgrounds in Illinois. It has 54 water and electric sites plus 35 tent camping sites, exceptionally clean bathrooms, shady sites, scenic vistas, boat rental, bait and tackle shop, and abundant fishing opportunities. **Devils Kitchen Campground** (9 tent sites), located on Devil's Kitchen Lake and managed by the U.S. Fish & Wildlife Service, is a small tent-only campground with showers that was also named by *The Best in Tent Camping: Illinois* as one of the best tent camping destinations in the state.

The Army Corps of Engineers manages four large and luxurious campgrounds around Rend Lake. **South Marcum Campground** (160 sites) is one of these four campgrounds and is my favorite Illinois camping destination because it is conveniently located about five miles west of I-57, has good overnight security, has exceptionally nice bathrooms, and offers beautiful lake vistas and sunsets. The campground is organized into five small spurs spread around a large central loop. Three of the small camping spurs extend down to the banks of the lake.

Eva and I arrived on a Monday afternoon in July and had the entire well-shaded pine campground almost to ourselves. We selected site #112 in the Covey Point loop on the lake's edge, set up our tent and hammocks, and enjoyed watching a beautiful sunset. After supper, we took our showers in one of the nicest shower buildings I have ever experienced. The next morning we explored the campground and discovered that some of the best sites are walk-in tent sites scattered along the lake's edge. The one limitation of this campground is that it does not have a large public swimming beach. Campers who want to swim must drive a few miles over to the South Sandusky beach.

South Marcum Campground is one of four campgrounds on Rend Lake managed by the U.S. Army Corps of Engineers. This is site #112.

South Marcum Campground's walk-in site #T8 is one of the best in the campground.

Other campgrounds located around Rend Lake are **South Sandusky Campground** (127 sites), **North Sandusky Campground** (118 sites), **Gun Creek Recreation Area** (100 sites), and **Wayne Fitzgerrell State Park** (283 sites). Regardless of their chosen campground, visitors in the area should plan to spend a few hours at the Rend Lake Visitor's Center on the west side of the lake.

County and municipal governments in the southern region manage three campgrounds that may be suited for tent camping. The **Du Quoin State Fair Park** (300 sites), located twenty miles north of Carbondale, is the largest of these local properties.

Useful Resources

After reading this chapter, readers should consult additional resources to determine specific destinations and campgrounds that best fit their family's particular interests and expectations. Some helpful resources are listed below.

- The Illinois Department of Natural Resources website (www. dnr.Illinois.gov) provides information about all state-managed properties.

- The official Illinois state highway map, available from the Illinois Department of Transportation (www.dot.state.il.us/) and at highway rest areas, shows approximate geographic locations of each state property. The map also has a table that summarizes phone numbers and amenities for each state property.
- *Oh, Ranger Illinois State Parks* (booklet), available at many state parks and rest areas, provides information about Illinois state parks, history, sights, and activities.
- *Illinois State Parks: A Guide to Illinois State* Parks (book) provides detailed descriptions of state properties.
- *Best in Tent Camping: Illinois* (book) provides detailed descriptions of Illinois' most secluded campgrounds, including a few county and municipal parks.
- Reserve America (www.reserveamerica.com/campgroundSearch. do, 800-246-5082) is a private organization that makes reservations for Illinois state parks and recreation areas. The website also shows photos of individual campsites.
- Recreation.Gov (www.Recreation.gov, 877-444-6777) is a private organization that makes reservations for all federal properties.

Illinois's Public Campgrounds

Campgrounds are listed by number of campsites available from most numerous to least. The following abbreviations are used to note public campgrounds that have been named by various authorities as among the best in the state:

FD   This property is one of my favorite camping destinations.

TB   This property was named by the *TripleBlaze* website as having one of the fifteen best campgrounds in the state.

YS   This property was named by *Yahoo Sports* as one of Illinois' top five parks for summer camping.

BTC This property was named and described by *Best in Tent Camping: Illinois* as having one of the fifty quietest and most private campgrounds in the state.

NG   This property was named and described by *National Geographic's Guide to State Parks in the United States* as one of America's most historic and scenic state parks.

(P = primitive)

Northern Region: Chicago Attractions

State DNR Parks, Recreation Areas, and Forests

Rock Cut SP
268 sites, showers, beach, fishing,
   bike trail, boat rental, hiking
7318 Harlem Road, Loves Park
5 m N of Rockford, 1 m W of I-39

FD
815-885-3311
42.36932, -88.97846

Illinois Beach SP
244 sites, showers, beach, fishing
Zion
On Lake Michigan, 40 m N of
   Chicago loop

YS
847-662-6433
42.43689, -87.81075

Mississippi Palisades SP
241 sites, showers, fishing, boating
16327A SR 84, Savanna
On Mississippi River, 40 m S of
   Dubuque

NG
815-273-2731
42.14908, -90.17517

Chain O' Lakes SP
238 sites, showers, boat rental,
   archery range
8916 Wilmot Rd, Spring Grove
40 m NW of Chicago, 2 m E of US 12

847-587-5512
42.45842, -88.21193

Lake Le-Aqua-Na SP
171 sites, showers, beach, fishing
8542 North Lake Rd, Lena
15 m NW of Freeport, 5 m N of US 20

BTC
815-369-4282
42.42378, -89.82393

Shabbona Lake SRA
150 sites, showers, fishing
4201 Shabbona Grove Road,
   Shabbona
65 m W of Chicago loop, 2 m S of
   US 30

FD, TB
815-824-2106
41.73220, -88.86378

Lowden Memorial SP
130 sites, showers, fishing, hiking
1411 North River Road, Oregon
20 m SW of Rockford, 15 m W of I-39

815-732-6828
42.03439, -89.32494

Prophetstown SP   TB
119 sites, showers, fishing, wildlife,   815-537-2926
   horseshoes   41.67167, -89.92583
Riverside Rd, Prophetstown
32 m NE of Moline, 3 m S of I-88

White Pines Forest SP   815-946-3717
103 sites, showers, hiking   41.99528, -89.47185
6712 West Pines Rd, Mount Morris
30 m SW of Rockford, 25 m W of I-39

Morrison-Rockwood SP   815-772-4708
92 sites, showers, fishing   41.85897, -89.94714
18750 Lake Rd, Morrison
40 m NE of Moline, 4 m N of US 30

Green River FWA   815-379-2324
50 P sites, hunting, equestrian trails   41.63819, -89.51653
375 Game Rd, Harmon
28 m NW of Peru, 18 m N of I-80

Apple River Canyon SP   BTC
47 P sites, fishing, hiking, wineries,   815-745-3302
   riverboat cruises, golf   42.44813, -90.05845
8763 East Canyon Rd Apple River
25 m NW of Freeport, 8 m N of US 20

Castle Rock SP   815-732-7329
Some P canoe-in sites, fishing   41.97824, -89.35663
1365 W Castle Rd, Oregon
On Rock River, 25 m SW of Rockford

Army Corps of Engineers *Campgrounds*

Thomson Causeway RA   815-259-3628
81 sites, showers, fishing, bike trail   41.95167, -90.11083
Great River Trail, Thomson
On Mississippi River, 40 m NE of
   Moline

Fishermen's Corner RA   815-259-3628
56 sites, showers, bike trail, John   41.56972, -90.39000
   Deere Pavilion, Black Hawk
   Historic Site
16821 N, Hampton
On Mississippi River, 3 m N of Moline

Blanding Landing RA   563-582-0881
37 sites, showers, fishing   42.28580, -90.40330
5720 S River Rd, Hanover
On Mississippi River, 20 m SE of
   Dubuque

Lock and Dam #13 RA   815-259-3628
6 P sites, no fee, fishing, bike trail   41.49843, -90.15429
Fulton
On Mississippi River, 35 m NE of
   Moline

County and Municipal Campgrounds

Sugar River FP, Winnebago CP   FD, BTC
92 sites, paddling   815-877-6100
10127 Forest Preserve Rd, Durand   42.46340, -89.23453
20 m NW of Rockford, 10 m N of
   US 20

Illiniwek FP, Rock Island CP   309-496-2620
85 sites, showers, fishing, eagle   41.56180, -90.39720
   preserve
Hampton
On Mississippi River, 5 m N of Moline

Burnidge FP/ Paul Wolff CG,   630-444-1200
   Kane CP   42.07158, -88.34914
100 P sites, rock climbing
38W235 Big Timber Rd, Elgin
35 m NW of Chicago Loop, 5 m S of
   I-90

Pecatonica River FP, Winnebago CP   815-877-6100
60 P sites, paddling   42.35307, -89.07344
7260 Judd Rd, Pecatonica
12 m W of Rockford, 2 m N of US 20

Hononegah FP, Winnebago CP   815-877-6100
60 P sites, fishing, paddling, wildlife   42.44130, -89.03970
   viewing
#80 Hononegah Rd, Rockton
10 m N of Rockford, 5 m W of I-39

Seward Bluffs FP, Winnebago CP   815-877-6100
60 P sites, hiking, equestrian trails   42.23888, -89.35777
16999 Comly Rd, Seward
15 m W of Rockford, 5 m S of US 20

Marengo Ridge FP, McHenry CP   **BTC**
46 P sites, hiking, wildlife viewing   815-338-6223
2411 SR 23, Marengo   42.28115, -88.60837
22 m E of Rockford, 5 m N of I-90

Lake De Pue MP   815-447-2177
25 P sites, fishing   41.31875, -89.28357
111 W 2nd St, De Pue
10 m W of Peru, 5 m S of I-80

West-Central Region: Lincoln Land

State DNR Parks, Recreation Areas, and Forests

Eldon Hazlet SRA   618-594-3015
364 sites, showers, pool, fishing,   38.66768, -89.32735
    nature programs
20100 Hazlet Park Rd, Carlyle
SW side of Carlyle Lake, 50 m E of
    St Louis

Lincoln's New Salem Historic Park   217-632-4003
200 sites, showers, historic buildings,   39.97856, -89.84347
    Lincoln sites
Petersburg
20 m NW of Springfield, 18 m N of
    I-72

Sangchris Lake SP   **TB**
185 sites, showers, fishing, hiking,   217-498-9208
    Lincoln sites   39.64167, -89.45694
9898 Cascade Rd, Rochester
15 m SE of Springfield, 5 m W of
    SR 29

Siloam Springs SP   **BTC, TB**
182 sites, showers, fishing, hiking,   217-894-6205
    boat rental   39.88501, -90.93429
938 East 3003rd Lane, Clayton
25 m E of Quincy, 10 m S of US 24

Jubilee College SP   309-446-3758
167 sites, showers, fishing, wildlife,   40.83218, -89.80835
    bike & equestrian trails
13921 West Route 150, Brimfield
10 m NW of Peoria, 4 m N of I-74

Argyle Lake SP
159 sites, showers, boating, hiking
640 Argyle Park Rd, Colchester
65 m SW of Peoria, 2 m N of US 136

309-776-3422
40.46424, -90.78656

Ramsey Lake SRA
159 sites, showers, fishing, boating,
    hunting
CR 600 E, Ramsey
70 m NE of St. Louis, 3 m W of US 51

BTC
618-423-2215
39.16937, -89.13487

Nauvoo SP
150 sites, showers, fishing, museum,
    LDS visitor center
Nauvoo
On Mississippi River, 10 m N of
    US 136

217-453-2512
40.54582, -91.38008

Big River SF
104 P sites, fishing
Keithsburg Rd, Keithsburg
On Mississippi River, 15 m N of US 34

309-374-2496
41.08951, -90.93540

Anderson Lake FWA
100 P sites, fishing
647 N State Hwy 100, Astoria
On Illinois River, 50 m SW of Peoria

309-759-4484
40.19394, -90.20464

Johnson Sauk Trail SP
95 sites, showers, fishing, round barn,
    historical sites
28616 Sauk Trail Rd, Kewanee
35 m E of Moline, 5 m S of I-80

BTC
309-853-5589
41.32596, -89.89260

Jim Edgar Panther Creek FWA
82 sites, showers, archery, fishing, bike
    & equestrian trails, Lincoln sites
10149 Co Rd 11, Chandlerville
25 m W of Springfield, 18 m N of I-72

BTC
217-452-7741
40.04810, -90.15511

Pere Marquette SP
80 sites, showers, fishing, bike &
    equestrian trails, wildlife
13112 Visitor Center Lane, Nauvoo
On Illinois River, 75 m SW of
    Springfield

YS, TB
618-786-3323
40.55004, -91.38487

Beaver Dam SP   BTC
77 sites, showers, fishing, archery,   217-854-8020
    wildlife   39.20896, -89.98834
14548 Beaver Dam Lane, Plainview
45 m NE of St Louis, 20 m W of I-55

Spring Lake FWA   BTC
70 P sites, archeological museum,   309-968-7135
    fishing   40.46212, -89.87005
7982 South Park Road, Manito
25 m SW of Peoria, 20 m W of I-155

Weinberg—King FWA   217-392-2345
60 sites, showers, fishing   40.23004, -90.95013
Augusta
35 m NE of Quincy, 12 m S of US 136

Delabar SP   BTC
56 sites, showers, fishing   309-374-2496
Delabar State Park Rd, Oquawka   40.96624, -90.93787
On Mississippi River, 10 m N of US 34

Horseshoe Lake SP, Madison   618-931-0270
48 P sites, fishing, boating, St. Louis   38.69780, -90.06683
    attractions
3321 Highway 111, Granite City
10 m E of St. Louis, 3 m N of I-55

Sand Ridge SF   BTC
35 P sites, hiking, hand trap range   309-597-2212
Forest City   40.41142, -89.86622
28 m SW of Peoria, 22 m W of I-155

Henderson County FWA   309-374-2496
35 P sites, fishing   40.85411, -90.98027
1150E Keithsburg
30 m W of Galesburg, 2 m N of US 34

Rice Lake FWA   309-647-9184
34 P sites, fishing, paddling, hunting   40.46179, -89.93466
19721 N US 24, Canton
25 m SW of Peoria, 1 m E of US 24

Marshall FWA   309-246-8351
28 P sites, fishing, canoe sites   41.02323, -89.40856
236 SR 26, Lacon
On Illinois River, 20 m NE of Peoria

Woodford County FWA
25 P sites
524 Conservation Lane, Lowpoint
On Illinois River, 15 m NE of Peoria

BTC
309-822-8351
40.87751, -89.43630

Army COE Campgrounds

Coles Creek RA
119 sites, showers, beach, fishing,
   laundry, visitor center
Carlyle
SE side of Carlyle Lake, 8 m NE of
   Carlyle

618-594-2484
38.65694, -89.26028

Dam West RA
109 sites, showers, beach, fishing,
   laundry, marina, tennis
Carlyle
SW side of Carlyle Lake, 1 m N of
   US 50

618-594-2484
38.62778, -90.35933

Boulder RA
83 sites, showers, fishing, laundry,
   marina
Boulder Marina Rd, Carlyle
E side of Carlyle Lake, 2 m N of US 50

618-594-2484
38.69167, -89.23306

McNair CG
25 sites, showers, fishing, boating
US Hwy 50, Carlyle
S side of Carlyle Lake, on US 50

618-594-5253
38.62843, -89.36342

East Spillway RA
15 P sites, fishing
Carlyle, below dam
S side of Carlyle Lake, near US 50

618-594-2484
36.61844, -89.35707

Bear Creek RA
40 P sites, no fee, fishing
Marcelline
On Mississippi River, 15 m NW of
   Quincy

217-228-0890
40.11182, -91.47949

Blanchard Island RA
34 P sites, fishing
Illinois City
On Mississippi River, 25 m W of
   Moline

563-263-7913
41.34810, -91.05570

Andalusia Slough RA   563-263-7913
16 P sites, fishing   41.43920, -90.7754
Andalusia
On Mississippi River, 5 m W of Moline

John Hay RA   217-228-0890
8 P sites, no fee, fishing   39.72976, -91.35098
East Hannibal
On Mississippi River, 3 m N of I-72

County and Municipal Campgrounds

Comlara CG, McLean CP   FD, BTC
144 sites, showers, fishing, boating,   309-434-6770
   visitor center   40.64286, -89.03032
13001 Recreation Area Dr, Comlara
10 m N of Bloomington, 2 m W of
   I-39

Spring Lake Park, Macomb MP   309-833-2052
120 sites, fishing, boating   40.50609, -90.71339
Macomb
60 m SW of Peoria, on US 67

Allison CG, Galesburg MP   309-344-1534
116 sites, beach, pool, fishing   40.98396, -90.39225
1351 S. Lake Storey Rd, Galesburg
40 m NW of Peoria, 2 m W of I-74

Loud Thunder FP, Rock Island CP   BTC
115 sites, showers, fishing, boating   309-795-1040
19408 Loud Thunder Rd, Illinois City   41.43437, -90.83423
On Mississippi River, 20 m W of
   Moline

Schuy-Rush Park, Rushville MP   217-322-6628
77 sites, showers, boating, paddling,   40.08377, -90.55296
   fishing
US 67, Rushville
50 m NW of Springfield, on US 24

Francis Park, Kewanee MP   309-852-2611
60 P sites, unique building   41.27872, -89.90332
N 900th Ave, Kewanee
38 m SE of Moline, 12 m S of I-80

Great River Road CG, Pleasant Hill MP
59 P sites, pool, fishing, bike trail, mini golf
Campground Rd, Pleasant Hill
70 m SW of Springfield, 8 m SE of US 54

217-734-2113
39.44338, -90.87235

Military Park, Scott Air Force Base
22 sites, showers, for military families
Bellville
20 m E of St. Louis, 1 m S of I-64

618-256-2067
38.55097, -89.84078

McCully Heritage Project CG
5 P sites, hiking, fishing, equestrian trails, wildlife viewing
Kampsville
65 m SW of Springfield, 10 m W of US 67

BTC
618-653-4687
39.29782, -90.60901

East-Central Region: Lake Shelbyville

State DNR Parks, Recreation Areas, and Forests

Wolf Creek SP
382 sites, showers, beach, fishing, boating, bridle trails
1750 N, Windsor
E side of Lake Shelbyville, 28 m N of Effingham

217-459-2831
39.48594, -88.68085

Clinton Lake SRA
308 sites, showers, beach, fishing, marina, horse & bike rental
7251 Ranger Road, DeWitt
20 m S of Bloomington, 10 m SW of I-74

217-935-8722
40.16316, -88.78925

Lincoln Trail SP
242 sites, showers, fishing, Lincoln Heritage Trail
16985 East 1350th Road, Marshall
45 m NE of Effingham, 4 m S of I-70

BTC
217-826-2222
39.33667, -87.72306

Kankakee River SP   815-933-1383
213 sites, showers, fishing, paddling,   41.20349, -87.97792
  hunting, horse rental
5314 W SR 102, Boubonnais
50 m SW of Chicago loop, 5 m W of
  I-57

Moraine View SP   FD, BTC
199 sites, showers, beach, boating,   309-724-8032
  fishing, horse rental   40.40907, -88.73496
374 Moraine View Park Rd, Leroy
15 m E of Bloomington, 8 m N of I-74

Kickapoo SRA   FD, BTC
184 sites, showers, canoe rental,   217-442-4915
  bike trail   40.14889, -87.73806
10906 Kickapoo Park Rd, Oakwood
28 m E of Champaign, 2 m N of I-74

Eagle Creek SRA   217-756-8260
174 sites, showers, fishing, golf   39.49359, -88.71245
Findlay
SW side of Lake Shelbyville, 30 m N of
  Effingham

Stephen A. Forbes SRA   BTC
136 sites, showers, beach, fishing,   618-547-3381
  equestrian trails   38.72202, -88.78048
6924 Omega Road, Kinmundy
30 m SW of Effingham, 10 m E of I-57

Starved Rock SP   FD, YS, TB, NG
133 sites, showers, hiking, fishing,   815-667-4726
  canoe rental, horse rental, visitor   41.31904, -88.99426
  center
2668 E 875th Rd, Utica
On Illinois River, 5 m E of Peru

Red Hills Lake SP   618-936-2469
129 sites, showers, fishing, trails,   38.72121, -87.83874
  wildlife, hunting
3571 Ranger Lane, Sumner
20 m W of Vincennes, IN, 1 m N of
  US 50

Illini SP
100 sites, showers, fishing
2660 E 2350 Rd, Marseilles
70 m SW of Chicago loop, 4 m S of
  I-80

815-795-2448
41.32250, -88.72083

Sam Parr FWA
80 sites, showers, fishing, hiking,
  hunting
13225 East SR 33, Newton
32 m SE of Effingham, 18 m S of I-70

BTC
618-783-2661
39.01088, -88.11852

Weldon Springs SP
75 sites, showers, boat rental, hiking,
  nature center, fall festival
4734 Weldon Springs RD, Clinton
25 m S of Bloomington, 3 m E of
  US 51

FD, YS
217-935-2644
40.12188, -88.93182

Walnut Point SP
60 sites, showers, fishing, nature
  center
2331 E CR 370N, Oakland
30 m SE of Champaign, 13 m E of I-57

FD, BTC
217-346-3336
39.69971, -88.03386

Fox Ridge SP
43 sites, showers, horse & bike rental,
  fishing, antique shops, pool
18175 State Park Road, Charleston
30 m NE of Effingham, 10 m N of I-70

217-345-6416
39.40025, -88.13722

Middle Fork FWA
45 P sites, archery, paddling, trap
  range, horse rental
10906 Kickapoo Park Rd, Oakwood
10 m W of Danville, 5 m N of I-74

BTC
217-442-4915
40.26046, -87.79416

Channahon SP
25 P sites, Illinois-Michigan Canal,
  fishing, paddling, biking
Canal St., Channahon
42 m SW of Chicago loop, 2 m S of
  I-80

BTC, TB
815-467-4271
41.42321, -88.22824

Gebhard Woods SP
25 P sites, Illinois-Michigan Canal,
    paddling, wildlife, hiking
401 Ottawa Street, Morris
On Illinois River, 55 m SW of Chicago
    loop

BTC, TB
815-942-0796
41.35685, -88.43736

Des Plaines FWA
22 P sites, fishing, hunting, archery,
    wildlife
24621 N. River Rd, Wilmington
45 m SW of Chicago loop, 2 m W of
    I-55

815-423-5326
41.37236, -88.20722

**Possum Creek CG, Hidden Springs
    SF**
Some P sites, fishing, hiking
Strasburg
16 m NW of Effingham, 12 m W of
    I-57

217-644-3901
39.31461, -88.69283

Army COE Campgrounds

Coon Creek CG
208 sites, showers, beach, fishing,
    laundry
Shelbyville
W side of Lake Shelbyville, 28 m SE of
    Decatur

TB
217-774-3951
39.45139, -88.76250

Lithia Springs CG
115 sites, showers, fishing, laundry,
    beach
1500 N, Shelbyville
SE side of Lake Shelbyville, 20 m NW
    of Effingham

217-774-3951
39.43444, -88.76000

Lone Point CG
92 sites, showers, fishing, golf
Findlay
W side of Lake Shelbyville, 30 m SE of
    Decatur

217-774-3951
39.45222, -88.74028

Whitley Creek RA   217-774-3951
84 sites, showers, laundry, paddling,   39.53917, -88.63016
  fishing
Kirksville
E arm of Lake Shelbyville, 30 m N of
  Effingham

Opossum Creek CG   TB
78 sites, showers, fishing   217-774-3951
Shelbyville   39.44556, -88.77250
W side of Lake Shelbyville, 30 m SE of
  Decatur

Forrest W. "Bo" Woods CG   217-774-3951
77 sites, showers, fishing, laundry   39.55139, -88.62222
1017 Illinois 32, Sullivan
On E arm Lake Shelbyville, 25 m SE of
  Decatur

County and Municipal Campgrounds

Mill Creek Park CG, Clark CP   217-889-3901
139 sites, showers, horse & bike trails,   39.43876, -87.81198
  boat rentals
10889 E Clarksville Rd, Marshal
50 m NE of Effingham, 2 m S of I-70

Prairie Pines CG, Rantoul MP   217-893-0438
95 sites, showers, laundry, aquatic   40.28454, -88.14926
  center
711 S Perimeter Rd, Rantoul
18 m N of Champaign, 3 m E of I-57

Forest Glen Preserve, Vermilion CP   BTC
58 sites, showers, paddling, hiking   217-662-2142
20301 E 900 North Rd, Westville   40.01198, -87.56506
5 m S of Danville, on US 150

Friends Creek Conservation Area,   217-423-7708
  Macon CP   40.02968, -88.78389
36 sites, showers, fishing, hiking,
  historic school
3939 Nearing Lane, Decatur
15 m NE of Decatur, 2 m N of I-72

South Park CG, Gibson City MP   217-784-8666
9 sites, showers, golf   40.45700, -88.37290
S Lott Blvd, Gibson City
30 m E of Bloomington, 13 m W of
    I-57

Lodge Park, Piatt CP   BTC
13 P unnumbered sites, old oak trees,   217-762-4531
    fishing   40.06678, -88.56349
1852 N Old RT 47, Montecello
25 m NE of Decatur, 1 m W of I-72

Southern Region: Rend Lake

State DNR Parks, Recreation Areas, and Forests

World Shooting & Recreational   618-295-2700
    Complex   38.18778, -89.75667
691 sites, showers, 310 overflow sites,
    shooting ranges, fishing, cowboy
    action
One Main Event Lane, Sparta
50 m SE of St. Louis, 22 m SW of I- 64

Wayne Fitzgerrell SRA   FD, BTC
283 sites, showers, beach, fishing, bike   618-629-2320
    & bridle trails, hunting, wildlife   38.11131, -88.93546
11094 Ranger Rd, Whittington
E side of Rend Lake, 10 m S of
    Mount Vernon

Fort Kaskaskia State Historic Site   618-859-3741
265 sites, showers, historic site, scenic   37.96617, -89.90762
    views
4372 Park Rd, Ellis Grove
On Mississippi River, 50 m S of
    St Louis

Washington County Lake FWA   BTC
150 sites, showers, boat rental   618-327-3137
    hunting   40.63312, -89.39852
18500 Conservation Drive, Nashville
22 m W of Mount Vernon, 8 m S of
    I-64

Ferne Clyffe SP
109 sites, showers, waterfalls, trails, fishing
S Broadway, Goreville
40 m NW of Paducah, between I-57 & I-24

BTC, NG
618-995-2411
37.53253, -88.96668

Giant City SP
99 sites, showers, fishing, horse rental, visitor center, rock climbing, wineries
235 Giant City Road, Makanda
10 m SE of Carbondale, 10 m W of I-57

YS, BTC, TB, NG
618-457-4836
37.60152, -89.18509

Randolph County SRA
95 sites, showers, fishing, hiking
4301 S Lake Drive, Chester
55 m SW of Mount Vernon, 48 m W of I-57

BTC
618-826-2706
37.97564, -89.80132

Sam Dale Lake FWA
93 sites, showers, beach, fishing, hiking
RR 1, Johnsonville
22 m NE of Mount Vernon, 20 m E of I-57

BTC
618-835-2292
38.54212, -88.58310

Horseshoe Lake FWA, Alexander County
88 sites, showers, fishing
Miller City
On the Mississippi River, 10 m W of I-57

618-776-5689
37.12625, -89.32481

Lake Murphysboro SP
74 sites, showers, fishing, hiking
52 Cinder Hill Dr, Murphysboro
10 m W of Carbondale, 25 m W of I-57

BTC, TB
618-684-2867
37.78043, -89.38424

Cave-In-Rock SP
59 sites, showers, hiking, river tours
#1 New State Park Rd, Cave-In-Rock
On Ohio River, 45 m NE of Paducah

FD, BTC
618-289-4545
37.46913, -88.15536

Fort Massac SP
50 sites, showers, visitor center,
    historical fort, fishing
1308 East 5th St, Metropolis
5 m N of Paducah, 2 m E of I-24

FD, NG
618-524-4712
37.14740, -88.71243

Dixon Springs SP
49 sites, showers, pool, hunting,
    Ohio River boat tours
Golconda
23 m NE of Paducah, 10 m E of I-24

BTC
618-949-3394
37.38317, -88.66030

Hamilton County FWA
71 P sites, fishing, hunting, hand trap
    range
CR 1025 N Mcleansboro
35 m SE of Mount Vernon, 15 m S of
    I-64

BTC
618-773-4340
38.05754, -88.39674

Pyramid SRA
54 P sites, fishing, boating, hunting
1562 Pyramid Park Rd, Pinckneyville
35 m SW of Mount Vernon, 28 m W
    of I-57

BTC
618-357-2574
38.02201, -89.41509

Saline County FWA
45 P sites, fishing, hunting, trails
85 Glenn O. Jones Rd, Equality
50 m SE of Mount Vernon, 30 m E of
    I-57

BTC
618-276-4405
37.69939, -88.37977

Beall Woods SP
16 P sites, fishing, hunting, trails,
    visitor center
9285 Beall Woods Ave, Mount Carmel
60 m E of Mount Vernon, Near
    Wabash River

BTC
618-298-2442
38.35452, -87.83041

Trail of Tears SF
Some P sites, equestrian trails,
    hunting, wildlife
3240 State Forest Rd, Jonesboro
20 m S of Carbondale, 15 m W of I-57

BTC
618-833-4910
37.50367, -89.34640

Army COE, National Wildlife Refuge, and National Forest Campgrounds

South Marcum CG
160 sites, showers, fishing
Benton
SE side of Rend Lake, 30 m NE of
    Carbondale

FD
618-724-2493
38.03369, -88.93984

South Sandusky CG
127 sites, showers, beach, laundry,
    bike trail, fishing
7820 Red Oak Lane, Sesser
SW side of Rend Lake, 25 m S of
    Mount Vernon

618-625-3011
38.06028, -89.00472

North Sandusky RA
118 sites, showers, fishing, bike trail,
    golf, laundry
Rend City Rd, Sesser
SW side of Rend Lake, 20 m SW of
    Mount Vernon

618-625-6115
38.07888, -89.00556

Gun Creek RA
100 sites, showers, fishing, laundry,
    bike trail, golf, marina
Golf Course Rd, Whittington
E side of Rend Lake, 20 m S of
    Mount Vernon

618-629-2338
38.07861, -88.93028

**Little Grassy Lake, Crab Orchard
    NWR**
115 sites, showers, beach boating,
    fishing
788 Hidden Bay Lane, Makanda
10 m E of Carbondale, 11 m W of I-57

BTC
618-457-6655
37.64351, -89.15163

**Crab Orchard CG, Crab Orchard
    NWR**
55 sites, fishing, boating, wildlife
    viewing, visitor center
Carbondale
10 m E of Carbondale, 10 m W of I-57

FD
618-985-4983
37.74083, -89.11833

Blue Heron CG, Crab Orchard NWR
40 sites, showers, marina, boat rental
Cartersville
8 m E of Carbondale, 8 m W of I-57

FD
618-985-2572
37.69118, -89.06839

Devils Kitchen, Crab Orchard NWF
8 tent sites, showers, fishing, boating
Tacoma Lake Rd, Makanda
15 m SE of Carbondale, 8 m W of I-57

BTC
618-998-5933
37.61960, -89.10168

Oak Point CG, Lake Glendale Rec.
    Area, Shawnee NF
56 sites, showers, beach, fishing
Lake Glendale Rd, Vienna
25 m N of Paducah, 13 m E of I 24

618-658-2111
37.40949, -88.66227

Buck Ridge CG, Lake of Egypt Rec.
    Area, Shawnee NF
37 P sites, fishing, boating
Harrisburg
20 m SE of Carbondale, 4 m E of I-57

618-253-7114
37.72640, -88.53706

Pine Ridge CG, Pounds Hollow Rec.
    Area, Shawnee NF
35 P sites, beach, fishing, paddling
Karbers Ridge Rd, Karbers Ridge
50 m NE of Paducah, 20 m SE of
    US 45

618-658-2111
37.61572, -88.27389

Tower Rock CG, Tower Rock Rec.
    Area, Shawnee NF
25 P sites, scenic view, hiking
Cave-in-Rock
40 m NE of Paducah, 25 m SE of
    US 45

618-287-2201
37.46056, -88.24175

Johnson Creek CG, Shawnee NF
20 P sites, beach, fishing
Johnson Creek Rd, Ava
20 m W of Carbondale, 35 m W of
    I-57

618-833-8576
37.83565, -89.51791

Red Bud CG, Bell Smith Springs RA,
    Shawnee NF
21 P sites, seclusion, hiking
Ozark Rd, Harrisburg
35 m N of Paducah, 13 m E of I-24

BTC
618-658-2111
37.73838, -88.54060

Pine Hills CG, Shawnee NF
13 P sites, fishing, hiking
Pine Hills Rd, Wolf Lake
20 m SW of Carbondale, 20 m W of
    I-57

BTC
618-833-8576
37.51532, -89.42259

**Pharaoh CG, Garden of the Gods
    RA, Shawnee NF**
12 P sites, hiking, scenic rock
    formations
Garden of the Gods Rd, Harrisburg
40 m NE of Paducah, 35 m E of I-57

BTC, TB
618-658-2111
37.60236, -88.37887

Camp Cadiz CG, Shawnee NF
11 P sites, hiking
Cadiz Rd, Elizabethtown
40 m NE of Paducah, 35 m E of I-24

BTC
618-658-2111
37.57725, -88.24513

County and Municipal Campgrounds

Du Quoin State Fair CG
300 sites, showers, fishing
DuQuoin
20 m N of Carbondale, 1 m E of US 51

618-542-9373
37.97987, -89.23084

**Arrowhead Lake CG, Johnson City
    MP**
53 sites, showers, laundry, fishing,
    paddling
1600 Peterson Ave, Johnston City
20 m NE of Carbondale, 1 m E of I-57

618-983-3535
37.81351, -88.93670

Burrell Park CG, Carmi MP
35 sites, fishing
Co Rd 1000 E, Carmi
45 m SE of Mount Vernon, 10 m S of
    I-64

618-382-2693
38.09765, -88.19924

Indiana

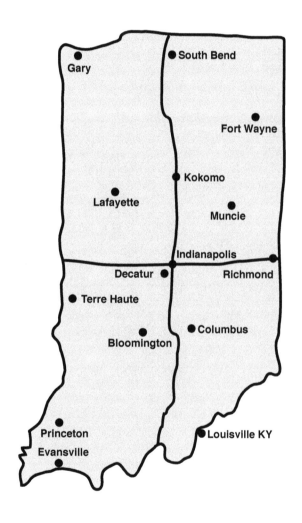

Gary

South Bend

Fort Wayne

Kokomo

Lafayette

Muncie

Indianapolis

Decatur

Richmond

Terre Haute

Columbus

Bloomington

Princeton

Louisville KY

Evansville

6

Indiana

The final stop on our tour of family camping and vacation destinations around Lake Michigan is Indiana. Since the early 1800s, Indiana has played an important role in the development of America's highway system. As early as 1806, Congress approved funding for construction of a National Road designed to connect the eastern states with the western settlements. The path of the road entered Indiana near Richmond on the eastern side of the state, stretched westward to Indianapolis, and then shifted in a southwesterly direction through Terre Haute into Illinois. Construction began in 1811 and the crude dirt road was completed in 1834. During its early years, this road was sometimes called the Cumberland Pike and National Pike but eventually earned the title of the Main Street of America. In the late 1800s, interest in the road faded when railroads emerged as a more efficient way to move people and goods out to the West but resurged in the 1920s when personal automobile ownership increased. In 1926, this National Road, or Main Street of America, became US Highway 40.

Another well-known road, built in the early 1900s, was designed to connect Chicago with the southern states. This road, originally named Indiana State Highway 10 ran down the western edge of Indiana through Hammond, Terre Haute, Vincennes, and Evansville. In 1926, this highway was renamed US Highway 41 and its intersection with US 40 in Terre Haute became known as the Crossroads of America. In 1970, I remember driving with my wife through Terre Haute on US 41 for the first time and seeing a large billboard proclaiming this intersection as the Crossroads of America. Today, US Highway 41 is a heavily traveled route through western Indiana that connects the Keweenaw Peninsula of Michigan with Miami, Florida.

A second north-south highway was planned in 1914. The main route of this highway connected the West Michigan Pike with South Bend, Indianapolis, and Louisville, Kentucky. Subsequently, other highways were added to make a network of highways, collectively known as the Dixie Highway, connecting the Midwest with the southern states. Several years later in 1926, the main route of the Dixie Highway was renamed US Highway 31 and Indianapolis officially became the center of Indiana's and perhaps the eastern U.S. Highway system.

Earlier in 1911, Indianapolis had gained attention as a center of automobile travel when Carl Fisher bricked an oval track in Indianapolis—called the Indianapolis 500—and this track became world famous as a testing ground for innovative automobile engineering. In 1913, the Lincoln Highway, running along the present U.S. Highway 30 from Fort Wayne to Gary, became one of the first transcontinental highways for automobile travel.

In 1937, the "The Crossroads of America" slogan was officially adopted by the state of Indiana as its official motto. Although the interstate system gradually replaced much of the old U.S. Highway system by 1980, Indiana continues to maintain its extensive highway system and merit the title of the Crossroads of America today. Indianapolis, located near the center of the state, is the hub of the highway system and seven major interstate highways extend out of the city like spokes of a wheel connecting it and other major cities throughout the eastern, southern, and midwestern United States. In total, fourteen interstate highways pass through the state and, every day, thousands of commercial trucks plus countless numbers of tourists travel into and through the state on the way to distant destinations. Along these interstate highways, travelers will find some of the cleanest welcome centers and rest areas in the country. Today, the Department of Transportation's official highway map proudly proclaims that the state's modern highway system has played an important role in making Indiana one of America's top states for economic growth and job development. In addition to its major interstate and U.S. highways, Indiana continues to maintain dozens of historic scenic highways and thirty-three covered bridges. It also actively promotes the Main Street Program to restore and revitalize main street business districts in dozens of small towns along major highways across the state.

The Indiana state parks system was also established in the early 1900s, largely by the efforts of a German immigrant and Indianapolis businessman named Richard Lieber. Competing with powerful lumber companies, Lieber used his negotiating skills and political capital to acquire the land needed to create McCormick's Creek and Turkey Run State Parks. In 1916 these two parks were established as Indiana's first state parks.

Today, the Indiana Department of Natural Resources (DNR) manages twenty-two state parks, nine state lakes, and eleven state forests with campgrounds, plus four fish and wildlife areas with campgrounds. Many of these state properties are conveniently located near major highways and cities for travelers who would like to spend a few nights in a public campground and save a few dollars. After visiting several of these DNR properties, I have discovered that their campgrounds vary considerably in terms of amenities. Many Indiana DNR campgrounds are spacious, well-groomed, grassy fields with gravel or paved parking pads and scattered trees, but a few, such as McCormick's Creek, are located in densely forested areas. Several properties have older, musty bathrooms but a few properties such as Brown County and Prophetstown have some of the nicest bathrooms found anywhere. A few such as Turkey Run and Indiana Dunes are very popular and require advance reservations for summer weekends but many are much less popular and rarely fill to capacity. When we traveled during late August, we found that several visitor centers and nature centers were closed and few educational programs were offered during the mid-week, but Prophetstown had a very interesting Wednesday evening program on resident animals. In many parks, staff and campground hosts were either not visible or too busy to talk with us, but in a few campgrounds, such as O'Bannon, the park manager and nature center staff were very eager to talk with us and answer our questions. The one constant across Indiana State Parks is that they all now charge a high entrance fee for out-of-state visitors (between $7 and $10 per vehicle) in addition to relatively high camping fees, making them some of the most expensive camping destinations of the Lake Michigan states. In past years, I bought an annual pass card but this annual pass now costs $60—twice as high as the out-of-state annual pass for Michigan or Wisconsin.

When we first began exploring Indiana DNR properties as potential camping destinations a few years ago, we discovered that anyone who is unfamiliar with the system may have a little difficulty becoming oriented and finding the names of campgrounds near intended destinations. The first problem is that some documents, such as the *Indiana 2012 Recreation Guide*, use the names of state reservoirs (or state lakes) while other documents, such as my highway map, printed the names of state recreation areas. When I tried to locate the Monroe Lake State Reservoir campground on my map, I could not find it. Only later did I learn that the Monroe Lake State Reservoir campground was located in the Paynestown Recreation Area. After a little research, I learned that Monroe Lake, like other state reservoirs, was constructed by the COE in the 1960s and continues to be managed by the COE. But the Paynestown Recreation Area campground has been leased to the Indiana DNR and the DNR refers to the recreation area and campground as "Monroe Lake

State Reservoir." To confuse things a little more, the COE also leases property on Monroe Lake to the U.S. Forest Service for the Hoosier National Forest's Hardin Ridge Recreation Area campground and a separate area for the Charles C. Deam Wilderness Area.

Similarly, when planning trips to Mississinewa State Lake, campers should know that the main campground is located in the Miami State Recreation Area. When planning trips to Cagles Mill Lake, visitors should know that the lake is sometimes called Cataract Lake and that the main campground is located in the Leiber State Recreation Area. And when planning trips to either Mounds State Recreation Area on Brookville Lake about 65 miles southeast of Indianapolis or Mounds State Park, located about 25 miles northeast of Indianapolis, visitors must pay special attention because it is easy to confuse the two and some books and websites occasionally use the terms "state park" and "state recreation areas" interchangeably.

A second problem is that Indiana has made several campground changes over the past fifteen years and, thus, names on older documents may not match with names on current documents. For example, O'Bannon State Park, located about twenty-five miles west of Louisville, appears as Wyandotte Woods State Recreation Area on older maps and brochures. Roush Lake Fish and Wildlife Area, located twenty miles southwest of Fort Wayne was previously named Huntington Lake and the once popular Kil-So-Quah Campground has been converted into a day-use area. The once popular Bass Lake State Beach and Campground, described in older publications and located in the northwestern corner of the state, is now managed by a private concern. Whitewater Memorial State Park is one of three state properties located on Brookville Lake, but is managed as a separate property from the other two Brookville Lake recreation areas. Allen's Creek Recreation Area on Monroe Lake still appears on the state website despite the fact that its campground closed in 2011. The rustic campground at Francis Slocum State Recreation Area, shown on many state highway maps on Mississinewa Lake, is no longer open for camping. And Prophetstown State Park, located just outside of Lafayette, does not appear on older highway maps and in older publications because it was only established in 2004.

When I first began researching Indiana state parks and recreation areas, I also had a little difficulty navigating through the official DNR website to locate camping destinations around the state. After a few mistakes, I learned that clicking the "Recreation" button on the left side of the page (rather than the "Destinations" button) opens a drop-down menu that contains a link for "Camping." Clicking this "Camping" button opens a page containing the names of all state managed properties with campgrounds. Clicking any property name will open a page that briefly describes the property and provides campground maps and brochures. To make reservations at a particular property, users must click the "Reservations" link at the bottom of the page and then enter the property name, arrival date, and number of days. After clicking "Submit," the user will be forwarded to the ReserveAmerica website where additional information about the property can be found and reservations can be made. This ReserveAmerica site also offers campground maps and individual sites photos.

Eva and I also had difficulty driving to two of the state DNR properties before we began using GPS coordinates. Our first effort to find Hardy Lake a few years ago ended prematurely when we missed highway directional signs and inadvertently took a wrong road leading to a dead end at the park boundary. I mistakenly concluded that the park had been closed due to budget cuts and decided to drive on to a private campground farther north on I-65. More recently, we had difficulty finding the state campground on Monroe Lake. On a state highway map, I saw four major perimeter highways around the lake but did not know which one led to the state campground. State roads 37 and 446 ran north-south on each side of the lake and were about ten miles apart. State roads 46 and 58 ran east-west on the northern and southern sides of the lake and were about 20 miles apart. As we approached Bloomington on state road 37 from the south, we saw several signs pointing to Monroe Lake and specific recreation areas but did not see any signs pointing to the campground and did not know to look for Paynestown Recreation Area signs. Consequently, we drove into Bloomington, around the northern side of the lake and then south on 446. After stopping and asking directions, we finally found the campground. Other campers who do not know that the campground is in the Paynetown Recreation Area and that the recreation area is located just off of State Road 446, may have to drive as many as sixty miles before finding the campground. Since newcomers could have similar problems finding campgrounds on other state reservoirs, this book provides both the recreation area name and the state lake name and includes GPS coordinates and addresses in the campground listings at the end of the chapter.

After learning how to identify state campgrounds, Eva and I have visited four state reservoir campgrounds (Monroe, Patoka, Mississinewa, and Hardy) and ten state park campgrounds over the past four years.

We found that the state reservoir campgrounds are typically large, well groomed, and grassy with small crowded sites and few trees. Although several RVs were parked in the campgrounds, we saw few children riding bicycles on the campground roads, few adults walking and visiting with neighbors, few people sitting around campfires, and few park employees. Reportedly, these campgrounds fill on summer weekends, but occupancy obviously drops considerably during the week and after mid-August. On the other hand, state park campgrounds seemed to have higher occupancy and more activities—even during the middle of the week and after mid-August.

Two federal agencies manage public campgrounds in the state of Indiana. The National Park Service manages the Indiana Dunes National Lakeshore with one campground, located in the northwestern corner of the state near Gary. The U.S. Forest Service manages the Hoosier National Forest, located in the southwestern corner of the state. This property has one large recreation area with five camping spurs on Monroe Lake plus four smaller campgrounds scattered through the southern part of the forest.

County and municipal governments manage sixteen public parks with campgrounds that may be suitable for tent camping families. In some areas of the state, these locally managed campgrounds may be the best choice for camping near specific tourist attractions or travel routes. For example, five county or municipal parks are conveniently located along the US Highway 41 corridor and provide acceptable camping options for campers traveling between Evansville and Gary.

Indiana also has one U.S. Wilderness Area for campers who prefer to camp in the backwoods. The Charles C. Deam Wilderness area, managed by the U.S. Forest Service, is located on Monroe Lake in the Hoosier National Forest between the Hardin Ridge Recreation area and the Paynetown Recreation Area.

In total, Indiana has 68 developed public campgrounds spread across the state. To summarize these campgrounds and their respective recreational activities, I divided the state into four geographic regions. Within each region, I summarized popular tourist attractions and public campgrounds. I also feature a few popular camping destinations that could be considered when planning a camping vacation trip to the region. At the end of this chapter, I list all of Indiana's public campgrounds along with key details needed to evaluate their location, popularity, amenities, and activities. Since Indiana, compared with other midwestern states, has fewer public campgrounds, campers traveling to or through the state may have to settle for private campgrounds in a few areas.

Northwestern Region: Indiana Beach

The northwestern region of the state will be defined as the area north of US Highway 36 and west of US Highway 31. Reference cities in this area include Gary located in the northwestern corner, South Bend located in the northeastern corner, Indianapolis located in the southeastern corner, Terre Haute located just south of the southwestern corner, Kokomo located on the eastern edge, and Lafayette located near the center. This area is characterized by large flat farms with numerous small lakes carved by the glaciers and several small rivers. Near the center of this region are Lakes Shafer and Freeman. The northwestern corner of the region is defined by the Lake Michigan shoreline. Major highways that pass through this region include I-65, I-74, I-80, I-90, I-94, US 6, US 20, US 24, US 30, US 31, US 36, and US 41.

This region offers several popular tourist destinations. One of the better-known destinations is Indiana Beach, located on Lake Shafer about half way between Indianapolis and Gary. This tourist area has an amusement park, swimming area, and lots of shops. Since no public campgrounds are located within twenty miles of this destination, tent campers may want to consider one of the four private campgrounds located in the resort area. Some choices would be Indiana Beach Camp Resort, Jellystone Park Camp Resort, Norway Campground, or White Oaks on the Lake.

A second popular tourist destination in this region is the shore of Lake Michigan found in Indiana Dunes State Park and Indiana Dunes National Lakeshore. Parke County, in the southwestern corner of this region, claims to be the covered bridge capital of the world with thirty-one covered bridges. Wine connoisseurs may enjoy visiting several wineries on the Indiana Wine Trail. In Delphi, about eighteen miles northwest of Lafayette, tourists may enjoy the Wabash & Erie Canal Museum. Other tourist destinations in this region include Purdue University in Lafayette and Notre Dame University in West Bend, which host a variety of academic, cultural, and sporting events. In the southeastern corner of the region, campers can enjoy many tourist attractions in Indianapolis, including the Children's Museum, the Indiana State Museum featuring a large transportation exhibit, the Indianapolis Zoo, the Indianapolis Speedway, and the Lucas Oil Stadium.

The Indiana Department of Natural Resources manages six state parks and one fish and wildlife area in this northwestern region. Tent campers planning vacations in this region may want to consider one of the following destinations.

Potato Creek State Park (287 sites plus 70 equestrian sites), about ten miles south of South Bend and I-80/90, is the largest camping destination in the northwestern region. After entering the main gate, campers will enjoy a leisurely drive around the lake to the campground. The family campground, grouped into six loops, is one of Indiana's more popular weekend camping destinations, but we found many vacant campsites, virtually no children, and little activity during our midweek visit in the third week of July. Inside the park, campers can enjoy hiking and bike riding on a variety of trails, swimming, renting boats, attending educational naturalist programs, and observing wildlife. Just outside the park, tourists enjoy a range of cultural and sporting events on the campus of Notre Dame University and in the South Bend area. Other popular attractions in the area include the Studebaker Museum, Potawatomi Zoo, Morris Performing Arts Center, College Football Hall of Fame, and Amish Acres.

Turkey Run State Park (209 sites), conveniently located on Sugar Creek and the US Highway 41 corridor, about thirty miles north of Terre Haute, was established in 1916 as Indiana's second state park and is one of my favorite camping destinations. The large family campground, located about a half mile west of the main property, is spread along a long winding park road. Here, campers will find any type of campsite imaginable, from small sunny sites in the middle of the large loops to large heavily forested sites out on the edges of the campground. Inside the park, campers and day visitors seem to especially enjoy hiking through scenic forest trails, glacial rock formations, sandstone ravines, towering bluffs, and waterfalls. Two short trails just behind the visitor center offer a few interesting geological features but the trails across Sugar Creek are considered to have the most interesting rock formations. Unfortunately, the suspension bridge over the creek to the trails was dam-

Turkey Run State Park's trail #2 just behind the nature center has impressive canyons and rock formations.

aged by a recent flood and hikers must now take a shuttle or hike a considerable distance to get to them. Campers can also enjoy swimming in the Olympic-size pool, fishing, paddling, riding horses, exploring the nature center, and visiting the Richard Lieber Cabin. Outside the park, tourists can enjoy a range of cultural and sporting events at Indiana State University in Terre Haute. I first camped in this park in 1970 and made several overnight camps here while traveling between Wisconsin and Alabama during the 1970s. Eva and I returned to this park in 2013 and enjoyed acquainting ourselves with the nature center and hiking trails.

Indiana Dunes State Park (140 sites), on the shore of Lake Michigan a few miles east of the intersection of I-65, I-80, I-90, and I-94, was established in 1925 as one of Indiana's early state parks and has been named by *National Geographic* as one of the most scenic and culturally significant state parks in the United States. The park has been named by other authorities as one of the best camping destinations in the state and is one of my favorite camping destinations. The large, shaded, grassy campground has four camping loops—two on the west side and two on the east side—with a camp store, potable water, and very nice comfort stations (bathrooms) located near the entrance road. Advance reservations are highly recommended since the campground fills to capacity many summer nights, even during mid-week. Visitors to this park can enjoy hiking over and among large sand dunes and relaxing on the sandy beaches that stretch for miles along the Lake Michigan shore. Campers should also visit the Indiana Dunes Visitor Center and adjacent Indiana Dunes National Lakeshore.

Indiana Dunes State Park's entrance gate is very impressive.

Indiana Dunes State Park's campground is clean, level, spacious, and partly shady.

Prophetstown State Park (110 sites), just off of I-65 near Lafayette, is the newest property in the system and is one of my favorite camping destinations because it is located near I-65 and has very nice bathrooms, a friendly family atmosphere, a great aquatic center, and a variety of interpretative programs. The campground has two oblong loops arranged end to end. The first loop (60 sites) was constructed in an old Christmas tree farm and has a dense stand of older fir trees providing privacy between most sites but little shade. The second loop has an exceptionally nice bathhouse but few trees and no understory. All sites in the campground are large with widely spread gravel pads that can accommodate both RVs and tents. Each site also has an impressive stone site marker. In fact, the park uses stones gathered from nearby glacial debris fields to build walls, bridges, and buildings.

Inside the park, campers can visit the working farm, ride bicycles or walk on a paved 3.2-mile trail, swim in the new aquatic center, attend ranger-led interpretive programs, and fish. Campers with children will appreciate the exceptionally nice playground. Outside the park, visitors should visit the Tippecanoe Battlefield Museum that describes efforts of Tecumseh and his brother—the Prophet—who tried in vain to unite native tribes throughout the Midwest and southeast to resist the westward insurgence of European settlers. After an ill-timed attack on the American troops in 1811, the Prophet's warriors were soundly defeated, Tecumseh's dream of uniting the tribes was dashed, and the native people living in Indiana were forced to move to Kansas. Campers in this park may also want to visit the Purdue University campus and explore the various cultural and sporting activities scheduled there. Or, they may want to ride up to Indiana Beach to spend the day.

Prophetstown State Park's first loop is situated in an old Christmas tree farm.

Prophetstown State Park's second loop is situated in an open field. Campsites are widely spread and each one has a beautiful stone marker.

Willow Slough State Fish and Wildlife Area (50 sites), along the US Highway 41 corridor near Morocco, has a rustic campground with 50 sites designed to serve sportsmen who want to fish and hunt in the wildlife area. But it could also serve as a convenient overnight camp for campers traveling between Terre Haute and Gary or Hammond.

The National Park Service manages the **Indiana Dunes National Lakeshore** (79 sites) located on the shore of Lake Michigan a few miles north of I-94 and I-80/90, and a few miles east of I-65. This campground differs in many ways from the adjacent state park and is also one of my favorite camping destinations. Two important differences are that the National Lakeshore campground does not accept reservations and camping fees are considerably lower. Other differences compared with the state park are: the National Lakeshore has more rustic campground with larger and more private campsites, older rustic but clean bathrooms, and friendly staff. The national lakeshore also features several trails through the dunes, long stretches of deserted beach, and an interesting 1830s French Canadian Homestead.

Indiana Dunes National Lakeshore's campground is more rustic and economical than its state park neighbor.

Indiana Dunes National Lakeshore has miles of deserted beaches.

County and municipal governments in the northwestern region manage two additional public campgrounds that may be suited for tent camping. **France County Park** (200 sites) is located about thirty-eight miles northeast of Lafayette near the intersection of US 24 and US 35. **Earl Park Community Municipal Park** (30 sites) is located about sixty miles south of Hammond along the US 41 corridor.

Northeastern Indiana: Fort Wayne Attractions

The northeastern region of Indiana is defined as the area that is north of US Highway 40 and east of US Hwy 31. Reference cities in the region are South Bend in the northwestern corner, Fort Wayne on the eastern edge, Richmond located in the southeastern corner, Indianapolis located in the southwestern corner, and Kokomo located on the western edge of the region. This region has several lakes including Mississinewa, Salamonie, Roush, Lake Wawasee, and Morse Resevoir. Major highways in this region are I-69, I-70, I-80, I-90, US 6, US 20, US 24, US 30, US 31, US 33, US 35, and US 40.

Several popular tourist destinations can be found throughout this region. The Fort Wayne area, for example, offers a dozen or so popular destinations. Tourists come to visit the Children's Zoo, Museum of Art, History Center, Science Central, the public library that houses one of the best genealogy collections in the country, and other attractions. Fort Wayne also hosts Indiana's Lincoln Highway Association that strives to preserve the old highway from Fort Wayne to Gary. The Huntington and Marion area, located a few miles southwest of Fort Wayne, has three reservoirs with large campgrounds that draw many campers every summer. This area also offers several nice restaurants, shops, and the Dan Quayle Vice-presidential museum. Other popular tourist attractions in the northern part of this northeastern region include the RV Museum and Amish Acres located near Elkhart, and the Trading Place of America (the Midwest's largest flea market) in Shipshewana. In the southern part of this region, history buffs may want to visit the early Adena-Hopewell era Indian mounds at Mounds State Park, located about thirty miles northeast of Indianapolis. In the southwestern corner of the region, Indianapolis offers a variety of concerts, museums, fine restaurants, sporting events, and other enjoyable attractions that were previously described in the northwestern region.

The Indiana Department of Natural Resources manages five state parks, three lakes, one state forest, and two fish and wildlife areas with campgrounds in this northeastern region. Tent campers planning vacations in this region may want to consider one of the following destinations.

Miami State Recreation Area on Mississinewa Lake (414 sites), about fifty miles southwest of Fort Wayne and about twenty-four miles west of I-69, is the largest camping destination in the northeastern region and has been named by *TripleBlaze* as one of the best campgrounds in the state. The beautiful grassy campground is organized into two large sections along winding roads and gently rolling terrain. A few trees are scattered throughout the campground but many sites have only partial shade or full sun. Sites 1 through 112 plus 400 to 418 are located in one section while sites 200 through 386 plus 450 to 470 are located in a second section. Despite the fact that several RVs were parked in the campground during our visit, we were a little disappointed to find that employees seemed too busy to talk with us, few children or adults could be seen in the campground, few activities were scheduled during the week, several campsite tables were damaged, and bathrooms had an unpleasant smell. Inside the park, campers can enjoy sunning on the large beach, swimming, boating, fishing, hiking, and disc golf. Outside the park, tourists can ride up to Huntington County or Fort Wayne and explore area attractions, shops, and restaurants. Or, they can ride a few miles to the south and visit the Automotive Heritage Museum or other attractions in the Kokomo area.

Miami State Recreation Area—Mississinewa Lake's campground had several RVs but few people during our late August visit. These are sites 151 to 155. The bathhouse can be seen on the left.

Miami State Recreation Area—Mississinewa Lake's beach area offers a refreshing dip on hot summer days.

Pokagon State Park (273 sites), on James and Snow Lakes in the extreme northeastern corner of the northeastern region just a mile west of I-69, was established in 1925 as one of Indiana's early state parks. Named for two Potawatomie Indian leaders, the park has a main campground control station, four electric campgrounds, one non-electric campground, and a youth camping area. Most sites are well shaded. Inside the park, campers can enjoy swimming, fishing, hiking, riding horses, viewing various glacial features, visiting the nature center, and enjoying special concerts and events scheduled throughout the summer. The park is also well known for its winter toboggan run. Outside the park, campers can enjoy winery tours, a windmill museum, buffalo preserves, golf, and a couple of old car museums.

Mounds State Park (75 sites), about twenty-five miles northeast of Indianapolis just off of I-69, has been named by *Lumberjack* as one of the best camping destinations in the state and is one of my favorite camping destinations because it is conveniently located near I-69, is close to Indianapolis, has an interesting visitor center, and has a popular family-friendly campground. The family campground has relatively crowded sites arranged in the shape of a square. About half of these sites are shaded while the remaining sites are open. Primary activities in the park include swimming in the pool, hiking the trails, and exploring the ten mounds or earth works that were constructed about 2,170 years ago. The largest of these mounds, called the Great Mound, measures about nine feet tall and sixty-three feet wide. Other activities in the park include visiting the nature center and fishing in White River. Outside the park, visitors can ride down to Indianapolis for a day trip and explore various cultural and recreational activities in the area. When driving to the park from the north, we discovered that a main road to the park has been closed for airport expansion and this closure was not recognized by our GPS receiver.

County and municipal governments in the northeastern region manage six properties that may be suited for tent camping. The **Elkhart 4H County Park** (288 sites), located about twenty miles southeast of South Bend, is the largest of these locally managed properties. The **Indiana State Fairgrounds** (170 sites) in Indianapolis, **White River County Park** (106 sites) a few miles north of Indianapolis and I-69, and **Bixler Lake** (103 sites) in Kendallville about twenty-five miles north of Fort Wayne, also have large campgrounds.

Southwestern Indiana: Cave Country

The southwestern region of Indiana is defined as the area south of US Highway 36 and west of State Road 135 running from Indianapolis down to the Ohio River. Reference cities in this region are Terre Haute in the northwestern corner, Indianapolis in the northeastern corner, Evansville in the southwestern corner, and Bloomington on the eastern border. The western border of this region is defined by the Wabash River and the southern border is defined by the Ohio River. This region has eight state forests, miles of rolling hills, numerous caves, a dozen small rivers, three large lakes, the Hoosier National Forest, and many popular camping destinations. Major highways include I-64, I-69, I-70, US 36, US 40, US 41, US 50, and US 150. In the near future, I-69 will be extended from Bloomington to Evansville.

Travelers passing through this region will immediately notice miles of rolling hills and dozens of highway billboards advertising various commercial cave tours and paddling outfitters in the area. These cave tours and canoe floats are popular tourist activities in the region as are boating, swimming, and winery tours. Holiday World Amusement Park, located in Santa Claus about seven miles south of I-64, features a variety of roller coasters and water slides while Bloomington and Indiana University offer a variety of historical, cultural, and sporting events. History buffs will probably enjoy Lincoln's Boyhood Home National Memorial and plays at the Lincoln State Park. And the Indianapolis area features a variety of cultural and sporting events previously mentioned in the northwestern region.

Lincoln's Boyhood Home National Memorial features a recreated log cabin and farm located a few feet away from Lincoln's original family home site.

The Indiana Department of Natural Resources manages twenty-three parks, lakes, fish and wildlife areas, and forests in this southwestern region. Tent campers planning vacations in this region may want to consider one of the following destinations.

Newton-Stewart State Recreation Area on Patoka Lake (495 sites), about twelve miles north of I-64 between Evansville and Louisville, Kentucky, has the largest campground in the southwestern region and has been named by *TripleBlaze* as one of the best camping destinations in the state. The largely open-field sites in the family campground are spread over a large hilly terrain with few mature trees. Very few campers were in the campground on the day of our mid-week visit but we were told that the campground fills on weekends. Primary recreational activities in this recreation area center on the lake. Swimming, fishing, and boating are popular but swimmers should be advised to avoid blue-green algae, which can cause headaches, diarrhea, and vomiting. Other popular activities in and around the park include archery, playing disc golf, touring caves, and visiting the Railroad Museum and Springs Resort and Casino in French Lick.

Newton-Stewart Recreation Area—Patoka Lake offers a picturesque entrance road with a nice multi-purpose paved trail.

Brown County State Park (404 sites), located between Bloomington and I-65, was established in 1929 as one of Indiana's early state parks and has been named by *National Geographic* as one of the most scenic and historically significant state parks in the United States. It was also named by *TripleBlaze* as one of the best camping areas in the state and is one of my favorite Indiana camping destinations. Nicknamed "The Little Smokies," this park is located on a high ridge with beautiful lookout points along the road. The park has three large campgrounds monitored by a single campground entrance control station. Of the three campgrounds, Buffalo Ridge is the most popular and centrally located. Although most sites are open and crowded, we found a large site in the back with a large tree that provided ample shade on a hot August day. And we discovered that the Buffalo Ridge campground has an exceptionally clean modern bathhouse. Raccoon Ridge is a smaller campground that seems to appeal more to tent campers. Taylor Ridge, the largest campground, is more wooded and isolated than the other two campgrounds. It would be my least favorite campground but campers wanting to find privacy may prefer to camp here. In addition to the electric campgrounds, Brown County State Park has an equestrian camp and several miles of bridle trails.

Within the park, campers will find a well-organized nature center with daily programs and activities plus a swimming pool that is open on weekends. Just outside the park, visitors will find dozens of quaint clothing and souvenir shops in Nashville. In fact, Nashville, Indiana, has become one of our favorite tourist and shopping destinations, having specialty shops that sell items we cannot find near our home and a thriving artist colony. A few miles to the west, visitors will find many cultural and sporting activities in Bloomington and on the Indiana University campus.

Brown County State Park's Buffalo Ridge Campground has several open sites but we found this large site (#47) with a large tree that provided shade on a hot summer day.

Brown County State Park, sometimes called the "Little Smokies," has several lookout points along a ridge top road.

Brown County State Park's covered bridge near the north park entrance is a frequently photographed landmark. Photo by Eva Douglass.

Paynetown Recreation Area on Monroe Lake (321 sites), about ten miles south of Bloomington, has been named by *Triple-Blaze* as one of the best camping destinations in Indiana. The family campground is spread across a mostly sunny open field located near the swimming beach and lakeshore. Despite the close proximity of the campground and beach area, few campers were in the campground during our mid-week visit. Primary activities within the park are swimming, fishing, boating, water-skiing, and other water-based activities. Visitors will also enjoy seeing various exhibits in the nature center. Outside the park, visitors can ride up to Bloomington to find cultural and sporting events at the University of Indiana or ride over to Nashville to explore dozens of unique shops and restaurants.

Paynetown Recreation Area—Monroe Lake's campground was almost deserted on the day we visited.

O'Bannon State Park (263 sites), on the Ohio and Blue Rivers about thirty miles west of Louisville, Kentucky, was originally established in 1980 as Wyandotte Woods State Recreation Area. It is one of my favorite camping destinations because it is conveniently located near I-64 and Louisville, Kentucky, its swimming pool and slides offer refreshing fun on hot summer days, and its staff was as friendly and helpful as any we have met in any other public park. The large camp-ground has four separate sections. Section A has fewer trees but seems to be the preferred section for most family campers. Sections B and C have more trees and more shade but seem to attract fewer campers. Section D is the equestrian campground. In the past, a popular activity was touring the Wyandotte Caves area but these caves were closed in 2012 when we visited the park. State biologists were concerned that cave visitors might accidentally infect local bats with Brown Nose Disease. Other popular activities in the park include riding horses, exploring the well-organized nature center, and swimming in the modern Olympic-size pool. I especially enjoyed sliding down the water slides and reminiscing about similar slides I enjoyed many years ago as a child. Outside the park, tourists can visit commercial caves in the area, canoe on local rivers, tour local wineries, and explore various cultural and recreational activities in the Louisville area. On the morning of our departure, we enjoyed a pleasant conversation with Ranger Bob, the park manager, who had just returned to the office after patrolling the bridle trails. To learn more about this camping destination, watch the Youtube video.

O'Bannon State Park's aquatic center provided a welcomed relief from the heat of a late August day. Photo by Eva Douglass.

Lincoln State Park (237 sites), on a small lake about thirty-five miles west of Evansville and six miles south of I-64, was established in 1932 as one of Indiana's oldest state parks. Although this park has not been named by other authorities, it is one of my favorite Indiana camping destinations. The park has a large electric campground with 150 sites and a rustic campground with 87 more sites. The electric campground has numerous trees but, as we discovered on a hot August stretch, most sites get full sun in the afternoon. Although the bathhouse is not as modern as bath houses in other campgrounds and although some sites are crowded with no privacy, the campground and park has an exceptionally comfortable family-centered atmosphere. Even during the mid week, families and children could be seen walking and playing in the campground, relaxing at the beach, paddling around the lake in rented

Lincoln State Park's bathhouse may be a little old but the campground has a warm family-centered atmosphere.

canoes and paddleboats, riding bicycles, playing games, and attending various park activities. During most of the summer season, plays are presented in the park's beautiful amphitheater and during the month of October children can enjoy trick-or-treating around the campground every Saturday evening while their parents relax and enjoy the fall colors. Across the highway from the park, campers will find Lincoln's Boyhood Home National Memorial with interesting exhibits and an authentic working farm. Within a few miles of the park, visitors can enjoy exciting rides at Holliday World Amusement Park, several commercial caves, and paddling outfitters.

McCormick's Creek State Park (222 sites), about 15 miles northwest of Bloomington, once served as a hunting ground for the Miami Indians and was established in 1916 as Indiana's first state park. It was named by both *Lumberjack* and *TripleBlaze* as one of Indiana's best camping destinations and is one of my favorite camping destinations. The family campground is divided into two large loops: Loop A has 118 sites and Loop B has 63 sites. The park also offers thirty-three primitive campsites, a youth camping area, two group camping areas, and fourteen family cabins. During summer weekends, the family campground fills almost to capacity but during the week, it is largely empty. Both loops of the family campground are set in a densely wooded area offering lots of shade and considerable understory vegetation. Large gravel sites on the outside of the loop typically offer more privacy while sites inside the loop, especially those in loop B, have less. On the late August midweek night we stayed there, Loop B was unusually dark and eerie with only two other campsites occupied in the loop. We could hear raccoons prowling near our tent, cicadas "singing" at deafening levels, occasional owl-hoots echoing in the darkness, and crows screeching before dawn.

Inside the park, campers can enjoy swimming in the Olympic-size pool open on weekends, renting horses for trail rides, fishing or canoeing in the White River, visiting the nature center, hiking on one of the ten trails featuring various rock formations and two nature preserves, attending naturalist programs, eating in the Birdhouse Restaurant, and attending one of the many festivals and special events scheduled during the summer. Outside the park, campers can enjoy various cultural and recreational activities in Bloomington, touring the covered bridges of Parke County, and visiting the Indiana State University campus in Terre Haute.

McCormick's Creek State Park's campground is situated in a dense forest. Our site #165 is just to the right of this road.

Spring Mill State Park (187 sites), located about thirty-five miles south of Bloomington between US 50 and US 150, was established in 1927 as one of Indiana's early state parks and was named by *National Geographic* as one of the most scenic and culturally significant state parks in the United States. It is also one of my favorite camping destinations. The large family campground, spread over rolling terrain, is small, crowded, and sunny. On the hot summer weekday we visited, few campers or park employees were visible in the campground but several people were enjoying other parts of the park. Reportedly, the campground fills to capacity on most summer weekends. Within the park, visitors enjoy touring the historically recreated mill and village with craftspeople dressed in period costumes. On the day we visited, we spent about three hours watching cornmeal being ground in the mill, pots being thrown in the pottery building, and rugs being woven in an old log cabin. We also enjoyed seeing the typical furnishings of several historic buildings

Spring Mill State Park features several historic buildings with craftsmen and women in period dress demonstrating pioneer activities and chores.

in the village. Other popular activities in the park include bicycle riding, touring caves on the grounds, strolling through Donaldson Woods (one of the few stands of virgin timber in the state), and visiting the nature center. Outside the park, visitors will find commercial cave tours and the Indiana Railway Museum.

The U.S. Forest Service manages the Hoosier National Forest and, in the forest, the Forest Service manages a large developed camping and recreational complex in the Hardin Ridge Recreation Area plus four smaller rustic campgrounds located in the southern half of the region. The **Hardin Ridge Recreational Area** (202 sites), located on Monroe Lake about fifteen miles south of Bloomington, has six ridge-top campground spurs in a densely wooded area. Ample understory vegetation provides privacy for individual sites but the sites seem to be small, sloped, rocky, and crowded for a national forest campground. Some sections of the campground have nice modern bathhouses while other sections have older bathhouses. Within the park, campers can enjoy swimming and relaxing at the Monroe Lake beach, renting boats, fishing, and visiting the nature center. My primary complaint about this recreation area is the distance between the camping and swimming areas. Campsites are located up a steep hill away from the swimming area. While campers could easily ride bicycles down to the beach, they would have considerable difficulty returning to the campground. Outside the recreation area, campers can enjoy many cultural and recreational activities in the Bloomington area, especially on the Indiana University campus.

County and municipal governments in the southwestern region manage seven additional public campgrounds that may be suited for tent camping. **West Boggs County Park** (222 sites), located on the

West Boggs Creek Reservoir about thirty-five miles east of Vincennes and five miles north of US 50/150, is the largest of these properties. **Fowler County Park** (53 sites), located about 10 miles south of Terre Haute, is one of my favorite camping destinations because all sites are situated on the banks of a small lake and it is convenient to the US 41 corridor. Although the sites are generally small and crowded, they are well shaded and located on a small lake that is stocked with plenty of catfish, bass, and other tasty fish. One of our neighbors apparently knew where and how to fish because he caught several for dinner. **Ouabache** (pronounced Wabash) **Trails County Park** (42 sites), located just north of Vincennes, is another favorite camping destination along on the US 41 corridor. The park has an entrance control station, on-site security, clean bathrooms, and an exceptionally nice playground. Sites 1 & F are exceptionally large and shady. **Vanderburgh 4H Center** (6 to 10 tent sites plus 67 RV sites), located about five miles north of Evansville, is a third county park along the U.S. 41 corridor to consider in a pinch. It has showers and a campground host, but few other amenities.

Fowler County Park near Terre Haute has a rustic entrance control station.

Fowler County Park's campsites are spread along the banks of a small, well-stocked lake.

Ouabache Trails County Park has a nice campground located near Vincennes.

Since Indiana, compared with other midwestern states, has few public campgrounds, I also want to mention **Horseshoe Lake Campground**, located near US 41 in Clinton about fifteen miles north of Terre Haute, because it was named by the *TripleBlaze* website as one of the best campgrounds in Indiana. This campground is one of ninety properties privately owned by Thousand Trails and Encore Campground Resorts—a campground membership club. From pictures and descriptions of this campground posted on the web, one can see that this property is immaculate and offers several enjoyable activities. It is one of nine Thousand Lakes properties located in the Midwest. In 2012, an annual tent camping pass cost $250 but it entitled members to unlimited camping in all twenty-four properties within the northeast zone (that includes Indiana and neighboring states). While most sites are reserved for members, non-members can sometimes book campsites in these properties. Anyone living in this region may want to check out the membership benefits.

Southeastern Indiana: Brookville Lake

The southeastern region of Indiana is defined as the area south of US 40 and east of State Road 135. Reference cities in this region are Louisville, Kentucky, in the southwestern corner, Indianapolis in the northwestern corner, Richmond in the northeastern corner, and Cincinnati, Ohio, just east of the region. Two large lakes in this region are Brookfield Lake and Hardy Lake. Major highways in the region include I-65, I-70, US 40, US 50, US 150, and US 52.

A popular camping destination in this region is the Brookfield Lake area located near the Ohio border. Two state recreation areas and one state park with large campgrounds on this lake offer a wide variety of water recreational activities. Nearby towns have a variety of unique shops and restaurants. Richmond and other small towns along US 40, for example, feature museums that preserve the history of the National Road and early automobile transportation. Metamora, farther south, offers several small shops, historic buildings, bluegrass music, and horse-drawn canal boat rides. Several towns in the area have concerts and festivals scheduled through the summer season. A few vineyards and wineries in the area offer tasty samples that will please the palate. To the south of this region, many tourists enjoy visiting The Falls of Ohio State Park. Although this park does not offer camping, visitors can enjoy seeing the fossil beds and visiting the interpretive museum. While in the Louisville area, tourists may enjoy visiting several museums, sports, and cultural attractions. In the northwestern corner of this region, Indianapolis offers a variety of attractions mentioned in previous regions, plus three early automobile assembly plants on Washington Street. And just a few miles east of this region, campers can enjoy various cultural, educational, and sporting events in the Cincinnati, Ohio, area.

The Indiana Department of Natural Resources manages four parks and two reservoirs with campgrounds in this southeastern region. Tent campers planning vacations in this region may want to consider one of the following destinations.

Mounds State Recreation Area on Brookfield Lake (388 sites), about twenty miles south of Richmond and US 40 on the eastern side of the lake, was established in the early 1930s as one of Indiana's early state properties and has the largest camping area of the state-managed properties in the southeastern region. This property has been named by *TripleBlaze* as having one of the best campgrounds in Indiana. The family campground is divided into two sections and each section has five to six smaller loops. For the most part, campsites have flat terrain, lots of grass, paved parking areas, few trees, and very little privacy. Swimming, boating, and fishing are three primary activities within the park. Several hiking trails are available but hikers are advised to wear blaze orange during hunting season. Outside the park, campers can ride over to Metamora and enjoy a variety of historic sites, restaurants, tourist shops, and the horse-drawn canal boat ride. Some families may prefer the smaller campground at the **Quakertown State Recreation Area** (75 sites) located on the western side of the lake.

Whitewater Memorial State Park (255 sites), on the northern shore of Brookville Lake about sixty miles east of Indianapolis, is the second largest camping destination in the southeastern region. The park has one large family campground with three main sections, an equestrian camp, a youth camp, and twenty cabins. The beautiful family campground has gravel parking pads, lots of grass, and many shade trees but fewer than half of the sites were claimed on the first weekend in August when we were there. Inside the park, campers can enjoy swimming, hiking, riding horses, fishing, and paddling in rented boats. Outside the park, campers can ride over to the Whitewater Valley Railroad in Connersville, canal rides and festivals in Metamora, or various cultural and recreational attractions in Dayton, Ohio.

Hardy Lake (167 sites), located on Hardy Lake about forty miles north of Louisville and eight miles east of I-65, was constructed in 1970 by the Army Corps of Engineers. It is one of my favorite camping destinations because of its proximity to I-65 and its raptor rehabilitation center. The family campground (Shale Bluff) has 150 sites and the primitive campground (Wooster) has 18 more sites. Most of the time, the primary activities at this property revolve around swimming, fishing, boating, and other water recreation, but high levels of blue-green algae that grows during hot summer months will limit those activities. All park visitors should plan to spend a few hours at the Raptor Rehabilitation Center and archery enthusiasts will be happy to know that the park has an archery range. As previously mentioned, my first attempt to visit Hardy Lake ended before I ever got inside the gates. In 2013, my wife and I returned to camp overnight at this property. The campground has large, level, grassy sites with a paved parking pad, few trees, and little shade. Only a few sites were occupied during the middle of the week but, reportedly, most sites fill on weekends.

No federally managed properties with campgrounds are located in the southeastern region of Indiana and only one county government in the region manages a public campground. **Muscatatuck Park** (50 sites) is a popular park located near US 50 about twelve miles east of I-65. Inside the park, visitors enjoy rock climbing, bouldering, hiking, and mountain bike riding.

Useful Resources

After reading this chapter, readers should consult additional resources to determine specific destinations and campgrounds that best fit their family's particular interests and expectations. Some helpful resources are listed below.

- The Indiana Department of Natural Resources website (www. in.gov/dnr) contains information about all state-managed properties.
- In addition to the DNR website, many state parks have their own website with more detailed information and more photos.
- The official Indiana state highway map, available from the Indiana Department of Transportation (www.in.gov/indot/) and at most highway rest areas, shows approximate geographic locations of each state and most federal properties. The map also has a smaller map showing the locations of all DNR property locations.
- *Indiana Recreation Guide* (brochure) available in rest areas lists the names of all state properties and provides brief descriptions of each one.

- *Indiana State Parks: A Guide to Hoosier Parks, Reservoirs and Recreation Areas* (older book) provides detailed descriptions of state properties. Some of the details are out of date but most are still current.
- *Indiana Travel Guide: Especially for Campers* (brochure), available at highway rest areas, briefly describes many private campgrounds in Indiana.
- *Indiana 2013 Travel Guide* (booklet), available at highway rest areas, describes major tourist attractions in the state.
- Reserve America (www.reserveamerica.com/campgroundSearch. do, 866-622-6746) is a private organization that makes reservations for Indiana state parks and recreation areas. The website also shows photos of individual campsites.
- Recreation.Gov (www.Recreation.gov, 877-444-6777) is a private organization that makes reservations for all federal properties.

Indiana's Public Campgrounds

Campgrounds are listed by number of campsites available from most numerous to least. The following abbreviations are used to note public campgrounds that have been named by various authorities as among the best in the state:

FD   This property is one of my favorite camping destinations.

LJ   This property was named by the *Lumberjack* website as being one of Indiana's best state parks for summer tent camping.

TB   This property was named by the *TripleBlaze* website as having one of the twenty best campgrounds in the state.

NG   This property was named and described by *National Geographic's Guide to State Parks in the United States* as one of America's most historic and scenic state parks.

(P = primitive)

Northwestern Region: Indiana Beach

State DNR Parks, Recreation Areas, and Forests

Potato Creek SP   574-656-8186
286 sites, showers, beach, canoe,   41.53576, -86.36087
  kayak, bike, & horse rental, nature
  center, golf
25601 S R 4, North Liberty
12 m S of South Bend, 5 m W of
  US 31

Turkey Run SP   FD, LJ, TB
209 sites, showers, pool, horse rental,   765-597-2635
  tennis, boat rental, golf, canoeing   39.87920, -87.21381
8121 East Park Road, Marshall
30 m N of Terre Haute, 2 m E of US 41

Indiana Dunes SP   FD, TB, NG
140 sites, showers, beach, dunes   219-926-1952
1600 N 25 E, Chesterton   41.65501, -87.06269
On Lake Michigan, 15 m E of Gary

Tippecanoe River SP   574-946-3213
112 sites, showers, paddling, fishing 41.11745, -86.60277
4200 N US Hwy 35, Winamac
50 m SE of Gary, 35 m E of I-65

Prophetstown SP   FD
110 sites, showers, working farm,   765-567-4919
  Tippecanoe Battlefield   40.50253, -86.82566
4112 E SR 225, West Lafayette
3 m NE of Lafayette, 2 m NE of I-65

Shades SP   765-435-2810
101 sites, showers, paddling, fishing 39.92932, -87.07226
7751 S 890 W, Waveland
38 m NE of Terre Haute, 10 m E of
  US Hwy 41

Willow Slough FWA   219-285-2704
50 sites, showers, target range, fishing   40.97266. -8748828
2042 S 500 W, Morocco
40 m S of Gary, 3 m W of US Hwy 41

National Park Service Campgrounds

Indiana Dunes National Lakeshore   FD
79 sites, showers, beach, hiking   219-926-7561
1100 N Mineral Springs Rd, Porter   41.63357, -87.05439
On Lake Michigan, 10 m E of Gary

County and Municipal Campgrounds

France CG, Cass CP   574-753-2928
200 sites, showers, beach, putt-putt,   40.76093, -86.45653
   disc golf
4505 W US Hwy 24 W, Logansport
38 m NE of Lafayette, near US Hwys
   24 & 35

Earl Park Community MP   219-474-6108
30 sites, showers, horseshoes,   40.68555, -87.42220
   volleyball courts, softball fields
Earl Park
60 m S of Gary, on US Hwy 41

Wabash & Erie Canal Park   765-564-2870
About 10 sites, showers, museum,   40.59272, -86.67912
   Indiana Beach
1030 N Washington St, Delphi
18 m NE of Lafayette, on US 421

Northeastern Region: Fort Wayne Attractions

State DNR Parks, Recreation Areas, and Forests

Miami SRA   TB
414 sites, showers, boat rental,   765-473-6528
   boating, fishing   40.69786, -85.95395
4673 S 625 E, Peru
W side of Mississinewa Lake, 10 m S of
   US 24

Chain O' Lakes SP   260-636-2654
380 sites, showers, 33 P sites, beach,   41.34140, -85.37847
   canoe & kayak rental
2355 E 75 S, Albion
20 m NW of Fort Wayne, 18 m W of
   I-69

Pokagon SP   260-833-2012
273 sites, showers, beach, boat rental   41.70792, -85.02934
450 Lane 100 Lake James, Angola
45 m N of Fort Wayne, 1 m W of I-69

Lost Bridge West SRA   TB
246 sites, showers, 38 P sites, boat   260-468-2125
    rental   40.76485, -85.62572
9214 W Lost Bridge W, Andrews
W side of Salamonie Lake, 35 m SW of
    Ft Wayne

Summit Lake SP   765-766-5873
125 sites, showers, beach, canoe   40.01872, -85.30267
    rental
5993 N Messick Rd, New Castle
40 m E of Indianapolis, 13 m N of I-70

Ouabache SP   260-824-0926
124 sites, showers, pool, canoe rental,   40.72854, -85.12922
    bike trail, Bison exhibit
4930 E SR 201, Bluffton
25 m S of Fort Wayne, 18 m E of I-69

Mounds SP   FD, LJ
75 sites, showers, pool, visitor center,   765-642-6627
    archeological site   40.09578, -85.62010
4306 Mounds Rd, Anderson
25 m NE of Indianapolis, 5 m W of
    I-69

J. E. Roush FWA   260-468-2165
25 sites, showers, 30 P sites, fishing,   40.83830, -85.46544
    hunting, shooting
517 N Warren Rd, Huntington
20 m SW of Fort Wayne, 5 m W of
    I-69

Pigeon River FWA   260-367-2164
44 P sites, fishing, hunting   41.68557, -85.26597
8310 E 300 N, Mongo
40 m N of Fort Wayne, 15 m W of I-69

Salamonie River SF   260-468-2125
21 P sites plus 15 equestrian sites   40.76485, -85.62572
9214 W Lost Bridge W, Andrews
N tip of Salamonie Lake, 35 m SW of
    Fort Wayne

County and Municipal Campgrounds

Elkhart 4H CP   574-533-3247
288 sites, showers, Amish shops,   41.58063, -85.80637
    tourist attractions
17746-D CR 34, Goshen
15 m E of South Bend, 8 m S of I-80

Indiana State Fairgrounds   317-927-7510
170 sites, showers, laundry,   39.79797, -86.11633
    Indianapolis attractions
1202 E 38th St, Indianapolis
Northeastern section of the city

White River CG, Hamilton CP   317-770-4430
106 sites, showers, paddling, concerts   40.12869, -85.96882
11299 E 234th St, Cicero
15 m N of Indianapolis, 12 m N of
    I-69

Bixler Lake CG, Kendallville MP   260-347-1064
103 sites, showers, beach   41.43775, -85.26256
211 Iddings St, Kendallville
25 m N of Fort Wayne, 12 m W of I-69

Johnny Appleseed CG, Fort Wayne   260-427-6720
MP   41.11583, -85.12061
41 sites, showers, Fort Wayne
    attractions, family friendly
    atmosphere
1500 E Coliseum Blvd, Fort Wayne
In Fort Wayne

Westwood Park, Henry CP   765-987-1232
38 sites, showers, fishing, horse trails   39.90404, -85.43749
1900 S CR 275 W, New Castle
35 m E of Indianapolis, 10 m N of I-70

Southwestern Region: Cave Country

State DNR Parks, Recreation Areas, and Forests

Newton-Stewart SRA   TB
450 sites, showers, 45 P sites, disc   812-685-2464
    golf, boat & jet ski rental   38.38432, -86.64690
3084 N Dillard Rd, Birdseye
SW side of Patoka Lake, 50 m NW of
    Louisville

Brown County SP
404 sites, showers, pool, special
  events, golf, horse rental,
  shopping, art studios
1405 SR 46W, Nashville
15 m E of Bloomington, 18 m W of
  I-65

FD, TB, NG
812-988-6406
39.15596, -86.23039

Raccoon SRA
279 sites, showers, 35 P sites, boat &
  jet ski rental, golf
1588 S Raccoon Pkwy, Rockville
W side of C.M. Hardin Lake, 30 m NE
  of T Haute

TB
765-344-1412
39.74127, -87.07864

Paynetown SRA
321 sites, showers, boat & jet ski
  rental
4850 South SR 446, Bloomington
E side of Monroe Lake, 6 m S of
  Bloomington

TB
812-837-9546
39.09003, -86.42856

**O'Bannon Woods SP (Wyandotte
  Woods SRA)**
263 sites, showers, 24 P sites, pool,
  water slides, caves
7234 Old Forest Rd SW, Corydon
30 m W of Louisville, 5 m S of I-64

FD, TB
812-738-8232
38.20593, -86.26076

Lincoln SP
237 sites, showers, beach, canoe
  rental, live theatre, concerts,
  museum
15476 N CR 300 E, Lincoln City
33 m E of Evansville, 10 m S of I-64

FD, TB
812-937-4710
38.11150, -86.99816

McCormick's Creek SP
222 sites, showers, 32 P sites, pool,
  horse rental, golf, special events
250 McCormick Creek Park Rd,
  Spencer
15 m NW of Bloomington, 15 m S of
  I-70

FD, LJ, TB
812-829-2235
39.28606, -86.7265

Lieber SRA
207 sites, showers, beach, pool,
  boat rental
1317 W Lieber Road, Cloverdale
E side of Cagles Mill Lake, 3 m S of
  I-70

TB
765-795-4576
39.48514, -86.88585

Harmonie SP
200 sites, showers, pool, water slide,
  Wabash River
3451 Harmonie State Park Rd, New
  Harmonie
25 m W of Evansville, 10 m S of I-64

TB
812-682-4821
38.12535, -87.93335

Spring Mill SP
187 sites, showers, 36 P sites, pool,
  historic village, bike rental, caves
3333 SR 60 E, Mitchell
50 m NW of Louisville, 35 m W of I-65

FD, LJ, NG
812-849-3534
38.72801, -86.41385

Shakamak SP
175 sites, showers, pool, horse & boat
  rentals
6265 West SR 48, Jasonville
25 m S of Terre Haute, 10 m E of US
  Hwy 41

812-665-2158
39.17456, -87.23044

Glendale FWA
121 sites, showers, fishing, hunting,
  wildlife viewing
6001 E 600 S, Montgomery
55 m NE of Evansville, 30 m E of
  US 41

812-644-7711
38.55184, -87.05122

Greene-Sullivan SF
100 P sites, fishing, hiking
2551 SR 159, Dugger
25 m N of Vincennes, 10 m E of US
  Hwy 41

812-648-2810
39.04459, -87.25964

Yellowwood SF
80 P sites, fishing, gold panning,
  horse trails
772 S Yellowwood Rd, Nashville
12 m E of Bloomington, 25 m W of
  I-65

812-988-7945
39.18432, -86.33803

Ferdinand SF   812-367-1524
77 P sites, beach, German heritage,   38.25215, -86.76916
  fishing, bike trails
6583 E SR 264, Ferdinand
60 m W of Louisville, 4 m N of I-64

Morgan-Monroe SF   765-342-4026
29 P sites, gold panning, fishing   39.32585, -86.41992
6220 Forest Rd, Martinsville
30 m S of Indianapolis, 28 m W of I-65

Martin SF   812-247-3491
26 P sites, fishing, hiking   38.70784, -86.72513
14040 Williams Rd, Shoals
45 m E of Vincennes, 1 m N of US
  Hwy 50

Owen-Putnam SF   812-829-2462
25 P sites, bike & horse trails   39.32083, -86.84556
2153 Fish Creek Rd, Spencer
30 m E of Terre Haute, 10 m S of I-70

Pike SF   812-367-1524
11 P sites, horse trails, fishing   38.35568, -87.19349
5994 E SR 364, Winslow
33 m NE of Evansville, 12 m N of I-64

National Forest Campgrounds

Hardin Ridge RA, Hoosier NF   FD, TB
202 sites, showers, beach   812-837-9453
6464 Hardin Ridge Rd, Heltonville   39.01787, -86.44972
E side of Monroe Lake, 15 m SE of
  Bloomington

Celina Lake, Hoosier NF   812-547-7051
60 sites, showers, fishing, bike trails, 38.19866, -86.59998
  interpretive programs
St Croix
45 m W of Louisville, 5 m S of I-64

Tipsaw Lake, Hoosier NF   812-547-7051
34 sites, showers, beach, boating,   38.13384, -86.63110
  fishing
St Croix
45 m W of Louisville, 8 m S of I-64

German Ridge, Hoosier NF   812-547-7051
20 P sites, bike trail, historic buildings,   37.95499, -86.58119
   fishing
Cannelton
50 m SW of Louisville, 20 m S of I-64

Saddle Lake, Hoosier NF   812-547-7051
13 P sites, paddling, fishing, hiking   38.05032, -86.64736
St. Croix
50 m SW of Louisville, 13 m S of I-64

County and Municipal Campgrounds

West Boggs CG, Daviess CP   812-295-3421
222 sites, showers, beach, boat rental,   38.69235, -86.91889
   miniature golf
16117 US Hwy 231, Loogootee
35 m E of Vincennes, near US Hwy
   50/150

Scales Lake CG, Warrick CP   812-897-6200
85 sites, showers, pool water slide,   38.05465, -87.25679
   beach, petting zoo
800 W Tennyson Rd, Boonville
15 m E of Evansville, 12 m E of I-164

Lynnville MP   812-922-5144
69 sites, fishing   38.19468, -87.32458
405 W SR 68, Lynnville
20 m NE of Evansville, 1 m N of I-64

Fowler Park, Vigo CP   FD
53 sites, showers, beach, pioneer   812-462-3413
   village   39.33213, -87.37189
3000 E Oregon Church Rd, Terre
   Haute
7 m S of I-70, 1 m E of US Hwy 41

Johnson CP   812-526-6809
50 sites, showers, golf   39.47694, -86.04733
Franklin
15 m S of Indianapolis, on I-65

Ouabache Trails Park, Knox CP　　**FD**
42 sites, showers, laundry, fishing,　　812-882-4316
    birding, mountain bike trails　　　　38.72410, -87.50850
    planned
3500 N Lower Fort Knox Rd,
    Vincennes
2 m N of Vincennes, 2 m W of US
    Hwy 41

Vanderburgh 4H Center CG　　　　812-867-6217
6 to 10 open field tent sites plus 67 RV　38.09361, -87.55995
    sites, showers
201 E Boonville-New Harmony Rd,
    Evansville
3 m N of Evansville, on US 41

Southeastern Region: Brookville Lake

State DNR Parks, Recreation Areas, and Forests

Mounds SRA　　　　　　　　　　**TB**
388 sites, showers, beach, golf, boat　765-647-2657
    rental　　　　　　　　　　　　　39.50019, -84.95690
14108 SR 101, Brookville
SE side of Brookville Lake, 60 m E of
    Indianapolis

Whitewater Memorial SP　　　　　765-458-5565
255 sites, showers, beach, canoe &　　39.61144, -84.94220
    kayak rental
1418 S SR 101, Liberty
N tip of Brookville Lake, 60 m E of
    Indianapolis

Versailles SP　　　　　　　　　　**TB**
220 sites, showers, pool, water slide,　812-689-6424
    canoe & kayak rental　　　　　　39.07468, -85.28318
1387 E US Hwy 50, Versailles
70 m NE of Louisville, 38 m E of I-65

Charlestown SP　　　　　　　　　812-256-5600
192 sites, showers, hiking trails,　　　38.44948, -85.64605
    waterfalls, fishing, interpretive
    programs
12500 SR 62, Charlestown
20 m NE of Louisville, 8 m E of I-65

Hardy Lake
149 sites, showers, 18 P sites, archery,
    beach, fishing, raptor center
5620 N Hardy Lake Rd, Scottsburg
45 m N of Louisville, 8 m E of I-65

FD
812-794-3800
38.77657, -85.70586

Deam Lake SRA
115 sites, showers, beach, boat rental,
    casino, aquarium, horse racing, golf
1217 Deam Lake Road, Borden
25 m N of Louisville, 9 m W of I-65

812-246-5421
38.46832, -85.86589

Starve Hollow SRA
113 sites, showers, beach, boat &
    canoe rental, golf
4345 South CR 275, West Vallonia
50 m N of Louisville, 15 m W of I-65

812-358-3464
38.81693, -86.08372

Clifty Falls SP
104 sites, showers, 59 P sites, pool
2221 Clifty Drive, Madison
45 m NE of Louisville, 25 m E of I-65

TB
812-273-8885
38.77079, -85.43618

Quakertown SRA
75 sites, showers, beach, boat rental,
    golf
Quakertown
NW side of Brookville Lake, 60 m E of
    Indianapolis

765-647-2658
39.57989, -85.00242

Jackson-Washington SF
54 P sites, fishing, archery, bike trails
1278 E SR 250, Brownstown
40 m N of Louisville, 15 m W of I-65

812-358-2160
38.86127, -86.00861

Clark SF
45 P sites, fishing, shooting range,
    horse & bike trails
US Hwy 31 N, Henryville
25 m N of Louisville, 5 m W of I-65

812-294-4306
38.55320, -85.76605

County and Municipal Campgrounds

Muscatatuck Park, Jennings CP
50 sites, showers, mountain bike trails,
    rock climbing, bouldering
North Vernon
55 m N of Louisville, 15 m E of I-65

812-346-2953
38.98785, -85.62164

Bibliography

Bailey, Bill (2000). *Wisconsin State Parks, State Forests, and Recreation Areas, revised edition.* Saginaw, Mich.: Glovebox Guidebooks of America.

___. (2003). *Illinois State Parks: A Complete Outdoor Recreation Guide for Campers, Boaters, Anglers, Skiers, Hikers, and Outdoor Lovers, revised edition.* Saginaw, Mich.: Glovebox Guidebooks of America.

Douglass, Frazier M. (2012). *The Tent Camper's Handbook.* Bloomington, Ind.: iUniverse.

DuFresne, Jim (2011). *Michigan's Best Campgrounds: A Guide to the Best 150 Campgrounds in the Great Lakes State,* 4th Edition. Holt, Mich.: Thunder Bay Press.

Duncan, Dayton, & Ken Burns (2011). *The National Parks: America's Best Idea.* New York: Alfred A. Knopf.

Finch, Jackie Scheckler Finch (2002). *The Unofficial Guide to the Best RV and Tent Campgrounds in the Great Lakes States.* New York: Hungry Minds.

Forster, Matt (2011). *Best Tent Camping: Michigan.* Birmingham, Ala.: Menasha Ridge Press.

Goll, John (1995). *Indiana State Parks: A Guide to Hoosier Parks, Reservoirs, and Recreation Areas.* Saginaw, Mich.: Glovebox Guidebooks of America.

Holding, Thomas H. (1908). *The Camper's Handbook.* Originally published by Simpkin, Marshall, Hamilton, Kent, & Co. Ltd. London, England. Reprinted by Kessinger Publishing LLC, Whitefish, Montana.

National Geographic (2012). *Guide to National Parks of the United States.* Washington D.C.

___. (2012). *Guide to State Parks of the United States.* Washington D.C.

Powers, Tom (2007). *Michigan State and National Parks, 4th Edition.* Holt, Mich.: Thunder Bay Press.

Revolinski, Kevin, & Johnny Malloy (2007). *The Best in Tent Camping: Wisconsin, 2nd edition.* Birmingham, Ala.: Menasha Ridge Press.

Roundabout Publications (2010). *National Park Service Camping Guide, 4th Edition.* Lenexa, Kan.

Schirle, John (2009). *The Best in Tent Camping: Illinois.* Birmingham, Ala.: Menasha Ridge Press.

Wolverton, Ruthe & Walt (1990). *Thirteen National Parks with Room to Roam.* Bedford, Mass.: Mills & Sanderson.

Woodall's Publishing Corporation (2011). *Woodall's North American Campground Directory.* Vista Del Mar, Cal.

Wright, Micah (2011). *Camping With the Corps of Engineers, 8th edition.* Elkhart, Ind.: Cottage Publishers.

Acknowledgments

I would like to begin by thanking all of my family and friends who have accompanied me on past camping trips. I am especially grateful to my wife, Eva Noveron Douglass, who has accompanied me on more than fifty camping trips over the past five years. From the first trip, she has been very comfortable with the tent camping routine and has become a very proficient companion. From working together many times, we are now able to set up and break down our camp in less than fifteen minutes without saying a word to each other. We each know our jobs and are able to perform them efficiently. In addition, I would like to express my appreciation to Peggie Weese (Douglass) Tucker and Robin Fain (Douglass) Moore, who accompanied me on many trips in past years. My two sons, Shel Douglass and Lyle Douglass have joined me on a few trips, as have my sister Jean Douglass Baswell and her husband Tom. Many more friends and family members have joined me on one or two trips to various destinations around the southeastern and midwestern United States.

I would also like to thank the people who have assisted me with various parts of this book project. Jean Baswell Douglass and Angela Jordan have read and critiqued several sections of the book. Tracy Hicks assisted me with the maps and photos. Gene Tiser read the Wisconsin chapter and gave me several good suggestions. Al Elmore helped me compose my initial book proposal. Harry Joiner helped me write the Overview. Steve Clarke helped me with my website; Damon Lares bailed me out when I ran into computer problems; and Ron Fritze helped me understand the publishing process.

Finally, I want to thank all the people who have listened to me babble about various camping and manuscript issues for the past six years. These people include my wife Eva, my sister Jean, my two sons Shel and Lyle, Susan Owen, and my regular lunch companion, James Gadberry.

The Author

Frazier Douglass was born in Birmingham, Alabama, educated at Auburn University and the University of Wisconsin-Milwaukee, worked as a clinical psychologist for ten years, and finished his career as a university professor for thirty years. Currently, he is retired and spends most of his time teaching a few graduate psychology courses at Alabama A & M University, camping, and writing books about camping. Although he was a teacher by profession, he is an engineer at heart and enjoys devising solutions to common camping problems.

Douglass began camping with his father when he was ten years old and has camped throughout the southeastern, midwestern, and western United States. His favorite camping destinations are Door County, Wisconsin; Michigan's western shoreline; southern Indiana; Rend Lake, Illinois; the Great Smoky Mountains National Park, Helen, Georgia; and the Florida Gulf Coast. In the mid 1990s, he served three summers as the campground host at Brigham County Park near Madison, Wisconsin. In 2011, he and his wife began taking two- and three-week-long campground touring trips through Illinois, Wisconsin, Michigan, and Indiana. Typically, these trips departed from north Alabama starting with a series of overnight camps in Indiana, Illinois, or southern Wisconsin, established a week-long base camp in Door County, Wisconsin, and culminated with a series of overnight camps in Michigan and Indiana on the way back home. Each year, he tries to visit at least ten new campgrounds in the four Lake Michigan states and experience more of the many attractions scattered around the region.